Also by Neil Chethik

FatherLoss: How Sons of All Ages
Come to Terms With the Deaths of Their Dads

*What Husbands
Really Think About
Their Marriages, Their Wives,
Sex, Housework, and
Commitment*

VoiceMale

Neil Chethik

Simon & Schuster
New York   London   Toronto   Sydney

SIMON & SCHUSTER
Rockefeller Center
1230 Avenue of the Americas
New York, NY 10020

SIMON & SCHUSTER and colophon are registered trademarks
of Simon & Schuster, Inc.

For information about special discounts for bulk purchases,
please contact Simon & Schuster Special Sales at
1-800-456-6798 or business@simonandschuster.com

Designed by Davina Mock

Manufactured in the United States of America

10   9   8   7   6   5   4   3   2

Library of Congress Cataloging-in-Publication Data
Chethik, Neil.
Voicemale: what husbands really think about their marriages, their wives, sex,
housework, and commitment / Neil Chethik.
p.   cm.
Includes bibliographical references.
1. Husbands—United States—Attitudes. 2. Husbands—United States—
Psychology. 3. Marriage—United States. I. Title.
HQ756.C436 2006
306.872'2'0973—dc22   2005051612

ISBN-13: 978-0-7432-5872-2
ISBN-10:   0-7432-5872-X

Contents

Part Four: How Men *Do* Marriage

For my wife, Kelly

Introduction

⚓

Marriage is like digging in the dirt. It's hard and messy, and there are treasures buried there.
—Forty-year-old school principal

AMERICAN HUSBANDS. Fifty years ago, it seemed the best of times for them. The heroes of World War II, they married their hometown sweethearts and busied themselves living the American Dream. The GI Bill educated them, corporations lavished job offers upon them, and their role in the American family was clear-cut and advantageous: bring home the money, discipline the children, and keep the lawn looking as good as the Joneses'. In exchange, they got security, sex, and their meals served up on time. With their wives economically dependent on them, some husbands even felt free to explore outside the marriage for sexual or emotional "add-ons," convinced that their wives wouldn't do the same.

A half century later, this portrait has gone the way of the Edsel.

Today, American husbands no longer dominate their relationships. And we know it. Twenty-first-century wives seek equality in their marriages and often exit those relationships if they don't get it. And the legislatures, courts, and media increasingly back up the women. At the same time, men no longer need to walk the aisle in order to have sex with a woman, live with her, or even have children with her.

And yet, American men keep marrying. We may wait a little longer than we did in the fifties; we may wed for different reasons; the dynam-

1

ics of the marriages may be vastly altered from marriages of the past. But those who argue that man's natural state is promiscuous detachment, serial monogamy, or some other form of isolationism haven't listened closely to the American husband. Despite fifty years of gender-role havoc, a husband's relationship with his wife remains the most important aspect of his life.

I come to this conclusion after fifteen years of interviewing men and writing about their personal lives. My first book, *FatherLoss*, focused on how sons of all ages come to terms with the deaths of their fathers. I found that, contrary to the stereotype, men grieve profoundly. We may not grieve like women, who tend to cry and talk when they grieve. But men's style of coming to terms with loss—a style that emphasizes action and thinking—seems to fit our character and get the job done.

Likewise, men's perspective on marriage has often been misunderstood. While hundreds of books have been written on marriage, virtually all come at the topic with a woman's sensibility, using female-oriented language, focusing on issues that mostly concern women and wives. Few authors seem to acknowledge the complexity and diversity of the male perspective.

This book aims to remedy that. Traveling from coast to coast, to cities and farms, ivory towers and factory floors, I have surveyed nearly 360 married American men of all ages, classes, religions, and ethnic backgrounds. To these men, I put every question that I could muster; with them, I explored every detail of marriage we could imagine.

And again, the stereotype falls: Rather than the "checked-out" male, I found that most husbands are keenly aware of, if at times utterly perplexed by and chagrined about, the state of their unions. While some men I interviewed acknowledged that they'd never before spoken about their marriages in such depth, virtually all had thought about the issues, and many had wrestled intensely with them.

They'd also wrestled, sometimes literally, with their wives. Husbands report that they disagree with their wives on issues ranging from money to in-laws to housework to children to sex. Physical violence—against husband or wife—had touched nearly one in five marriages. A third of husbands reported that they had considered getting a divorce from their current wife, and almost one in ten had actually separated from her for some period of time.

And yet, in one of the many striking findings of my survey, more than 90 percent of currently married men said that if given the choice today, they'd marry the same woman again. The vast majority of husbands consider themselves happily married. They recognize that marriage takes work, and work pays off. From unimaginable low points, for reasons practical, emotional, and prideful, American husbands seem determined to weather the rough times of their relationships and keep their marriages intact.

I'm one of those men. Born in the center of the postwar Baby Boom, I am, in matters of marriage, a member of "the Straddle Generation."

One of my feet is planted in the era of *Father Knows Best*. My parents married in 1953, just days after graduating from college. My father's military service, education, and career choices dictated my parents' travels in their early years together. When their kids were young, my father made the money, my mother the meals. He left home each morning; she stayed home all day. Thus, I got a taste of the traditional American family that in some circles is so lovingly remembered today.

But as I came of age in the late 1960s and early 1970s, I found myself stepping into a fresh, feminist world. My mother returned to graduate school, then launched a professional career. My female classmates in high school and college competed with me for grades and jobs. "A woman needs a man like a fish needs a bicycle" one popular bumper sticker trumpeted at the time. And I occasionally found it hazardous to disagree.

It was in the echo of this era that I met my wife, Kelly. We crossed paths on the job in 1983, both in our mid-twenties. I was lured by her luminous smile and optimism. Our differences in personality, sexuality, and family background made for a tumultuous courtship. But something told us not to give up, and after four years of struggle, we pledged ourselves to each other for life.

And then our troubles *really* began.

I remember a particularly rude awakening in the first year of our marriage. The bedside clock blazed 3:02 A.M., but it was Kelly who was in a state of alarm. Pushing at my shoulder, she said: "We've got to talk *right now*." I extracted myself from the arms of sleep and rolled to face her. It was the third night in a row she'd awakened me this way. As before, she was sitting back against the headboard, sheet pulled to her waist. "I realize now that we have to get divorced," she said steadily. And then she concluded, "The sooner the better."

I have never been a morning person. But I tried nonetheless to catch on to the rhythm of this conversation. "Yes, we're having problems," I thought to myself. We'd been sexless for weeks. Finances were tight. And worst of all, I was not meeting her standards of affection; cuddling, hand-holding, and little nothings, it turned out, did not come readily from the married me.

Despite my haze, I knew that my response in that bed would be momentous. And so I paused before I launched. "It may be so," Kelly remembers me finally saying. "It may be that we've made a huge mistake. It may be that our life together is over. But"—and here is where I got to the crux of my response—"I am not going to talk about it right now. I'm not going to talk about something this important in the middle of the night."

Then I dove back into the mattress and fell asleep.

Eighteen years of marriage later, Kelly and I can look back and smile at that moment. Since that wake-up call, we've grappled with our physical needs, spending habits, household chores, and a laundry list of other differences and disagreements. Some of these issues could actually be labeled as "solved." The great majority of them have resulted in hopeful accommodations, wobbly compromises, and agreements to disagree.

And yet, buoyed by my research on this book, I've learned to trust those compromises, to celebrate those temporary agreements. They're really all a married couple has. While marriage may be a venerable institution with a history many thousands of years old, each bond remains fragile.

It appears to be wives who most often call attention to this fragility, to the struggles and shortcomings of their marriages. But most husbands are well aware that difficulties exist. In the past forty years, they just haven't felt comfortable in speaking. My hope was to change that. From mid-2003 until late 2004, I crisscrossed the country, determined to talk about marriage with as many and as varied a collection of husbands as I possibly could.

Using my contacts from years of writing about men, I found husbands in their living rooms, kitchens, backyards, dens, and workplaces. I met with jobless men in downtown parks and inmates in jail. Sometimes, we talked for hours in our first meeting as I explored the man's "relationship history": the marriages they had seen as children; their own early love relationships; their initial meeting with their wives; the decision to marry; and the arc of the marriage itself. After this initial conversation, we often spoke or e-mailed frequently in the months that followed.

Not surprisingly, many men were wary at first. I assured them of anonymity (the names used in this book are pseudonyms, and some details are changed), but most did not know me well enough to trust me at first. Some wondered aloud whether it was appropriate to reveal details of this most intimate relationship in their lives. But in the end, virtually all of them did. Ultimately, they came to believe that I was there not to judge them, but to listen to their stories. They also recognized that they might be able to help other couples by sharing those stories in detail.

As I listened, I was struck by both by the vulnerability and the astuteness of their responses. We've been led to believe that men are emotionally disabled, relationally inept. Yet most of the husbands I interviewed were nothing like this stereotype. They could identify the troublesome dynamics in their marriages, their marital strengths, and the series of trade-offs they had made to maintain their relationship.

I also heard about one of the pervasive differences between them and their wives: the way they experience intimacy. Women, having grown up with talking as the currency of communication, often define intimacy as face-to-face conversation on important topics. "How do you feel?" is a common conversation starter for women. For many husbands who hear those words, they are a conversation killer.

Men grow up in a boy culture that emphasizes action and teamwork, so it made sense to me when they said they felt closest to their wives when they were not face to face, but side by side. Working on a home project, attending a ball game together, sitting in the front seat of a car on a long drive—these (along with the activity of sex) were the men's most commonly mentioned moments of marital closeness.

In my in-depth conversations with seventy husbands, I also was struck by some trends and tendencies among them. I noticed, for example, that men who spoke highly of their fathers tended to be in good marriages, a connection that had rarely been analyzed. It also emerged from these in-depth interviews that husbands who felt that housework was shared fairly—and whose wives felt the same way—had happier sex lives.

In an effort to objectively test these and other observations, I contracted with Dr. Ronald Langley at the University of Kentucky's Survey Research Center to conduct a national telephone survey of close to three hundred husbands. The results of the VoiceMale Survey confirmed the connection between good fathers and good marriages. It confirmed the relationship between housework and sex. And it offered scores of other insights into men's attitudes and activities in marriage. (See "A Note on the Research," at the end of the book, for more details.)

In the following pages, you will find the results of both the VoiceMale Survey (288 husbands) and my in-depth interviews (70 husbands) blended together through four sections. In Part One, "Why Men Marry," you'll learn what men are looking for in potential wives, why they make the decision to marry, and what impact the wedding itself has on them.

In Part Two, "The Arc of the Relationship," you're invited to follow the husband's perspective through four major phases of marriage: the honeymoon phase (the first three years of marriage); the family phase (years four to twenty); the empty-nest phase (years twenty-one to thirty-five); and the mature marriage phase (years thirty-six and beyond).

Part Three of the book, called "VoiceMale," will focus on several of the most important findings from my survey, including the link between sex and housework; the impact of fathers on shaping men into husbands; the willingness of husbands to change; the impact of affairs; and how a man's second marriage tends to differ from his first.

Finally, in Part Four, "How Men *Do* Marriage," I'll outline what I came to see as the masculine style of loving. It's a style that emerges from the combination of men's biology and training.

In the course of the chapters ahead, you will meet, up close, husbands of all ages, races, religions, and backgrounds. You will hear words that will both inspire and appall you. You will see couples in the throes of lovemaking and mischief-making. You will smell the anger, feel the blows. And, if you are like me, you will be uplifted by the time you finish this book. That's because you'll discover that despite our many differences—in expression, aggression, and emotion—most husbands and wives ultimately want the same thing: a safe, caring fellow traveler in their journey through life.

N.J.C.

Part One

WHY MEN MARRY

Chapter One

<small>—꩜—</small>

THE SPARK

I was going through some dark times. All of a sudden, here came this girl.
She was bubbling, extroverted. I got the enthusiasm.
—Thirty-nine-year-old electrician

I<small>T BEGAN WITH THE FLASH</small> of an ankle.

On an unseasonably mild midwestern day in January 1989, Rob Reilly gathered up the dirty clothes in his apartment, stuffed them into a cloth bag, and hauled them through the student ghetto toward the local Laundromat. He was in a gloomy mood. In his first five months of graduate school, he'd already had his heart broken once. Then, just as things seemed promising with a second woman, she'd exposed a bigoted side that offended Rob. He'd determined to break it off with her this very night.

At thirty-two years of age, Rob was becoming "disappointed and discouraged, even pessimistic" about finding a woman to marry, he recalls. Approaching the Laundromat, "I was thinking: 'Maybe I'm just one of those guys who's destined to be alone. I'll become a career man.'"

This thought was particularly distressing because Rob had returned to school in part to find a life partner. After six years as an actor and waiter in New York City, he wanted stability. He'd even written down the attributes of a potential wife: She should be "smart, opinionated, independent, and sexy."

Was he expecting too much? Did he have what it took to attract such a woman? In part to take his mind off such questions, he had brought with him to the Laundromat his first draft of a letter to the governor of the state. Rob opposed capital punishment and planned to hone an anti-death-penalty argument while his clothes got clean.

The Laundromat was abuzz when Rob arrived, but he found a vacant washer and emptied his laundry bag. He plugged in the requisite number of quarters, then deposited himself on one of the anchored yellow plastic chairs that lined the room. Elbows on knees, he focused on the letter at hand.

A few minutes later, the ankle flashed into view. It was attached to the woman sitting two seats to his left. Wearing black pants and brown sandals, she crossed her left knee over her right to reveal, as Rob recalls, "several inches of leg, beginning just below the calf and narrowing to this perfect ankle. I've never been very interested in thin women, and this ankle wasn't thin. But it was the perfect shape. . . . I caught it in my left periphery, and I thought to myself, 'Now that is nice. That is a *really* nice ankle.'"

For a few moments, Rob hovered over his letter, stealing occasional glances at the woman's lightly bouncing foot. Then, feigning interest in the status of his laundry, he glanced up to see the rest of the woman. She was dark-haired, dark-eyed, full-lipped, and broad-shouldered. His interest was in no way dampened.

Rob scoured his mind for something to say, but as is the case with many men, the fear of sounding trite asserted itself. A few minutes went by, and two children on plastic riding toys clambered across the floor in front of him. That's when Rob's first noncommittal words emerged. "Boy, those kids have a lot of energy," he said aloud. The woman didn't hesitate: "Actually, I wish I knew who the parents were." Then, gesturing toward the kids, she added, "They ought to have some limits on them."

Rob was intrigued by this response. But before he could say more, the woman was inquiring about his letter. Soon they were in a friendly debate over capital punishment. During the next forty-five minutes, with interruptions only for washer-to-dryer transitions, the two ranged over politics, education, feminism, and other topics. He learned that her name was Sandy, she was a teacher, a year older than he was, recently divorced, childless, and full of energy and opinions. He found her very stimulating.

Eventually, the bedspread Sandy had brought to the Laundromat was dry. She folded it and prepared to leave. Rob recalls, "A red light started flashing in my mind. I kept telling myself, 'Ask her out now, or forget it.'"

Finally, he summoned the courage: "Maybe we could go out and have a beer sometime."

Sandy replied: "Why not tonight?"

Within weeks of their meeting, Rob and Sandy were dating exclusively. Less than a year later, they exchanged vows in the home of a friend. Today, fifteen years into their marriage, the couple lives in a college town in the Southeast, raising two middle-school-aged children. As one might imagine from that initial meeting, their relationship has been both passionate and occasionally volatile. Through it all, however, the legacy of the Laundromat lives on. As Rob says: "It was there that I saw the essence of who she is. Yes, I thought she was beautiful. But it was her assertiveness, her intelligence, her energy that captured me."

There's little debate that a woman's physical appearance is a crucial factor in attracting a man. Influenced by his culture's focus on the female form, and by his biology too, the typical American man responds to physical cues: a tapered ankle, a narrow waist, shapely calves, silky skin over high cheekbones. Indeed, 55 percent of the men in the VoiceMale Survey said that they had initially been drawn to their future wife by some aspect of her looks.

This focus on physical attributes may have biological roots. Evolutionary psychologists remind us that the most basic drive of all creatures is to perpetuate their genetic line. Recent research indicates that women with thin waists and full hips—attributes that men across cultures name as desirable—are most likely to have successful pregnancies. Thus, a man's attraction to a curvaceous woman apparently gives him the best chance of healthy children to carry on his genes. (Similar studies indicate that women are initially drawn to tall men with strong builds, indicators of the man's ability to provide for the woman and her children.)

But biology is not destiny. Even in a culture where curves and cleavage are fully exploited by marketers, the vast majority of men marry women who are less than physically ideal. Numerous studies show that men, in fact, tend to approach women who are comparable to them in physical attractiveness. *Rather than seeking to meet women of unattainable beauty, they tend to seek out the beauty in the women they meet.* It turns out that this is a good strategy. According to the VoiceMale Survey, men who say they were initially attracted to their wife by her physical attributes alone are less satisfied in their marriages than those for whom personality was key.

"Most men would not consider my wife a ten," one forty-seven-year-old teacher told me. "She's a little bigger than average. But she has dagger-like eyes . . . . She's always been attractive to me." Another man, who said that neither he nor his wife "would ever be mistaken for a model," added, "She has a smile that puts the sun to shame." Even for this man, however, physical attraction to his future wife "only opened the negotiations. It didn't close the deal." Rather, when a man is seeking a long-term relationship (as opposed to a short-term liaison), he tends to look beyond her physical attributes to a host of less tangible assets, including her attitude, bearing, and character.

Before we examine more closely what men say they look for in a potential wife, it's important to emphasize that men entertain the idea of marriage only when they're ready. And readiness is different for men of different eras. Among husbands I interviewed who married in the 1930s through the early 1960s, readiness tended to come when they had a job that would allow them to support a wife and family. Men who married in more recent years usually judged their readiness by their flagging interest in the singles scene. "One morning, I woke up next to a woman who could have been a Playboy model," one man told me, "and I didn't want her." That's when he realized that sex alone would not truly satisfy him, and that marriage might.

David M. Buss, a professor of psychology at the University of Texas, has discovered that both women and men distinguish between short-term and long-term potential mates. In a study of ten thousand people from thirty-seven countries, Buss found that when seeking a short-term mate, as compared with a potential wife, men cared less about education, devotion, social skills, generosity, honesty, independence, kindness, intellectuality, loyalty, sense of humor, wealth, responsibility, spontaneity, courteousness, and emotional stability.

In short, a man who is looking for short-term connection is usually satisfied with someone who looks good enough. But when he begins the search for someone with whom to build a life, his standards change dramatically.

Every husband has a unique story to tell of meeting his wife. Over the past three years, I've had the chance to hear scores of them. And when I examine what personality traits men describe as initially most attractive about their wives, one attribute stands out: *a positive temperament.* Men measure the *mood* of the women they might marry. And not surprisingly, they prefer a woman who is in a generally positive frame of mind.

Here's a sampling of what husbands said they noticed first about the personalities of their future wives:

- "She was the life of the party. She just generated energy in a gathering."
- "I found her so vivacious and alive. I remember saying to myself, 'I'm going to take that woman out sometime.'"
- "She was outspoken and enthusiastic. She had this openness and joy."
- "I was going through some dark times. All of a sudden, here came this girl. She was bubbling, extroverted. I got the enthusiasm."
- "I look people in the eyes. I looked into her eyes and saw merriment."

Men emphasize mood because they recognize that marrying a woman means being permanently within the sphere of her energy. Indeed, many of the men I spoke with said they had spent their childhoods in homes where their mother's temperament dominated. If she was angry, bitter, or depressed most of the time, others in the house tended to feel that way too. If, on the other hand, she radiated optimism and warmth, that attitude permeated the home.

In addition, since males tend to be discouraged in childhood from freely expressing their emotions (except, in some cases, anger), many are attracted to women who are vibrantly expressive. "I wanted someone who could bring me out," one sixty-three-year-old engineer told me. "I'm a social animal, but I'm shy. I thought [my wife] would bring some excitement into my life."

Of course, first impressions can be deceiving; women who seem initially upbeat are rarely that way all the time. And men acknowledge that it's unrealistic, and probably unhealthy, to expect a woman to be perpetually cheerful. Nonetheless, based on my conversations with scores of husbands, when a man in search of a wife meets a woman who is drawn toward the positive, he tends to be drawn toward her.

Close behind physical beauty and an optimistic outlook in initially attracting a man is another personality trait: self-confidence. Rob Reilly, the man who met his wife in the Laundromat, remembers that after Sandy agreed to the date with him, she headed for the Laundromat door, then suddenly wheeled around and returned to him. "I have just one question," she told him. "Do you have a drug or alcohol problem?"

The question (to which Rob answered no) signaled to him that Sandy would not compromise her integrity just to date him. While some men might have been scared off by Sandy's assertiveness, Rob, who was looking for a long-term relationship with an independent woman, says he was turned on by it.

This emphasis on a woman's self-confidence was especially prevalent among men who were married in the last thirty years or so. According to my in-depth interviews, men who married prior to 1975, and particularly those who married before 1965, tended to judge a potential wife in good part on her domesticity—her apparent ability to take care of a home and children. Since then, men seem to show increasing interest in whether a potential wife can earn a decent share of the family income. As a result, recently married men have tended to seek a woman who is strong and confident, someone who can handle herself in the working world.

Self-confidence is such a strong attraction for some men that even when they are not looking for a wife, they may suddenly change their mind when they meet a woman who exudes strength.

One afternoon in the spring of 1988, Porter Williams, then aged thirty, was driving down a busy boulevard near his Baltimore home when he noticed a Grand Prix parked on the shoulder. Passing it, he caught a glimpse of two women leaning over the engine compartment. "Honestly," Porter told me, "what I saw was a pair of yellow shorts and two fine legs. I decided to make a U-turn."

Porter, a middle-school teacher, was not handy with cars but hoped the problem was merely a dead battery or a loose wire. Unfortunately, he couldn't fix the problem. But while tinkering unsuccessfully under the hood, Porter learned that the car was rented and offered to ferry the women back to the agency where they'd picked it up.

Unlike Rob Reilly, Porter was not shy when flirting with women. He'd been a high-school football star, and he remained handsome and muscular more than a decade later. He believed in his ability to charm. And he'd had plenty of practice. Porter, an African-American man, told me he grew up in the inner city with a father who was prone to infidelity. In his father's mold, Porter also came to objectify women, he said. Throughout his twenties, Porter hung out with a group of friends at strip clubs and bars, looking for sexual relationships. Before meeting the woman in the yellow shorts, Porter told me with regret, he'd had two children by two different women.

Sex, he acknowledged, was on his mind as he drove to the rental agency. In the car, he began the seduction of Sara, the woman in the yellow shorts. He flattered her, let it be known that he was unmarried and available, and eventually asked for her phone number. A week later, he took her to dinner on their first date. Then he invited her back to his apartment, poured drinks, filled the room with soft music, and, in his words, "tried to get her to spend the night."

That's when she rebelled. "If you think I'm a one-night stand, you can forget it!" Porter remembers Sara declaring. Then she did something that floored him. She opened her purse, counted out the $80 that he'd spent for dinner and drinks, and thrust the cash toward him. "If [having sex] is why we went out, I'll pay for my dinner," she said, "and I'll pay for yours too."

Porter refused the money and apologized. As he now recalls, "I didn't try anything else that night, and she did go home."

It took some convincing to get Sara to date him again, but gradually, Porter gained her trust. Two years after meeting, the couple married. Today, they're parents of a twelve-year-old daughter; they're raising one of Porter's other children too. Sara's offer to refund his meal money on that first date "made me respect her," Porter says. "I've never lost that respect."

While in this case self-respect and chastity were linked, they are not the same thing. Most men, in fact, are not looking for virgins to marry. Indeed, several told me that they specifically did *not* want to marry a sexually inexperienced woman. A survey of couples that has been repeated several times over fifty-seven years confirms the relatively low priority that American men place on having a virgin bride: The survey showed that among eighteen "mate characteristics" that men desired, chastity was 10th most important in 1939, 13th in 1956, 15th in 1967, 17th in 1977, 17th in 1984, and 16th in 1996.

Beyond physical beauty, a positive outlook, and self-respect, the men I surveyed named a handful of other attributes that initially attracted them to women they would later marry. Here are the most common of those:

Brains. Like Rob Reilly of the Laundromat, John Karl was one of several men I interviewed who, when they were single, put down on paper a list of attributes they sought in a wife. At the top of John's list was intelligence. John, a fifty-four-year-old marketing specialist, had been married once in his twenties. Intellectually speaking, he recalls, his first wife could not keep up with him. In arguments, he would overwhelm her with logic and mental gymnastics.

The woman who would become wife number two was different. When he met her, John was in his early forties and one of the top professionals in his field. She was the new woman in the office. As he recalls upon first setting eyes on her, "She looked graceful and floating, lithe and ethereal, just beautiful." Only on their first date did John realize that in addition to being physically attractive "she was one of the smartest people I'd ever met. I could talk with her about my work. I couldn't put anything over on her. She was absolutely brilliant."

In fact, in what he acknowledges has been an up-and-down twelve-year marriage, John counts his wife's intelligence as a top reason for sticking it out.

Another man in his mid-forties told me the following story about his intellectual connection with his wife-to-be. He was working for an environmental protection agency. Lori, a female teacher from a local community college, asked him to lead a field trip for her students to a local stream. That day, during a conversation with him and two other people, Lori said, "You know, getting people out to the creek like this would be a great way to develop public support for infrastructure financing."

Several years later, the man told me: "Her technical vocabulary, insight, and understanding of one of my key professional goals caused a visible, physical reaction in me. My heart melted." The other two people in the conversation, he recalls, "immediately noticed my change in respiration rate, temperature, and skin color, [but] she was oblivious. It took me two years to get a date with her, and two years after that, she said yes to my proposal."

Motherliness. Some of the husbands I surveyed said that before they married they were not interested in dating a woman who already had children. But a few said exactly the opposite. "Her sons were a plus to me," recalls a fifty-three-year-old business consultant, married twenty-four years. "I was kind of looking for a ready-made family." When this man first discussed marriage with his then girlfriend, she warned him, "My sons will always come first." He took that as an indication of what a loyal person she was. "I understood it, and I accepted it."

Another man, now forty-nine and married for seventeen years, said he was first attracted to his future wife when he saw her at a pool with her three young children. "She was very attentive to the kids; she looked them in the eye; she smiled at them; she didn't let them run wild; she kept talking to them," he remembered. "I could tell she was a really responsible person."

Still another man, forty-three and recently married, told me by e-mail: "For me, having a built-in family was very attractive, as I had lost a baby during my previous marriage. Her son has filled a space in my life that had been previously empty." This man also wrote that he feels closest to his wife when "we do things that involve our boy."

Devoutness. Peter Kahana, at age twenty-six, had recently given up alcohol after several years of almost daily partying. A day laborer and native
Hawaiian, he decided to seek spiritual nourishment and new friends by attending a Christian church. There, he met Barbara during the postworship
coffee hour. For many weeks, they saw each other only on Sunday morn-
ings. Then he asked her out.

Twenty-three years into their marriage, Peter, now a records clerk at a
small hospital in Oregon, remembers what drew him to Barbara: "I was attracted to her character. She would talk about God. Other women I knew
wouldn't do that. . . . She was real, not trying to flaunt anything. She accepted people where they're at. Everybody was valuable to her." Peter adds,
"I was a good person, but she made me want to be better."

Peter's attraction to Barbara gradually grew over several months; it was
not love at first sight. This is typical. Most husbands reported some level of
attraction at first, followed by a long, slow buildup of connection. In 5 percent of cases, according to the VoiceMale Survey, husbands said they had
been *not at all attracted* to their wives on first meeting. Only over time did
a spark kindle.

But every now and then, a man knows almost immediately that he's
met his match. According to my survey, 8 percent of husbands knew they
wanted to marry their wife within a week of meeting her; an additional 5
percent said they knew within a month.

Kevin O'Leary had "a sense of something big" the day he met his wife-
to-be. The meeting occurred one evening in 1976, as Kevin and a group
of twenty-something young-professional friends gathered in one of their
homes for their daily beer and banter. Kevin had moved to Southern
California from the East Coast a year earlier to escape the influence of
his parents but was continuing his father's legacy of drinking too much.
His recent relationships with women, he recalls, had tended toward the
short and disastrous.

And then Carolyn walked into the room. Fresh from the Midwest,
where she'd grown up and attended college, she was new to the group.
Kevin involuntarily sat taller on the couch as Carolyn was introduced

around. He noticed her deep blue eyes and trim figure. But it was "the subtle bend in her nose, and a chipped front tooth" that particularly intrigued him. "At the time, I had no idea what was so compelling about her." But he knew he was attracted.

In the moment, Kevin did what many men do when they are drawn to a woman: He searched for "a flicker of interest" in Carolyn's face. To his dismay, he found none.

Weeks later, Kevin learned that Carolyn had begun dating one of his best friends. He accepted this grudgingly—"I was used to disappointment," he told me—and gradually became friends with Carolyn too. A couple of years later, he was an usher in her wedding to his friend.

Then, just a week before Carolyn and her husband were to move permanently back to her home state, Carolyn told Kevin, in a fit of honesty, that she'd always been interested in him. Kevin's response: "I'm going to kiss you now." And he did.

Thus began an affair that lasted, off and on, for the next six years. Carolyn and her husband went through with their move to her home state. After that, Kevin saw Carolyn once a year or less, when she came to California alone. Each time she left Kevin to return to her husband, Kevin recalls, "I was miserable. I'd always had a drinking problem, and it got worse."

Finally, in his mid-thirties, after a DUI arrest, Kevin quit alcohol and decided to bring the Carolyn issue to a conclusion. On Carolyn's next visit, Kevin was determined not merely to fall in bed with her. Rather, handing her a half-dozen red roses—"one for each year I'd been in love with her"—Kevin made the following statement: "I won't accept the crumbs anymore. I love you and I want to be with you. It's one way or the other."

Carolyn never returned to her husband. Eighteen years later, Kevin and Carolyn are happily married, he reports, raising a teenaged son, and running an advertising business together. Now aged fifty-three, Kevin still remembers that first glimpse of Carolyn in vivid detail. "There was something in her face that told me I could trust her with who I am," he says. "I could bare my soul. I just knew that whatever I brought to her—all my fears, all my vulnerabilities—they would be safe. . . . The best part is that what I thought intuitively has since unfolded."

Interestingly, my survey shows that a man who knows within a month of meeting a woman that he wants to marry her is likely to be happier in the marriage than a man who takes longer to decide. Three-quarters of those who knew within a month described themselves as "very happy" in their marriages compared to 56 percent of those who took a year or longer to make a decision. Not surprisingly, the only area where men who decide quickly had more problems was in their relationships with their wife's parents. Apparently, some women's parents are skeptical of short courtships.

Kevin O'Leary met his future wife at a casual gathering of friends. Rob Reilly happened upon his at the Laundromat. Porter Williams needed a U-turn to get his first close-up look at his wife-to-be. When we think of the "singles scene" in today's America, many of us may imagine raucous bars or alcohol-drenched nightclubs. But, according to the VoiceMale Survey, it's a rare marriage that begins that way.

- 24 percent of husbands met their wives in school, some as early as elementary school. Those married more than thirty-five years were most likely to have met their wives in school (36 percent).
- 18 percent met their wives at a social event, such as a dance, party, or wedding.
- 18 percent were introduced to their wives by friends or family members.
- 14 percent met their wives at work. This figure has changed dramatically since the middle of the last century. Among those married more than thirty-five years, only 2 percent met their wives at work. This compares to 23 percent of those married in the past three years. This change is no doubt due to the influx of women into the workplace.

- 6 percent met their wives at a bar.
- 4 percent met their wives at church, at synagogue, or in another religious setting.
- 1 percent met their wives online.

Which kind of meeting results in the best marriages? My survey suggested that husbands who were introduced to their future wives by friends and family members were most likely to pronounce themselves happy in their marriages later on. The size of my survey sample was not large enough to confirm this as statistically significant, but my personal interviews supported the theory: Those who know us best may know what—and who—is best for us.

Because of the newness of online dating, no studies have yet been completed on whether marriages that begin online are more or less successful in the long term than those that start in more traditional ways. Online matchmaking tends to rely less on physical attractiveness (photos are usually available, but self-selected) than on résumés and self-descriptive abilities. I interviewed two men who had met their wives online, and the evidence was mixed.

One fifty-eight-year-old man who had left a long first marriage met his wife through an Internet dating service. "I put my set of criteria out there, and her name came up. I sent her my profile," he told me. Both were on spiritual quests, and they e-mailed back and forth on that and other subjects for four months before meeting at a restaurant. In person, they gradually warmed to each other. After several months of dating, they decided to move in together, and a year later they married.

When I spoke with the man, however, he and his wife had separated after three years together. He told me that his wife had been living alone as an adult for twenty years before marrying him; she could not get comfortable with sharing decision-making. In addition, he added, "I had difficulty expressing emotions." The fact that they'd met online, he believed, wasn't a factor in the split-up.

Another man, a fifty-one-year-old artist who had been twice divorced, told me he had met his wife in a chat room four years earlier. He found that "she was willing to go deep" in their e-mail conversations. When they met at a neighborhood bar after a few weeks, "I felt a spark immediately."

Now, two years into the marriage, the man says he's in this relationship for life. "We made all our mistakes in our previous relationships," he told me. He said that meeting online had been efficient because he hadn't wasted time dating women with whom he had little in common.

One question I'm often asked about mate selection is whether opposites attract. There is some evidence that they do. As noted at the beginning of this chapter, men often seek women who are open and expressive to complement their own less animated personalities.

But most of the evidence supports the theory that "like attracts like." Research over the past twenty years shows that men marry women who are comparable to themselves in age, height, socioeconomic status, political and religious orientation, even nose breadth, earlobe length, and consumption of cigarettes. My survey supported the likes-attract theory. For example, even though interracial marriage has been legal throughout the United States for more than two generations, the VoiceMale survey showed that, even today, only 5 percent of men marry someone of a different racial background.

Another question I often hear about selecting a husband or wife is: When is the best age to meet a spouse? According to my survey, the *most common time* is between the ages of nineteen and twenty-four; more than a third of men reported meeting their future wives in this age period. But the survey showed that overall, the age at which a man meets his wife does not predict his level of happiness in the marriage. The age that a man meets his wife does apparently affect the *subjects of disagreements* that arise in these marriages. Couples that meet before the age of twenty-five tend to have more disagreements about sex, and more affairs, than those who meet at later ages.

One trend that is disturbing to social observers is the increasingly high expectations that both genders—even *before* meeting their spouses—place on marriage. The National Marriage Project at Rutgers University published a survey in 2001 in which 94 percent of 20-to-29-year-olds agreed with the statement "When you marry, you want your spouse to be your soul mate, first and foremost."

The authors of the survey, Barbara Dafoe Whitehead and David Popenoe, said these results are troubling. "While marriage is losing much of its broad public and institutional character," they wrote, "it is gaining popularity as a SuperRelationship, an intensely private spiritualized union. . . . Other bases for the marital relationship, such as an economic partnership or parental partnership, have receded in importance or disappeared altogether."

I interviewed Popenoe in 2004. At the time, he was seventy-one years old and had himself been married for forty-four years. He said that he believed men and women in today's marriage market would be more successful if they focused "less on finding the right mate than on being the right mate."

He worried that the soul mate expectation was feeding the high divorce rate. He said: "A surprising number of young people believe that there's one person out there who can complete them, one person who is chemically perfect for them. Once they get into a marriage and things go bad—as they do at times in almost every marriage—they think they've picked the wrong person." Their manner of dealing with this disappointment, Popenoe laments, is often to leave a marriage that may be salvageable.

Popenoe went on to say that the goal of having a soul mate is a good one, but "it's a lifetime goal. It's not a realistic goal in *pursuit* of a spouse. What *is* a realistic goal is to find someone who shares as many values with you as possible, so that you can become best friends." Ultimately, he believes, an enduring friendship is the foundation of an enduring marriage.

First Kisses

Computer programmer, fifty-four, married twelve years: *"It was in my car. We had taken a ride. It was a fairly warm summer evening, and we drove at night through the back roads and villages of New England. The longer we drove, the more I thought about kissing her and finally couldn't stand it anymore, and pulled the car over to the side of the road. She said, 'What's wrong?' 'Nothing's wrong. I just really want to kiss you.' And I did."*

Minister, forty-three, married six years: *"It was on Valentine's Day the year we met. After a very nice evening out, I felt sparks flying and asked her if I could kiss her. She said yes. I felt a very strong emotional connection. [She] told me later that she knew on that night she was going to marry me."*

Electrician, fifty-six, married thirty-five years: *"Wow, that was a long time ago, but I can remember it like it was yesterday. We had gone out 'for a Coke,' which I spilled on her, at a local drive-in restaurant. When we got back to her home, we planned a double date with my then future sister-in-law and my high-school friend who had fixed us up. We went to the Moonlite Drive-in movie theater to see the original McHale's Navy. I drove my '56 Chevy, and the other couple was in the back seat. I know they were not watching the movie, so I thought I'd try my luck with a first kiss. She seemed sincere and caring when we kissed, and I liked that. Both drive-ins are long, long gone now, but the kisses are still the same."*

Graphic artist, forty-eight, married sixteen years: *"My future wife gave me a 'coupon' for a kiss in a birthday card that she gave me just before we seriously started dating. I remember that kiss vividly. It was electric! That kiss promised a lot."*

Technical writer, forty, married six years: *"I remember it well. I found her to be just so beautiful. The more I knew her, the more I was attracted to her and knew she was the one. She lived in a tiny apartment. There was a small 'hall' that was really a place to enter two bedrooms, a bathroom, and a linen closet. One day, I found us both in this place. I kind of couldn't help myself. A bit roughly, I pinned her to the linen closet and kissed her. As she fell back a few inches into the linen closet doors, her body made a thud sound. I planted a big kiss on her lips. She tasted like nothing I had ever experienced. I was maybe fiftyfold more in love with her in those few seconds."*

Chapter Two

⌇

THE DECISION

There was no thunderclap, no parting of the clouds.
We were both moving in that direction for a long time.
—Forty-year-old college administrator

H E HAD SEEN IT PLAYED OUT in the movies many times: A smitten man searches for the perfect diamond ring, invites his beloved to a swanky restaurant, arrives for the date with bouquet in hand. Later, perhaps between the appetizers and entrée, the man rises from his seat, bends to one knee, and asks the woman to be his bride. As tears flow down her reddening cheeks, fellow diners rise to applaud.

Growing up in Los Angeles in the 1960s and 1970s, William Suzuki, a second-generation Japanese-American, imagined that he would propose in this, or an even more dramatic, way. Years later, as a thirty-year-old management consultant, he still envisioned a stirring proposal in his future. By then, he had been with his girlfriend Rachel for two years and had begun "chewing on" the idea of marriage, he recalls. Still, he adds, "I hadn't gone through the whole spreadsheet in my head—the pluses and minuses—and how it would all work. I didn't think I was ready to ask her."

But it happened anyway. In the wee hours of a summer's night in the first apartment they shared, William and Rachel made love in their bed. As they lay in the darkness afterward, the question seemed to arise on its own.

"Do you want to get married?" William said.

There was a pause and then her near-whisper: "Are you asking me?"

And his response: "Yes, I'm asking you."

"I had always imagined something out of Hollywood," William told me eight years later. "Maybe we'd be at the Super Bowl. I'd point to the scoreboard, and our names would be there. Thousands of people would be looking on. It turns out we're in bed, in a tiny apartment, in the wrong part of town, with a mishmash of furniture, in the middle of the night, just the two of us. . . . I have no regrets."

The conventional wisdom is that men run from commitment. Threatened with "confinement" in a marriage, it is alleged, males become Houdini-like, scrambling to shed their chains. Yet this image doesn't square with two simple facts: First, the U.S. Census Bureau reports that nearly nine out of ten American men will marry at least once in their lifetime. And secondly, according to the VoiceMale Survey, men do the marriage-proposing 85 percent of the time. (Women propose 3 percent of the time; in the rest of the cases, couples agree to marry without a proposal.) At least formally, it is overwhelmingly men who initiate the marital commitment.

Certainly, some men propose under pressure. Several husbands told me their girlfriends had threatened to break up with them unless they committed to marriage. But among the men I surveyed, those reluctant husbands were in the minority. Rather, for a variety of practical, cultural, and emotional reasons, most American men seek a committed relationship that will go on for the rest of their lives.

In his groundbreaking book *Who Will Marry Whom?* psychologist Bernard I. Murstein tells the story of the son of a French aristocrat, living several hundred years ago, who heard that his father had offered the son in marriage to a certain young woman. The younger man asked his father whether this was true. "Son," the father is said to have replied, "mind your own business."

Arranged marriages like this one are almost unheard of in American culture today. But they were commonplace in the early days of the American republic. At that time, families, particularly fathers, took charge of matchmaking, joining with other clans for economic, political, and social advantage. Romantic love existed, but it generally grew after the wedding or occurred outside the marriage bond.

By the early 1800s, the fundamental American values of consent and individual choice began to invade the marriage realm. While men still held legal rights far beyond those of women, including the right to own property and have sex with their wives against their will, both partners became increasingly involved in the mate-selection process. This right of consent applied to Americans of all classes, but not to the millions of slaves, whose marriages went unrecognized by the U.S. government until the Civil War.

Even in the first half of the twentieth century, love and romance continued to be less than primary motives for men to marry. More than a dozen of the men I interviewed had married prior to 1950. Here's a sampling of what they said about why they had asked their wives to marry them:

> Retired milkman, ninety-three years old, married in 1937: "I met her at a dance. We went out a couple of times. She was a sturdy woman. [Marrying her] seemed like a good idea."
>
> Retired factory worker, eighty-two years old, married in 1948: "We grew up together, lived on the same street. I was friends with her older brothers. When it was time to hitch up, I figured she was a nice girl. She was a homelike girl. . . . So far, I got no complaints."
>
> Retired teacher, ninety-two years old, married in 1938: "She had a good family background. She was a Baptist. We liked each other, and liked what we did together."
>
> Retired engineer, ninety-five, married in 1940: "There was no infatuation. There was just something right about it. . . . I wonder about this infatuation business. I'd lived with ups and downs. I wanted a stable life, and she was a stable girl."

Some of these men acknowledged another reason for marrying that is rarely cited by today's new husbands: they wanted to have sex for the first time. Prior to 1967, according to the VoiceMale Survey, just 22 percent of men had sexual intercourse with their wives before marriage. Women were often considered loose or coarse if they weren't "pure" on their wedding day.

Several older men told me that their future wives set clear sexual boundaries before marriage. Thus, wanting to consummate the relationship, some of these men proposed. "I know it's not a good reason, but I was very, very eager" for sex, said one man, who has been married to the same woman since 1945. "We even chose the wedding date so she wouldn't be on her period."

Beginning in the early 1960s, male-female dynamics in America underwent an enormous upheaval. Emboldened by the black civil-rights movement of the fifties, the 1963 publication of Betty Friedan's *Feminine Mystique,* and the popularization of the birth-control pill, women began claiming their full freedoms. One result was that women increasingly had sex before marriage. It's no coincidence that men in my survey who married after 1960 rarely said they had done so to have sex with their wives.

The year 1965 was a watershed; marriage rates tumbled, while the number of cohabitations, divorces, and out-of-wedlock births soared. By 1999, living together before marriage had become the norm in America. Among men married three years or less, according to my survey, more than 62 percent lived with their future wives before exchanging formal vows. By contrast, among the forty-nine men I surveyed who had married before 1965, *none* had cohabited with their future wives.

It could be—and was—argued that these societal changes made marriage obsolete, particularly for men. Why would a man who could live with a woman, have sex with her, and even have children with her choose to take the additional step of marrying her? Why would he legally bind himself to a woman, share his (usually larger) income, restrict his (usually greater) freedoms, if he didn't have to?

These are the questions I posed to the men for this chapter. Their responses challenge the myth of male commitment phobia and show that even in an era when marriage is no longer culturally necessary, it is something nonetheless that most men want.

Men may have acquired the image of commitment phobia because it takes considerable time for some to decide to marry. According to my survey, 47 percent of husbands said that at least a year had elapsed between the time they met their future wife and the time they decided they wanted to marry her. Fifteen percent of those men didn't decide for three years or more.

These meeting-to-proposal times have remained about the same for the past sixty years. While men tend to marry later than they used to—at age twenty-seven, compared to age twenty-two in 1960—it's generally because they go through more relationships before settling on a wife. In my survey, 49 percent of men who married in the past three years had at least three serious relationships before meeting their wives. Among men married thirty-five years or longer, only 13 percent had three or more serious relationships; 42 percent had no previous serious relationships.

Through the generations, some men undoubtedly delayed marriage because they were afraid of commitment. But most of the men I interviewed rejected the fear factor. They delay, they say, because they're doing what they've been trained to do: logically evaluate a situation before making a major decision. And this evaluation takes time.

Remember William Suzuki, the man at the beginning of this chapter who made his proposal in the middle of the night instead of planning a Super Bowl proposal? It took about eighteen months from the time he met Rachel until he proposed. His progress toward proposing marriage was typical among the husbands I interviewed.

William and Rachel first met at a church gathering, where he was attracted by her smile and intelligence. When she volunteered at that meeting to help create a new membership database, William decided that he liked databases too and quickly volunteered to join her committee. On subsequent phone calls to discuss church business, the couple seamlessly veered off into personal conversations. William thought early on that "she could be a very significant person in my life."

Prior to his relationship with Rachel, William, then thirty, had tended toward nervousness in his interactions with women. "My experience was to obsess back and forth: Should I call the girl? Should I not call her? What should I say on the phone? How should I say it?" After each phone call, William would judge his performance: "Did I say it right? Oh, I know I didn't say it right." Calling Rachel inspired no such emotional turmoil. He found her receptive and nonjudgmental.

In the first year of their relationship, while living apart in nearby cities, William gradually became comfortable with Rachel's values, sense of humor, sensuality, and vision of her future life. For the most part, they were in synch; where they diverged, William noticed, Rachel seemed willing to meet him halfway.

A year into the relationship, the couple encountered their first major jolt. Rachel got a job offer in another state and asked if William would be willing to move with her. At first he was reluctant and asked for time to think about it. After several days, he still hadn't decided, and she became angry. They even had a blow-up at a restaurant. The experience was difficult, but William learned that they could fight and make up. And he realized that beneath Rachel's external toughness, there existed a vulnerable core. At first, her insecurity scared him, but he came to see it as a positive, a glimpse into the emotional depth that awaited him.

In the end, William chose to quit his job and move with Rachel. He remembers how good it felt the day they blended their CD collections. In the first weeks of living together, however, they struggled to bring their daily rhythms into harmony. William remembers becoming angry one day when Rachel used one of his expensive kitchen knives and broke off the tip. Yet he found that he could forgive her. They enjoyed debriefing at the end of the day, making love, and waking up in the morning together.

After several months of living in the same home, William, who had landed a job as a college administrator, started thinking about marriage. He recalls: "There was no thunderclap, no parting of the clouds. We were both moving in that direction for a long time. . . . Like so much else about our relationship, it felt like a natural progression."

As I mentioned earlier, William hadn't planned to propose to Rachel the night he asked her to marry him. He was inspired by the affection and love he experienced in the moment. He never regretted asking her. As he told me: "I wanted a partner. I wanted a companion. She was my choice. The way I make decisions is I live with something for a while, and then gradually, it becomes clear."

Indeed, that's the way a lot of men make decisions. Among the scores of husbands I interviewed, I heard again and again about a spirit of gradualness: "There was a growing sense of closeness." "It was building up." "I had a feeling of partnership." "It was a slow and steady process." One man told me: "I could be myself with her. I didn't have to watch myself." Another said: "It was a combination of a lot of little things. There were no stars and fireworks. There was an ease." Still another man said: "It was a realization that settled in over time. There was no big epiphany. We both grew comfortable and happy. We had a lot of interests in common and a lot of different interests that would keep us fresh."

If there were few thunderclaps or fireworks when it came to a man's decision to marry, many men claimed specific *reasons* behind the decisions. I asked husbands to reflect on what made them decide to marry.

Forty-two-year-old accountant, married seventeen years: "I was really happy with her. She's good company. We both enjoyed outdoor stuff. We both liked throwing parties. She's easy to talk to. She has a spontaneity that I enjoy. And the sex was great. It still is."

Thirty-year-old teacher, married six years: "She was caring, thoughtful, genuinely interested in me and my interests. We were quick friends. She wasn't one of those types of women I had been avoiding for so long: someone who was vain, materialistic, sexually promiscuous, or empty-minded."

Thirty-five-year-old physical therapist, married four years: "She forced me to think about [getting married] or else end the relationship. This was after four years of dating and two years of living together. It turned out to be a good thing. But I definitely was made to think about it sooner than I naturally would have—which according to her would have been *never*."

Thirty-four-year-old computer programmer, married seven years: "It was very difficult for me [to decide to marry]. I was living in a house with two other bachelors, and the thought of leading a bachelor's life was very appealing. I knew that a wife would surely mean the end of that free-spirited lifestyle. At the same time, I also liked female companionship, and I felt as though family life was the more satisfactory long-term goal."

Thirty-nine-year-old occupational therapist, married six years: "We dated for six or seven years. I decided to take the plunge after speaking with my best friend, who asked me if there was anything I could see myself doing that wouldn't involve [my future wife]."

Forty-seven-year-old attorney, married twenty-five years: "After about six months, I saw her praying fervently in church and decided, 'That's the girl I want to be the mother of my children.' "

As is clear, men's reasons for marrying tend to weave together the practical and the emotional. And in the cases of about 20 percent of the men I interviewed, it was the practical that provided the final push. For these men, while marriage might have happened anyway, they made the decision sooner than later because circumstances convinced them that now was the time.

The most common practical reason for deciding to marry was children, or the prospect of them. As many as 10 percent of the men I interviewed said they had been spurred to marry because their future wives were pregnant. Even in an era when out-of-wedlock births are common and often don't result in marriage, many men chose to give their children a home with two parents from the start.

A typical example is Kenneth Royce of Pittsburgh. He met his future wife, Katherine, in 1989, when he was twenty-six and working for a city sanitation department. Katherine was a twenty-three-year-old store clerk. Kenneth told me that he had been raised by a single mother and considered marriage only when one of his girlfriends brought it up. Then he tended to find a way to end the relationship.

When he first started dating Katherine, he had no intention of marrying her. But when she became pregnant, Kenneth reassessed the situation. As he told me fourteen years later: "My father abandoned me. He threw me away." Having experienced that, Kenneth found that he could not do the same thing to his own son. So he asked Katherine to marry him.

Kenneth says he now realizes that he loved Katherine even at that early point in their relationship and surmises that he would have married her eventually anyway. The pregnancy speeded up his decision. He and Katherine now have three children, ages five to thirteen, and remain strongly connected.

For Adam Masters, a mechanic from Minnesota, it was not a premarital pregnancy but the desire to have children in the future that brought him to a judge's chambers in 1982. Adam and his artist girlfriend, Kate, had been together for three years, attracted by mutual respect and "an ability to gab." Their relationship was losing steam, however, until they began to discuss having kids. Adam loved children and had always wanted to be a father someday. Kate was game, so they decided to marry. Three years later, they had a son. For the next eighteen years, Adam and Kate shared the child-care, housework, moneymaking, and other family obligations.

When I spoke with Adam in 2003, their son was a well-adjusted, high-achieving college freshman. And Adam and Kate had just separated. From the beginning of their relationship, both had considered themselves bisexual, a fact they shared with each other. But Adam's yearnings to be with men had strengthened through the years, and when their son was preparing for college, Adam asked for a separation.

At the time of our interview, Adam and Kate were still legally married but lived several hundred miles apart. Adam reflected on his relationship with Kate: "I do have a sense that to some degree I wasted a couple decades of my life. On the other hand—which does seem to be a much larger hand—I've been in a shared project that has been remarkably successful. We created an extraordinary child. We can celebrate that for the rest of our lives."

Some would argue that marrying Kate primarily to have a child was problematic. But Adam contends that trust is the pillar of any relationship, and that he and Kate remained faithful to each other throughout their years together. While he initiated the breakup, Adam says he did not abandon Kate. "In some ways, I see her now as another sibling; she's an important, ongoing relationship in my life," he told me. As they were splitting up, Adam recalls, they discussed whether to continue to serve as "a safety net" for the other if the need arose. They agreed to do so.

In addition to having kids, men told me they had made the decision to marry for other practical reasons. One said he married while in college in the late 1960s so he could begin a family and avoid being drafted into the Vietnam War. Others said they married for immigration reasons.

Born in Miami to Cuban exiles, Jesus Cardona was twenty when he met a Colombian woman while working at his college's campus newspaper in 1988. "It was love at first sound," Jesus recalls. Chatting with a colleague in his office one day, "I heard this voice, this beautiful voice, in the hallway. . . . It was sultry, sexy."

Jesus was an editor at the paper. The woman, Sofia, a fellow student who was in the United States on a temporary student visa, eventually came to work closely with him. They began a romance. But within a few months, a problem arose: Sofia's mother didn't like Jesus—he was not ambitious enough, in her view.

Jesus told me that he had no interest in getting married at the time. He believed that he was too young. But when Sofia's mother threatened to take Sofia back to Colombia if they continued to date, he responded: "You can't take her away. I'm going to marry her." And he did.

At the time, he was motivated by a "sense of chivalry, honor, and love," Jesus told me. But looking back on the wedding—conducted in three minutes in a "dingy little office" in a courthouse—he is less impressed. "It was a legal maneuver. There was never a proposal, never any rings, never a wedding, never any music, never a honeymoon, and we didn't even tell our friends or most of our relatives. It was cold and unromantic."

Eight years into the marriage, for reasons that Jesus says had less to do with Sofia's mother than his differences with Sofia, the couple divorced.

Another man I interviewed, a sixty-year-old Pennsylvanian, said he and his girlfriend had been living together, unmarried, for four years when they decided to make their union legal for a different kind of practical reason. It was 1996, and the firm where they both worked had just been sold to another, larger company. She had lost her job; his was in jeopardy. As they began looking for new work, they realized that if one of them got a job with health-insurance benefits, the other might not be covered.

As this man tells it, he asked his would-be bride to marry him with these words: "Let's do it as an insurance scam!" The couple remains happily married.

At the beginning of this chapter, William Suzuki spoke about how he had imagined for years what his marriage proposal would be like. Indeed, if women tend to invest their creative energy in wedding planning, many men do the same in preparing their marriage proposals.

Here is a selection of the more imaginative approaches:

A Wisconsin social worker asked his girlfriend to close her eyes, then slipped a ring on her finger made from a twist tie and a glass doorknob. "I told her it was 300 carats and that it would have to do until the real ring was ready." He adds: "She thought it was funny and kept the doorknob to show her coworkers the next day. Eventually, I had to get a new doorknob because she wouldn't give it back."

A California student teamed up with a local newspaper editor to create a Sunday crossword puzzle that spelled "Dear Leslie, will you marry me?" in the center of it. She solved the puzzle and said yes.

An Illinois psychologist who is Jewish learned just enough Punjabi—"*Ma thera nal vya kurna chanda ha*"—to tell his Indian-American girlfriend in her native tongue that he wished to marry her.

Asking a woman to marry him is often one of the most memorable, and nerve-wracking, moments in a man's life. But in some cases, the fear of asking the question pales in comparison to having the proposal accepted.

Three of the men I interviewed told me that in the weeks after their proposals were accepted they had panic attacks, insomnia, and other adverse reactions. One man, a twenty-one-year-old recent college graduate when he married in the 1960s, recalls a night a few weeks after he proposed: "I woke up screaming, like somebody was going to kill me," he recalled.

For several weeks, this man said, he felt "loneliness, despondency, and depression." He continued: "It was a cold, horrible feeling. . . . It was wintertime, things were bleak, my wife[-to-be] was a hundred fifty miles away. There was this gloom. I felt like I was in a muck that I must climb out of." The man went for help to a minister, who told him that "lots of people feel like this" before getting married.

The minister's words didn't ease the turmoil. But the coming of spring, a sympathetic letter from a childhood friend, and reuniting with his fiancée, did help. Looking back four decades later, he offers this analysis: "I was making this big change. Not only was I getting married, but I was becoming a [professional]. I was growing up. But I had all these negative messages about myself [from childhood]. I was trying very hard to suppress them, but they wouldn't go away."

Years later, he would deal with those messages in therapy. Today, he remains married to the woman he proposed to forty years ago.

There continues to be disagreement about why men choose to marry. Evolutionary psychologists suggest that biology plays the biggest role; they say marriage still provides a man the best chance of survival and reproduction. Economists see marriage as a practical trade-off in which each partner balances the pros and cons and makes a logical decision. And psychoanalysts say that marriage is a man's subconscious way of trying to return to the state of unconditional love that he experienced—or wished to experience—as an infant.

To some extent, my research supports all of these theories. But it invites a simpler analysis as well: *Men marry primarily because they like company*. Yes, men are trained to be independent, and, compared to women, they may seem hermitlike at times. But the strong message from the three hundred–plus husbands I surveyed is that they married because they wanted the physical, emotional, and intellectual companionship of a woman.

On one of my trips around the country, I happened to sit next to a fifty-year-old married businessman on an airplane. We began talking about why men marry. He told me his thoughts on the topic: "I travel a lot, and I'm with men who are away from their homes for weeks or months at a time. We may enjoy the freedom at first, but being alone gets old fast. For me, there's nothing better, nothing more assuring, than knowing my wife is waiting for me at home."

Bachelor Parties

Business consultant, fifty-three years old, married twenty-four years: *"I never had a bachelor party. I don't think it ever even occurred to me to have one, and none of my friends proposed it. It's always seemed like a rather silly and childish thing to me."*

Technical writer, forty, married six years: *"My dad and my boss handled it. I felt tremendous pressure to have the party. I did not want one. We all met in the bar of the hotel where the wedding was going to be. There was my dad, my boss, a good friend who I also went to high school with, my bride's stepdad, and two or three others who slip my mind. We started out by drinking and playing pool. I hate alcohol. I was pretty bombed pretty quick. My boss had found a nightclub that was walking distance. We danced a bit with some of the females. I remember one woman danced with me quite a bit. It turns out my dad was trying to pay her to take me home with her. I hated the whole experience. I remember feeling very angry at my dad."*

Historian, forty-seven, married seventeen years: *"The bachelor party went on for a whole day—plenty of cards, movies, and food. About midnight, we headed over the state line to crash the girls' bachelorette party at a hotel. We got there and they had left to raid our cabin. They decided to strip me to my underwear and a fedora and leave me in the hotel parking lot. Just as they went out one exit, a Tennessee Highway Patrol car entered. It's amazing how far you can crawl up under a pickup truck. Lots of hangovers the next morning, but the wedding went off well. It was a great time and the only really big bachelor party from our small group."*

Lab manager, thirty-three, married four years: *"I did have a bache-lor party. I wasn't expecting it since I was married in Palm Beach but liv-ing in Los Angeles, plus all of my groomsmen lived out of state. Much to my surprise, my best man spoke to the doorman and found a strip joint near the airport. As we walked in, there was another bachelor party going on, and the bachelor was on stage with two strippers doing their thing. So I turned to my best man and said, 'Please do not do that to me—any-thing but that!' So, for the first few hours, I was getting lap dances and all. Then, suddenly, I hear my name. My best man did what I asked him not to do! They placed me on a chair center stage and started to strip. I drank champagne from their breasts and thighs and everywhere else. Then she ripped my underwear lining with her teeth."*

Minister, forty-three, married six years: *"I did have a bachelor party. One of my best men put it on for me. We gathered in a friend's basement and played pool and bullshitted. We got drunk and just hung out. It was what I wanted."*

Chapter Three

THE WEDDING

BEDECKED IN BLACK TAILS and a bow tie, Noah James, twenty-four, tries to still the thumping in his chest. Just minutes earlier, two altar boys had escorted Noah and his groomsmen from a choir room in a Minneapolis-area Catholic church to a "staging area" directly behind the altar, just out of sight of the one hundred assembled guests. While lingering for forty minutes in the anteroom, Noah had declined his best man's offer of a sip of booze from a silver flask.

The best man may have known something about Noah. Now, behind the altar, Noah senses a tingling in his legs and left arm. His breath grows short, and his face dampens. Then the tingling arm goes completely numb. For a moment, Noah worries that he might collapse.

The priest, eying Noah, is quietly alarmed. "Do you need a chair?" he whispers.

"Yes, I do," Noah replies.

The respite appears to help. A few minutes later, though still wobbly, Noah moves out in front of the altar where he will take his marriage vows. He is wearing "one of those perma-grins on my face, almost to the point of pain," he recalls. But as his fiancée enters to the strains of "Here Comes the Bride," Noah senses his breathing returning to normal. When she reaches him at the altar and takes his hand, he relaxes.

"A lot of it was purely the unknown," he says. "Neither of us had experienced living away from home. We didn't know what to expect or even
what to worry about. How would the dynamics [of the relationship]
change? How would our relationships with other people change? Suddenly,
we'll be together all the time. How would we handle that?"

Weddings are for women—or so it is said. Thumb through any get-ready-
for-marriage magazine, and you'll find images of future brides, brides'
mothers, aunts, grandmothers, and (usually female) wedding planners.
From the earliest years of their lives, girls are encouraged to dream about
their wedding days. The bride's family is tasked with planning the wedding
and paying for it. "Bridal registries" are peppered with home-oriented gifts:
towels, sheets, Crock-Pots. Rarely does a power tool make the cut.

For the most part, men accept this emphasis on the bride. But the
image of impassive, uninvolved grooms is a misleading one. According to
the VoiceMale Survey, six in ten husbands say they are equally or more involved than their wives in planning their weddings. And even when their
fiancées take the lead, grooms know that their wedding day is no ordinary
one. Indeed, while some men may know, or care, little about the *mechan-
ics* of their wedding, they fully understand its *meaning*.

"When I stood up there with her, I made a promise," a forty-eight-
year-old hospital administrator told me. "I was choosing love over everything else that's working against it. And I was choosing it forever." This
man adds: "Getting married was heroic for her and for me. It required
courage and action. I know guys who went to Vietnam, who were jumping
out of helicopters. That was much easier than jumping, open-eyed, into
marriage. Whether [it's compared to] Vietnam, a hurricane, a lightning
storm, or climbing Everest, to be available to a woman while staying true to
yourself—that's the ultimate challenge for a man."

No wonder men are nervous as they make their vows. Like Noah
James, who nearly collapsed behind the altar, many husbands I interviewed
readily acknowledged their fear. They used words like "quivering," "trem-
bling," "jittery," and "scared to death" when recalling their wedding days.
And previous experience didn't make it easier; grooms on their second or

third wedding days, in fact, were particularly apt to tremble. One second-time husband told me: "We'd lived together for two years. We'd written the vows and planned the wedding together. But it was still frightening. . . . What if I fail again?"

While these men said the source of their anxiety was largely internal, others pointed to complicated life circumstances surrounding their wedding. One man, an electrician married in 1982, said his wedding represented the first time his divorced parents had been in the same room for several years. "It was extraordinarily tense for me. My parents were not always cordial to each other." This man remembered how he showed his anxiety: "[My wife] has a big family, and I had crammed up on all their names so I'd remember who was who. I was so nervous and intent on introducing people to each other that at one point I introduced my brother to my parents." Nonetheless, he recalls, the wedding "was one of the best days of my life."

Planning a wedding has been called "boot camp" for marriage. Couples must make decisions together and begin to blend their sometimes divergent styles. Often, husbands told me, they were surprised at the intensity of their fiancée's focus on wedding details. At the same time, many couldn't seem to find a way to help.

"She kept wanting me to do my share" of the wedding arrangements, one man told me. When he offered suggestions, however, his fiancée tended to grimace and say she'd "consider" his idea. Then she did things her own (or her mother's) way, the husband recalls. In an attempt to prevent clashes with his wife-to-be, this man eventually decided to simply rubber-stamp his fiancée's decisions.

Another husband told me that seven years into his marriage, he still has a sour taste from his wedding. Like the previously mentioned husband, this man stepped back from the planning when his wife's "body language" conveyed that that would be a good idea. Thus, in the days leading up to the wedding, while his fiancée prepared furiously for the wedding and reception, the husband-to-be hung out with his friends. He says he tried to be supportive by assuring his fiancée that the wedding would be perfect no matter how it turned out.

For some reason, that didn't comfort her. And on the wedding day, when the caterer failed to handle her duties according to plan, the man's bride became exasperated—with her new husband. "I had a no-big-deal attitude" about the wedding problems, the groom recalls. "She was really wore out." The husband adds: "I remember that we had some discussions on the honeymoon" about his nonchalant attitude. "When we got the photos back, we had more discussions. And when we were doing thank-you notes, there were still *more* discussions."

Marriage counselors Patrick and Michelle Gannon have put together a list of the most-fought-over wedding-planning issues. These echo the problems that husbands named in my interviews. In addition to the groom's lack of interest in the wedding's color scheme, hot-button wedding problems include:

- Cost. Men generally prefer to spend less than their wives on the wedding day and more on the honeymoon. (Weddings now cost an average of nearly $25,000.)
- Location. Men generally prefer to have the wedding where the couple currently lives, while many brides lean toward having it in their hometown.
- Formality. Men are more apt to want a casual event, while brides tend to want tuxes and elegant bridesmaid dresses.

In my own relationship, Kelly and I struggled mightily during the wedding planning. Like most men in their twenties, I had not thought much about my wedding day prior to our engagement. I didn't resist when Kelly started planning, but since I was paying a significant part of the wedding costs, I did request a say in the major money decisions. As Kelly brought me ideas, however, I began to feel like a veto machine. I kept saying no. On the occasions that I offered an alternative idea, she was no-oriented as well.

Soon we sensed a dangerous pattern. So we adopted what we have come to call the "Just *Don't* Say No" rule. (We got married during the Reagan administration, when one of the popular antidrug phrases was "Just Say No.") We agreed that when one of us brought the other an idea, it was the listener's job *not to reject it* for at least twenty-four hours. At that point, if the listener still didn't like the idea, he or she had to offer an alternative that preserved the spirit of the initial suggestion.

Interestingly, as often as not, the person who made the initial suggestion backed away from it during those first twenty-four hours. Equally telling, when the other considered the idea carefully, he or she usually found the germ of a *good* idea there. Through this approach, we were able to create a wedding that we both embraced and that represented a merging of our two different personalities and heritages.

To this day, when we're facing an important decision in which we might disagree, one of us will often resurrect the Just *Don't* Say No rule.

In my survey of husbands, I heard about three basic types of weddings. These styles seem to occur in roughly equal numbers, though many men tended to like the first style best. Regardless of what style was ultimately chosen, husbands said, it was important to ensure that the style of wedding matched the personality of the couple.

The first style of wedding was what might be called the **Express**. This style is designed to move a couple from unmarried to permanently bonded with few stops along the way. It tends to take place in the home of one of the betrothed, a judge's chamber, a pastor's study, or Las Vegas. The upside is obvious: An Express wedding is easy to plan, relatively inexpensive, completed quickly, and as legally binding as any other.

When couples chose this style freely, my interviews showed, they tended to be happy with their choice. For example, a forty-three-year-old Washington State paralegal told me that he and his wife had gotten hitched in Las Vegas eight years earlier because neither liked to be the center of attention. They now have two daughters and no regrets. "It was no muss, no fuss," the man says of the wedding, "and that's basically who we are."

Many Express wedding couples, however, felt forced into this style by external circumstances, including unplanned pregnancies. Particularly prior to the 1970s, it was scandalous for a woman to marry while carrying a child. It was equally disgraceful for a man to refuse to marry a woman whom he'd gotten pregnant. The solution for these couples was to get married quickly and quietly. Husbands I interviewed who had these kinds of weddings usually acknowledged that they had been less than satisfying. "Sometimes I wish I could look back on our 'big day' with pride," one man, married fifty-one years, told to me.

A Texas librarian, now forty-eight and divorced from his first wife, recalls that their unexpected pregnancy preceded a quickie wedding. "We called our parents on Mother's Day to tell them that we were pregnant," he recalls. "A couple of days later, my mother calls back and says, '[The wedding] is all arranged.' " This man recalled that a tornado struck his hometown the day before he got married there; he was happy just to have the event behind him.

A second style of wedding mentioned by husbands is the **Establishment** wedding. Establishment weddings generally take place in a church, synagogue, or other religious facility, with family and friends numbering in the scores or hundreds. A clergyperson usually presides. And the pastor's religious traditions tend to dictate the specific content of the wedding.

This style was most common among couples who married young, particularly those who were living with their parents at the time of the wedding or whose parents were paying for the wedding. The parents of the bride and groom tended to play an important role in the engaged couple's life, and the couple sought to honor their parents by marrying in their tradition.

A few men who had Establishment religious weddings told me years later that they regretted it because they had not been believers themselves. Thus, while they may have relished being with friends and family, as well as having the chance to seal their relationship with their beloved, they experienced, in the words of one man, "a void" when it came to the spiritual significance of the event.

But most Establishment weddings were remembered with abiding fondness. "Being in the presence of God, my family, my friends, and my wife—there is nothing else like it," a twenty-eight-year-old salesman told me. "I cried when she came down the aisle. . . . It was the best, most amazing day I ever had."

Catholic couples were particularly likely to marry in their church, with a priest presiding. One man who'd left the Catholic Church in his late teens told me that he had been living with his girlfriend in his mid-thirties when he asked her to marry him. To the man's own surprise, he was drawn to the idea of marrying in a Catholic church. He had spent years exploring Eastern religions and now, in his mid-thirties, had "developed a renewed appreciation for the Catholic mystical and saintly traditions."

He spoke with a priest about getting married in the church. But when the priest learned that the man was living with his fiancée, he refused to perform the ceremony. "I'm not going to make a mockery of the sacrament," the priest told him.

The groom-to-be, however, was "dead set on a Catholic ritual," he told me. And he negotiated a compromise with the priest: He and his girlfriend would continue to live together (they already had bought their home together) but would have no "genital contact" in the four months remaining before the wedding. They also would attend a weekly course, designed by the priest, to reacquaint them with Catholicism.

During this period, the man recalled, the priest performed what he described as "a minor exorcism" on him, placing a hand on the man's forehead and reciting an incantation. When I spoke with the husband two years after the wedding, he said: "It was a magical ritual. It wasn't just the celibacy [leading up to the wedding]. It was the process of reaffirming my faith. It felt like a really blessed time."

The third style of wedding that men mentioned might be called **Eclectic**. Eclectic weddings tend to blend different religious traditions, or jettison religious tradition altogether, in favor of rituals that the bride and groom create themselves. These types of weddings have increased dramatically since the 1970s as secularism has grown and prohibitions against interracial and interreligious marriages have fallen.

Lars Persson, a forty-four-year-old engineer originally from Sweden, met his American wife, Kathy, when she was a high-school exchange student in Europe in the late 1970s. They were platonic friends during her stay, and remained in touch through letters as they both attended college an ocean apart. When Lars visited the United States in 1982, he spent time with Kathy in California. On a visit to the Magic Kingdom at Disneyland, they kissed for the first time. As he recalled: "That was for me the moment the relationship changed."

The couple, who now live in Wisconsin, communicated by phone and letters over the following year as they finished their schooling. Then she moved to Sweden, and they set up a house together. Two months later, Lars sat down with Kathy one day and "laid out a time line" that included their engagement the following Christmas. "I think she was moved" by his matter-of-fact proposal, he recalls. "She started crying."

A hundred people came to their wedding, including thirty friends and family members who traveled from the United States to Sweden for it. Kathy and Lars baked their own bread for the reception, and Kathy and her four sisters prepared Swedish meatballs and a variety of salads.

Kathy had grown up Episcopalian but no longer attended church, and Lars had never had a religious affiliation. They chose to hold the wedding in a liberal Christian church because, Lars told me, they liked its architecture. They hired the church's minister to officiate and "gave some concessions" on the vows and his message, Lars recalls. The minister mentioned God in his remarks but primarily spoke on the theme of "unity," which led into the couple singing a song together. They chose John Denver's "Perhaps Love." The singing was a major risk for Lars, who said singing in public was "something I never thought I'd dare to do."

Kathy wrote most of the ceremony because they decided to do it in English. After the wedding, the couple toured Sweden and Denmark "with a traveling circus" of friends and relatives, Lars recalled.

Looking back on the wedding nearly twenty years later, Lars said he might do things a little differently, particularly since he and Kathy started attending a different church after they moved to the United States. But overall, he says, "I see a couple who was fairly young, fairly idealistic, fairly romantic. I have very pleasant memories around it."

Three of the men I interviewed said they had more than one marriage ceremony with their current wives. In two cases, the husbands renewed vows with their wives at a milestone anniversary. One man, married during the Depression, took vows again sixty-eight years later in the same Catholic church in which he and his wife had originally said "I do."

But perhaps no second ceremony was as meaningful for the men I interviewed as that of Eric Gilliland, a recovering drug addict, to his wife, Leandra. Eric was fifty-one years old, tall and easy to laugh, when I spoke with him in his psychotherapy office on the fifth floor of a gray-glass building in a southern state. Water gurgled in a small fountain in a corner; a lava lamp glowed near a tray of coffee essentials. Live plants and flowers danced about the room in the air-conditioning breezes.

Eric told me he had grown up Irish Catholic in the midsized city where he now lived. His father was a machinist who worked fourteen hours a day, and his mother was "an angry housewife," Eric recalled. He learned from them not to trust people who claimed to love him. At sixteen, he started using hard drugs and continued doing so all the way through his twenties. He made a "geographical escape" at the age of thirty. Having been fired from "my umpteenth" job, he borrowed a friend's car and drove to Florida. From there, he took a plane to the West Indies, where a few days earlier "a drunken friend had called me and asked me to come."

His first night on the island, Eric went to a bar and saw Leandra, a young woman native to the islands. She was dancing. "My guts knotted up," Eric recalls. "I got terrified. I was enthralled, but I couldn't even speak to her." He returned to the bar every night after that hoping to see her, but she never came back.

Convinced that "my soul had found its match," Eric got a restaurant job on the island and kept an eye out for Leandra. One day, she came into his restaurant for lunch. From a fellow waiter, he found out who she was and where she lived and started "prowling" her neighborhood. A mutual friend later told him that Leandra had seen Eric near her home and "wondered who was that nice-looking white guy with the good ass."

On New Year's Eve 1982, Eric was at a bar, drunk on champagne and high on mushrooms, as he recalled, when Leandra walked in and approached him. Her first words: "You look lonely." He was thirty-one, she was seventeen.

A few weeks later, they were living together. For the next two years,

Eric recalls, they earned just enough money to get by. They traveled from the islands to Nantucket, Massachusetts, to Palm Beach, Florida, and back to the islands, working where the tourists were. As she matured, however, Leandra tired of Eric's drug use. She left Eric on numerous occasions, only to return to him. "I was her project," Eric recalls.

In the summer of 1985, at a party in Palm Beach, Eric finally proposed to Leandra. Inside, he felt a swirl of love and fear. "Something in my gut was gnawing at me: I better lock this girl down. I gotta make it harder to leave me," he remembers. He told her that they would go back to his hometown, where he'd get clean and start over. Shortly thereafter, they married, with a judge officiating, in the living room of Eric's parents' home. Eric acknowledges that of the nine people in the room, only four were sober. Leandra was one of them; Eric was not.

At this point, Eric's parents agreed to pay off his debt—Eric had embezzled money at a job in Palm Beach—if he'd go to a drug-treatment program. He said yes, but he was using drugs again almost immediately. That's when Leandra left him, apparently for good. Eric reentered treatment "to get my wife back." And finally, the therapy took hold. For three months, Eric attended Alcoholics Anonymous meetings twice a day, while Leandra lived with friends in Florida. Then she returned. And Eric stayed clean. Eventually, Leandra started attending Al-Anon, a support group for relatives and friends of alcoholics, to help her deal with her own unhealthy relationship patterns.

For two years, the couple grew gradually closer as they excised the "third lover" from their lives: drugs. "We'd have great fights, then we'd make great love," he recalls. Eric returned to school, and she did too. Then, in 1988, Leandra asked Eric if he'd be willing to have another wedding ceremony. At first, he was reluctant. What would people think? But he finally agreed. "She said she wanted to do it clean. The first time, we were two desperate people hanging on."

They got remarried in an auditorium. The chaplain from Eric's drug-treatment center officiated. About 150 family members and friends, mostly people from their recovery programs, came to celebrate. The Phil Collins song "Take a Look at Me Now" played in the background. Eric's father was his best man.

Eric surprised Leandra during the service with a diamond ring. Eric also recalled: "During one moment in the service, I began to tear up. [My wife] reached across and wiped a tear from my cheek. You know, she continues to do that."

The second wedding, Eric now says, was "an affirmation and dedication to recovery" that both needed. It was "a celebration of us as a couple, an honoring of our love, and a time to rejoice that we had survived the hell of addiction." These days, Eric and Leandra's volunteer work includes mentoring younger married couples.

Mythologist Michael Meade, author of *Men and the Water of Life,* says that American weddings have lost much of their transformative power in recent decades. Meade has studied marriage rituals in an array of cultures. While many tribal rituals are similar to those in modern marriages, there is a key difference when it comes to the bride and groom: In the tribal cultures, Meade told me in an interview, young men and women who want to marry must go through rites of passage that test them and welcome them into adulthood. Before marrying, they must have proven themselves ready for it.

Not so in modern-day America, Meade says. Often, the wedding itself serves as the first significant rite of passage for the American bride and groom. The only aspect of the couple that may have been tested is their blood. Meade laments: "What we have now is a dress-up performance that is closer to a ball . . . a debutante ball."

Nonetheless, the fear and awe that so many grooms experience leading up to and during their weddings, Meade says, are an indication that the impact of a wedding—even in its diluted state—can never be fully denied. Men are anxious at the altar, he said, because they know the ultimate promise they are making in that moment. It's the promise to sacrifice their personal needs and desires for something greater than themselves. The struggle to follow through on that promise is the challenge of virtually every married man.

Honeymoons

Social worker, sixty-three, married thirty-nine years: *"We drove a hundred miles to the nearest bigger city in North Dakota the first night. We did not get into our motel until 2:30 A.M. We did not have the wisdom to restrain from our first sexual experience—both of us were virgins—until we were less exhausted. It was probably the least pleasurable sexual experience for either of us, but we made our way through it. The subsequent sexual experiences were very pleasurable until my wife developed a urinary tract infection and was too tender for sex on about day four of our honeymoon."*

Police officer, forty, married nine years: *"We went to Northern California to meet family that could not make it to the wedding. We had several fun moments. First, I borrowed my brother's van and locked the keys in it on top of Mount Diablo. Later, on the same van, the water pump went out. We traveled to Napa Valley and camped out. Of course we had to roast marshmallows. It was dark and I found a nice straight stick. Unfortunately, it was poison oak. Taken internally, you get it everywhere."*

University professor, forty-seven, married sixteen years: *"Our honeymoon was contentious and passionate. We went to Spain for three weeks. The ups were sharing the beauty of Spain. The downs were our fights at learning to travel together. We have very different vacation styles. I go into 'monastic' mode—eating little, meditating, physical exercise. She's into laying back and drinking piña coladas."*

University administrator, sixty-five, married thirty-seven years: *"Our honeymoon was notable in part because we did it on the cheap. I was teaching part-time and also still a grad student. My wife was a part-time grad student assistant. Money was very scarce. We had friends in Muskegon, Michigan, who had moved out of their home and were going to put it on the market. It was still fully furnished, and they offered it to us for our honeymoon. We were there for about five days. We went out for dinner, but otherwise most of our time was spent in Energizer-bunny screwing. Our most embarrassing moment was when we realized we had actually moved the bed halfway across the room in our energetic activities."*

Part Two

THE ARC OF THE RELATIONSHIP

Chapter Four

———⚘———

Newlyweds: The First 3 Years

I'm waiting for her to act right, and she's waiting for me to act right.
—Thirty-three-year-old schoolteacher

E D AND PATRICIA GRIFFITH had been married less than two
months when a filet of catfish came between them.

To that point, in mid-1995, Ed's relationship with Patricia had
gone as well as either might have expected. Both were thirty-eight years old
when they met, and previously unlucky in love. Ed's two most recent relationships had ended after the women, having first accepted his marriage
proposals, changed their minds. Patricia's relationship past was similarly
difficult.

Ed and Patricia met through a personal ad he placed in an alternative
newspaper in a city in the Southwest. Ed says he and Patricia were brought
together by a love of music, a desire for companionship, and "a weird sense
of humor."

But tensions existed, and shortly after the wedding, they boiled over
in the kitchen. For nearly two decades, living alone, Ed and Patricia had
made their own meals. Both enjoyed the relaxation of cooking, and, upon
moving in together, neither was willing to give it up. So they agreed to
share the kitchen duties. On this day, as Ed chopped vegetables on the
counter in their cramped kitchen, Patricia prepared fresh catfish filets just
to his left.

That's when Patricia did the unimaginable, at least as Ed saw it. Instead of dragging the filets through the flour mixture to bread them, she laid the fish on the pan and sprinkled flour on top of them.

Witnessing this, Ed couldn't stop himself from pointing to the breaded-catfish recipe in the magazine on the counter nearby. "It says to *dredge*," he informed his new bride. Ed is an engineer and, as he told me years later, "It's an article of faith that you follow the directions."

Patricia was puzzled at first by her husband's reference to dredging, then realized what he was referring to.

"Oh, it doesn't really matter," she responded.

Which was not what Ed wanted to hear. "Yes, it *does* matter," he countered.

Startled, Patricia stared at Ed for a moment. "Okay," she said, "then *you* do it." She wiped her hands and marched out of the room.

Ed and Patricia's "flour struggle" may be unique in its details, but its elements are well known to newlyweds. Virtually all of the husbands I interviewed acknowledged that they had gone through similar conflicts as part of a complicated transition to married life. At least from the husband's point of view, the period of marriage most often described as the honeymoon phase is second only to the child-raising years as the most difficult in a marriage.

Not that new husbands are miserable. According to the VoiceMale Survey, about two-thirds of husbands say they're "very happy" during the first three years of their married lives. Their love is fresh, and the excitement of blending lives dominates. Yet these men, particularly those who did not live with their wives before marriage, acknowledge that they have a lot of adjusting to do. Among the top issues: sharing money; balancing family with outside interests; getting along with the in-laws; maintaining mutual interest in sex. It's not surprising that, according to the Centers for Disease Control and Prevention, 5 percent of marriages end within two years of the wedding day.

Underlying all of these particular issues is a critical relationship challenge: how to move from the stage in which passion dominates to the one in which practical daily issues become paramount. Husbands say there's an almost inevitable crash for both partners. In the earliest times of a relationship, couples are on their best behavior. They keep themselves physically fit and try to impress and romance. They are chemically drawn to one another. Of course they want this idealized life to continue.

But they must let it go. In fact, *disillusionment* appears to be a necessary and beneficial stage in any relationship. Couples must renounce the fantasy of perfection and accept the reality of difference. Unless a couple can negotiate this transition effectively, the relationship stagnates or falls apart. As the author Michael Gurian writes in *Love's Journey,* "We must understand infatuation as only a first step toward mature love."

Power struggles have always been a part of the American marriage. But prior to about 1965, such struggles were largely unacknowledged. During the pre-1965 period, the larger culture dictated who had the power in marriage.

Women were awarded authority over the kitchen and, to some degree, the children. Men held most other power. In fact, as late as the 1970s, laws in many states still allowed a man to "discipline" his wife and to have sex with her against her will. "It was assumed that whatever I wanted was the rule for the household," one man, married in 1963, told me. He added that expecting to dominate the home was "like expecting the sun to come up. I didn't know there were other options."

Not so for men married in more recent years. Today, husbands say, the key issues in their marriages are fully negotiable.

The most common issue of contention for newly married husbands, according to my research, is sharing financial authority and responsibility. In my survey, 28 percent of newlywed husbands listed money as the topic most likely to cause disagreement between them and their wives.

Michael Bernstein, a social worker married thirteen years, told me his story of early-marriage money conflict. It's a typical one for many couples. Michael met his wife, Rebecca, in 1991, just after graduating from college. He was still working on campus, and Rebecca was an entering freshman. Ten months later, they married in a Jewish ceremony.

Their attitudes about money were vastly different. Michael's parents had divorced when he was nine, and he remembers them as "shortsighted and into instant gratification." He recalls that after his parents divorced, his father sometimes gave him money and advised him to keep it secret from his mother.

Michael started earning his own money at twelve years of age and, a few years later, discovered that he'd have to pay his own way to college. That's when the trouble really began. He accepted student loans and credit cards but did not rein in his spending. By his senior year, he'd run up thousands of dollars in debt. He suspects now that buying things "was fulfilling in me something that I wasn't getting elsewhere."

Michael recalls a particularly telling incident in college: He was at a mall, shopping with a friend, when it neared the time that the mall would close. Michael hadn't bought anything to that point, and suddenly felt he could not leave until he did. For fifteen minutes, he "ran around like a crazy man," pulling on clothes, trying to find something to spend his money on. He finally purchased an orange polo shirt. Later, he recalls, after he "came off my high," he returned the shirt. "There was some kind of compulsion going on," he admits.

He discussed none of this with Rebecca when they first started dating. And Rebecca didn't ask where he got the money—on his $12,000-a-year salary—to take her out, buy himself nice clothes, and pay the rest of his bills.

Rebecca, in fact, was naïve about money. She had been sheltered. Michael told me that she came from an upper-middle-class home and hadn't worked much in high school. Even during the first two years of their marriage, her parents paid for her tuition, books, and room and board at college.

In the second year of their marriage, however, Rebecca learned about the severity of Michael's debts and became alarmed. "For her, the issue was security," Michael told me. She wondered how they would be able to buy a home, raise children, and take care of emergencies if they were in such deep debt. "I just basically didn't worry as much about money," Michael said. "I didn't lose sleep over it."

Soon Rebecca took over the family finances. And not surprisingly, the clashes intensified over Michael's spending, particularly his use of credit cards. "I was accustomed to doing things without permission," Michael recalls. "It wasn't so much that I thought this was *my* money. I just thought: 'If I'm on the street and I'm hungry and I see a burger, I want to be able to buy it.' I saw her as someone who would say, 'Wait a minute.' " And that's exactly what she did. Repeatedly. There were times, Michael told me, that he'd hide his spending from Rebecca by using a check or debit card to buy necessities, ask the cashier to add $10 to the total, and take the change back in cash.

Now married thirteen years, with three children, Michael says things are much better. The more secure he's become in his marriage and professional life, he's found, the less intense is his need to buy things. He also believes that Rebecca has "loosened up" as she's come to trust him more. Occasionally, Michael says, she'll even buy something frivolous for herself.

But even today, the issue remains a sensitive one. A few days before I talked with Michael, a collection agent called their home about an old debt. Michael told me that after the phone call, he and Rebecca had an intense conversation about the importance of using credit cards responsibly.

While Rebecca is the "spending brake" in this marriage, the tug-of-war over money finds husbands and wives about equally on each side of the spending-saving equation. Regardless of who's doing the spending, however, the issue can be explosive. Several men told me that their earlier marriages had ended because money issues could not be settled, and that their current marriages were threatened.

Some couples tried to mitigate the money problems by setting up separate bank accounts. Among those in my survey who were married three years or less, 23 percent kept their money in separate accounts, the highest percentage among the four phases of marriage.

Almost as big an issue as how newly married couples spend their money is how they spend their time. In my survey, balancing work and family ranked second on just-married men's list of topics that cause disagreements.

Jean-Luc Gaillard offers a classic example. Jean-Luc was born in Haiti and immigrated with his family to the United States when he was four years old. When I spoke with him, he was thirty-three and married two years, with a year-old daughter. Things were not going particularly well in his relationship.

One frustrating problem, according to Jean-Luc, was that he and his wife could not agree on how much time he should spend working. Jean-Luc had "always been a success-driven person," he told me. In high school, he thought he'd have a career in sports, but when that didn't pan out, he went to college and got a teaching degree. Then he took a job at an urban high school in Alabama.

Even while teaching full-time, he attended night school to become a real-estate broker. It was during this period that he met his future wife, Victoria. He admits that he was attracted to her beauty primarily, but adds: "I felt that I had the personality to the point that I could successfully change her."

Soon after they married, Victoria became pregnant. Jean-Luc wanted to be involved in the child-rearing, but he also wanted to continue his work at the same intensity. So he laid out a schedule: The child would be in day care until Jean-Luc got home from his teaching job. He'd stay with the baby for a couple of hours until Victoria came home from work. Then he'd set out on his second job: buying, fixing up, and selling homes.

Victoria agreed at first, but soon found that Jean-Luc was out late into the evening and spent many of his weekends on his real-estate business. She urged him to cut back. He resisted. The arguments escalated, and they were continuing when I interviewed Jean-Luc two years into the marriage. Jean-Luc told me that he wanted to focus on work so that he and Victoria could retire in their forties. "My goal is to get this [money making] out of the way now," Jean-Luc told me. "She would rather it take longer. . . . I tell her to give me five years. To her, five years is an eternity."

Jean-Luc says he doesn't know why making money is so compelling to him, but adds, "I find that I *must* be financially successful. I just can't turn away from it." When I spoke to him, he and Victoria were at a standoff: "I'm waiting for her to act right, and she's waiting for me to act right."

This couple's work-family disputes seem intractable, and they may have been fueled by disagreements in other areas, including when to start their family. Jean-Luc told me that he would have preferred to wait a few more years. But even if a couple's overall values are similar, newly married husbands and wives often have very different expectations of the amount of time they'll spend together after they marry and what they'll do during that time.

I noticed two things in talking with men about this issue: First, for many husbands, success at work remains the greatest, and clearest, measure of their worth. And *particularly after they marry,* men often feel powerful internal pressure to be financially successful. In the majority of cases, men still are the primary breadwinners in the marriage, and they want to secure the financial stability of their families. Job security seems tenuous everywhere, and most husbands seem willing to work harder and longer if it means a greater chance of keeping their job and fulfilling their "duty" as a husband.

Second, for some husbands, it's *the fact of being married,* not the amount of time spent with their wives, that gives them a sense of security and satisfaction. Just having a wife and a home is comforting to many husbands. A dentist who works sixty hours a week put it this way: "I don't have to be with my wife to feel good about her. I feel good just knowing she's there."

It's not only work that causes balance problems for newly married couples. Several men I spoke with said their wives objected to the amount of time they spent with male friends, often playing or watching sports. And one man, who was twenty-two when he got married, acknowledged that early in his marriage, he was out four nights a week rehearsing and performing in a local band.

He remembers a conversation with his wife after returning home at 2 A.M. after a rehearsal.

> *His wife:* I never see you.
> *Him:* We're young. If you're not happy, find someone else.

Eventually, she took him up on his offer. She had an affair that led to their divorce. Ten years later, remarried, this man lamented: "The mistake I made in my first marriage was neglect."

In a smaller, but significant, number of cases, it is the husband who wishes the wife would spend more time with him. Work and friendships occasionally take wives away, but a more common distraction for a wife is her family of origin.

One husband, married since 1962, told me that in his first year of marriage, spending time alone with his wife "was bliss. I wanted more of it. But she felt pressured to be with her family." For him, being with her family meant "pretending to be Mr. and Mrs. Nice." He recalls: "I found out I could be angry and jealous."

Another man, a dry-wall hanger married in 1978 at age twenty-four, had a somewhat different in-law problem: "Any time we had a difficult argument, [my wife] would say: 'I'm going home.' And she'd leave." Fortunately, this husband told me, his mother-in-law refused to let her daughter stay. The mother-in-law would say to her daughter: "You married him. He didn't hit you. He didn't abuse you. You go back and work it out." This man said that, after a quarter century of marriage, he still gets along fabulously with his mother-in-law.

According to my survey, about half of recent marriages involve at least one partner who has been married previously, and an almost equal number involve children from a previous relationship. Not surprisingly, dealing with those children is another significant issue for newly married couples.

Most husbands did not have permanent custody of their children from previous relationships, and they often felt torn about what to do with their free time: They wanted to spend some of their evenings and weekends with those children, but they did not want to slight their new wives. In some cases, husbands were able to spend time with their children and new wives at the same time. But this was often uncomfortable, and occasionally disastrous, because of the emotions surrounding the various relationships.

The most common problem regarding children from previous relationships involved men who were in-house stepfathers for the children of their new wives. The adjustment was almost always difficult, husbands told me. The children tended to resent the new man in the house, and frankly, the feeling was mutual for many stepdads.

A business executive who married a woman with two grade-school daughters remembers: "I jumped into the pool of parenting. There were no lessons." He acknowledged making major mistakes. Once, he gave a Valentine's Day card to his twelve-year-old stepdaughter with the inscription: "Thank you for being my daughter." The girl gave it back to him. "Don't ever call me your daughter," she warned him. "I have a father!"

In about a quarter of marriages, a child is born to the new couple in the first three years. This accelerates the couple's transition to the next stage of marriage—coparenting—which I will deal with in depth in the next chapter.

Not surprisingly, most newly married husbands are happy in their sex lives. In my survey, 92 percent said they were sexually satisfied, and, perhaps not coincidentally, 92 percent reported having sex at least once a week. About one in twelve new husbands said they had sex every day. Husbands generally wanted more sex than their wives, the men told me, but the disparity in desire between husbands and wives was smaller in this phase of marriage than in any other.

There does seem to be an all-or-nothing aspect to newly married men's sex lives. In my survey, the 8 percent of husbands who did *not* have sex at least once a week all reported that they had sex less than once a month. According to my in-depth interviews, this lack of early-marriage sex was most common in those who had lived together before marriage; many already had gone through a high-frequency sex phase.

For a small percentage of newly married men, impotence was a problem. "After we got married, I had trouble" maintaining an erection, one man told me. This man's wife had gained about twenty pounds in the first few months after the wedding, and that bothered him. But, mostly, he told me, he had trouble transitioning from sex with a girlfriend to sex with a wife. "Knowing that this person was the only woman I'd ever have sex with again kind of freaked me out," the husband said. For a while, he kept Viagra around the house just in case. Now, six years into the marriage, he no

longer needs medication, he says, and enjoys sex with his wife. He's still attracted to other women but doesn't act on the feelings.

While sex is usually a strong bond for newly married couples, it is occasionally a deal breaker. A few men told me that after their weddings, their
wives were far less interested in sex than before marriage. One said he had
felt "betrayed" by this change in his first marriage, and the relationship did
not survive. Another man said that he hadn't slept with his first wife before
marriage and found afterward that they were sexually incompatible. "She
was not active" in bed, this man said. "I lost interest." Despite counseling,
this marriage eventually broke up.

Only 3 percent of newly married men in my survey acknowledged having had an affair, but one man I interviewed, married just two years, told
me he'd already had sex with two other women since his wedding. Ironically, the man, who was thirty-four, had married in hopes of bringing
some stability to his life. He said he had a tendency "to thrive on excitement" and had chosen as his bride a stable, financially secure woman
who had her own career and home.

Almost immediately after marrying her, though, he felt uncomfortable. "I don't want to be controlled," he told me. "I don't want to be told
what to do."

Several months later, he met a woman whom he was attracted to "in a
primal way." He slept with her and, soon after, with another woman.
When I spoke with him the first time, this man was agonizing about
whether to try to make the marriage work. A year later, he told me he'd
ended the marriage and was determined not to marry again.

Ultimately, husbands said, the key to the first three years of marriage is
not to try to agree on everything, but to learn how to disagree.

This can be difficult. As other researchers have uncovered, American
men and women emerge from different childhood "cultures." Girl culture is oriented toward feeling and talking, while boy culture tilts toward
action. Healthy marriages seem to require a meshing of the different

customs in a way that both partners maintain a level of comfort and dignity.

Almost inevitably, this meshing process results in moments—or eras—of disagreement. According to my survey, 27 percent of couples in the first three years of marriage argue at least once a week. Only 12 percent of newlywed husbands said they never argued with their wives.

And solutions don't often come easily for these couples. All of the husbands in our survey who were married three years or less said they or their wives express anger toward the other at times. In 3 percent of cases, newly married men acknowledged that they had hit their wives in anger; 8 percent said their wives had hit them. (For more on physical and emotional violence, see Chapter Twelve.)

Violence during arguments remains the exception, however. More often, when things are going badly, husbands and wives are defensive, critical, blaming, or condescending to the other. Many husbands told me that their biggest problem during early marriage was their lack of skill in arguing. Only years into their marriages did many come to believe that the key to a successful arguer is the ability to be introspective, to look at one's own motivations with both discernment and compassion.

One fifty-something computer programmer, married twelve years, told me that at the beginning of his marriage he irritated his wife with his "senior-management style" in arguments. He would speak with an air of authority and dismiss her point of view. If she became emotional in the conversation, he would take advantage by intellectually outdueling her on the merits of the argument. His anger, he said, "came out in snide remarks and disrespect. It was never direct and clean. It was not about the issue at hand."

This husband entered therapy after his marriage foundered. And after six months of regular visits to the counselor, an important life experience came to light: At the age of four, this man had been diagnosed with a disease that required him to stay away from other children. Because his mother was divorced and had to work, she left him home with his grandmother; he had to stay in a darkened room for most of the day.

He recalls being terribly afraid during this period of his life. The experience, he discovered years later in counseling, led him to "create a shield" against outside threats. As an adult, whenever he believed the shield might be pierced—for example, when arguing with his wife—he lashed out. "I realized there was a boatload of fear inside me," the husband told me. "I had stuffed it."

Learning about a key source of his emotion "brought down the temperature" in the marriage, the husband said. Both he and his wife, aware of his vulnerability, interrupted arguments when they threatened to get out of hand. "I'm finally getting some control over my emotions and reactions," he said.

Many men said that the best arguing strategy for them was to give in to their wife's wishes. "The two most popular words in my vocabulary are 'Yes, dear,'" one man told me. Another man put it this way: "I learned what matters and what doesn't. I often ask myself: Is it worth a ruckus?"

Husbands rarely said that their wives regularly gave in to them during arguments. While my survey did not determine whether men or women were more likely to give in during arguments, a 2000 study by Creighton University's Center for Marriage and Family sheds light on this. The survey of 457 couples married five years or less found that *husbands and wives disagree even about who most often gives in during disagreements*. Husbands say they give in five times as often as their wives. Wives, meanwhile, say both they and their husbands give in equally as often.

Chapter Five

~~

FAMILY TIMES: YEARS 4 TO 20

All of a sudden, I was in second place. I was almost jealous of the kid.
—Thirty-six-year-old plumber

W HEN THE CONTRACTIONS BEGAN at home at noon on a Friday, Matt Luzon was surprisingly calm. It was the day that Matt and his wife, Belle, who had struggled with fertility, had literally prayed for. Belle's labor pains intensified throughout that day until Matt, a twenty-six-year-old lab technician, decided the time was right. Then he helped a wobbly Belle into the front seat of their Honda Accord and drove gingerly to the suburban Kansas City hospital, taking the turns at low speed. Finally, at two the next morning, he breathed encouragements into Belle's ear as their daughter's head crowned. "I wasn't panicked or anything," Matt, who is a second-generation Filipino-American, recalls of the moment of birth. "I was just doing what needed to be done."

But the serenity wouldn't last. The new family left the hospital two days later. And from the moment Matt carried the bundled newborn over the threshold, he could not contain his emotions. As he remembers it: "Whenever I was with my wife and daughter, I'd cry. I couldn't keep back the tears. When I tried to speak, I would get so choked up that I couldn't go on." Friends and family started asking Belle if something was wrong with Matt. She didn't know.

The tears continued for two weeks following the birth; then they stopped abruptly and never returned. Looking back seven years later, Matt told me he still couldn't account for his heightened sensitivity. The recent death of his mother-in-law might have been a factor, or relief that Belle and the baby were well. He might have been experiencing, in his own words, "the baby blues"—postpartum depression that strikes some husbands too—or simply "nerves run raw."

Then again, perhaps unknowingly, Matt might have been grieving for his marriage. From sex to housework to balancing home and family, the birth of a first child forever ends the marriage relationship as it was. And the changes that come are not always for the better.

Indeed, if there is a low period for husbands in an otherwise happy marriage, the birth of a couple's first child is its harbinger. According to the VoiceMale Survey, men consider the child-raising years the least happy of the four major phases of marriage. Having survived the difficult adjustments required of the honeymoon phase, husbands discover that they must adapt all over again. And this time, another human being, with almost endless needs and demands, dictates many of the changes.

More than a few husbands told me that they found it difficult to watch their children become the center of their wives' relationship world. "All of a sudden, I was in second place," one thirty-six-year-old plumber remarked. He recalled that in the months after their first daughter was born, his wife immediately interrupted whatever she was doing whenever the baby cried. "I was almost jealous of the kid," this husband said. "Selfishly, I missed those times of just having my wife and me."

Given the potential for marital upheaval caused by a new child, the surprise is not that arguing, infidelity, domestic violence, and divorce tend to increase during this phase, but that so many marriages actually thrive. Half of the husbands in my survey who were married between four and twenty years reported being "very happy" in their relationships. And, by a three-to-one margin, they said that their marriages had gotten better rather than worse after the birth of a child. Most were able to come to terms with the end of their child-free years and celebrate their new role of fatherhood.

The plumber mentioned above is one of those. Now wed fourteen years, with two middle-school daughters, he continues to miss having uninterrupted time alone with his wife. "It's still an issue. We just talked about it last night," he told me in an interview. He acknowledged that he looks forward to the day when he and his wife are without children in the home. But he adds: "There are certain sacrifices you make as a couple. No, I don't have as much time with my wife, but I have more with my family. . . . There are different phases of life, and different ways of being satisfied."

When to begin having children is often among the first major decisions a couple makes. And it doesn't always go smoothly.

The conventional wisdom is that men want to wait longer than women do. I found this generally true. Husbands I interviewed tended to equate having children with losing freedoms. Not surprisingly, then, husbands wanted an equal say in reproductive decisions, and when they didn't get it, they felt betrayed.

Donald Craft's story demonstrates this poignantly. In the first two years of their marriage, Donald and his wife, Lori, argued numerous times about when to start trying to get pregnant. The conversation tended to repeat itself. Lori would tell Donald that she was ready to start a family. They were both in their mid-twenties, she'd point out, plenty old enough. Their marriage was solid, and they were doing well financially. But Donald was reticent. "I'm just not ready," he'd tell Lori. "I don't feel mature enough yet." Frustrated, Lori would ask: "When *will* you be ready?" And Donald would end the conversation: "I don't know."

One evening in their third year of marriage, however, the discussion began in a new way. Donald recalled it fifteen years later.

> *Lori:* I've got something to tell you: I'm pregnant.
> *Donald:* You're what?
> *Lori:* I'm pregnant.
> *Donald:* But you're on the pill. What happened?
> *Lori:* Well, maybe I haven't been so good about taking my pills.
> *Donald:* Maybe?
> *Lori:* Okay. I haven't been.

When I interviewed Donald, he was a thirty-nine-year-old corporate controller, still married to Lori, and the father of two young teens. But he could still touch his anger about that first pregnancy. "What she did felt like the equivalent of rape," Donald told me. "[Having children] was a committee decision, and I wasn't on the committee." Donald recalled that his resentment was most intense in the early months. "I treated her badly during the whole pregnancy," he acknowledged. "If she said, 'I've got a craving for ice cream,' I'd say, 'Well, I guess you better go out and get some.'"

Donald's reaction illustrates just how seriously today's husbands take parenthood. Like Donald, newly married men generally say they want to be fathers someday. But they are more cautious about it than ever. That's because they know that the birth of a child will bring new pressures to every aspect of their lives: their careers, their free time, their social contacts, the family budget, their marriages.

Such pressures were less often a problem in the 1940s and 1950s. In that era, when a man's wife was pregnant, her husband rarely attended her obstetrician visits. When she delivered, he was rarely in the room. And paternity leave was not even in the lexicon. Many fathers spent the day after having a child the same way they had spent the day before: working at an office or other job site.

This is not to say that fathers of that era loved their children less. But little was expected of them on the home front except providing a paycheck and, often, producing even more children. A retired chemist who had married in 1946 told me he had felt an obligation to have a large family. World War II had taken a bite out of the American population. Children restocked the economic system and restored hope. Like so many other couples, the chemist and his wife had the first of their children within a year of getting married. They had three more in the next four years.

Younger men rarely have such large families. According to the Voice-Male Survey, 56 percent of men married in 1967 or before have at least three children. That compares to 22 percent of men who have married since 1967. A recent Gallup poll found that 79 percent of those in their twenties now disagree that "the main purpose of marriage is having children."

Younger husbands shared with me several reasons for wanting fewer children than their parents had. Here are three:

Advancing age. Men are marrying on average five years later than they did in 1960. Thus, the window of opportunity for having children is smaller. One father of two said that at age forty, he considered having more children until he "started doing the math. I realized that I'd be a fogy" by the time any subsequent children reached high school.

Financial limitations. In the mid–twentieth century, one wage-earner generally could support a family of five or six. Today, for a variety of reasons, many families feel they need two wage-earners to support a family. A number of husbands told me they wanted more children but either could not afford them on their current income or could not count on having their current jobs for the long haul.

Psychological reasons. Many of today's younger men grew up with absent fathers and don't know what it takes to be a dad. One thirty-three-year-old paralegal told me, "I question my skills." Other men said they figured that the fewer children they had, the more attention they'd be able to focus on each one.

Even when a husband is gung ho to have children, the reality can be a shock to the marriage. A few husbands told me ruefully how they had made the mistake of competing with their children over their wife's affection. Looking back thirty years, one man remembered the intense feeling of jealousy he had as their first child breast-fed. "On some level, I had played the child in the family before that," this husband acknowledged. "My needs had always been met. Now there was a child with *real* needs." In retrospect, he added, "I was frightened of the responsibility [of parenting]. It was overwhelming."

He said that his wife was "enough of a stoic or a masochist or a trooper" to try to meet both his and the child's needs for a while. But eventually, after she bore a second child three years after the first, she focused on the kids to the relative exclusion of her husband. He gradually came to see his family not as allies, but as adversaries. During the child-raising years, he told me, "I felt very alone."

* * *

Naturally, with these kinds of dynamics asserting themselves, conflicts tend to escalate during the child-raising years. And a new topic of marital conflict often emerges: sex. Based on my survey, the news about sex in the child-raising years of marriage is anything but uplifting:

- The number of couples having sex at least once a week falls by almost 30 percent from the honeymoon phase.
- Seven in ten husbands in this phase want sex more often than their wives do.
- The percentage of husbands who admit to having sex outside their marriage rises fivefold from the honeymoon phase.

Jorge Cruz spent the first eight years of his life in Colombia, South America. During most of that time, his father was gone, having traveled to the United States to pave the way for the family to immigrate. Jorge arrived in New York City with his mother and siblings in the early 1970s. Thirteen years later, as a young Army officer, Jorge first set eyes on his future wife, Anita, at a friend's house. He was drawn to her beauty. "Think of a young flower," he told me. He described Anita approvingly as "moral, religious, and willing to learn how to cook."

As a self-described "traditional Hispanic male," Jorge said, he adhered to the standard that "the male is the breadwinner, the male makes decisions." Anita got pregnant almost immediately after their wedding. Over the next five years, the couple had three children. Jorge expected Anita to be the primary child-raiser in the early years. He believed the children should get "psychological support . . . from their mother until they were older and better able to deal with my sternness."

As the workload on the couple intensified—Jorge worked seventy hours a week for a building contractor, Anita stayed home with the kids— their relationship began to fray. Sexual differences were particularly stark. "I used to chase her around the house," Jorge recalled. "That was the game we played. But it wasn't a game. I'm chasing her, and she's running away."

This angered Jorge. In his mind, "by providing shelter, support, and a

safe environment, I've done my job." He hoped that Anita would be interested in having sex with him, but she claimed fatigue when he approached her and refused to hire a babysitter so they could go out
together.

About a decade into the marriage, while attending night school in
Brooklyn, Jorge met a woman and began an affair. For Jorge, the sex was
important. Mostly, though, he said, he cherished "finding someone who
would communicate, where I could close the door and have a sheltered
place." He added that his girlfriend knew when he was having a bad day
and asked about it. "That didn't happen with my wife."

The affair went on secretly for five years, at which point Jorge told his
wife about it, moved out of his family home, and began living with his
lover. But it turned out not to be the fantasy life he had expected. His girlfriend was a heavy drinker. He also felt guilty about leaving his children,
who were then between the ages of seven and twelve. "I grew up without a
father. I grew up without a family. I couldn't let my children do the same,"
he told me. So after six months out of the house, Jorge moved back home.

When I spoke with Jorge, he was forty-four years old, married twenty
years, with three teenaged children. After ending his marital separation, he
stopped seeing his lover for a few months. Then he went back to her. Then
they broke up again. Jorge said the relationship is now permanently nonsexual.

Ironically, as his children got closer to leaving the nest, Jorge said he
was more likely than ever to stay married to Anita for good. That's because
she'd been diagnosed with diabetes. Staying with her is a matter of honor.
"You don't take a person who you've been with for twenty years, and when
she gets sick, just ditch her," Jorge said.

Jorge's story illustrates, among other things, the power of culture in
defining marital norms. Jorge told me that it's accepted, at least among
his generation, for Latino husbands to have affairs and even longtime
girlfriends. However, according to the Latino custom, husbands must
continue to financially support their wives and children. Jorge, who is
Catholic, did acknowledge some moral tension over his infidelity but be-

lieved that if a wife is not willing to have sex with her husband, the husband is not required to remain true to her.

Husbands of European descent, who made up the majority of my interviewees, generally were not as self-accepting about infidelity. Those I interviewed who did stray described themselves as "tormented," "ashamed," or "scared shitless" that they would be found out. Nonetheless, about one in eight husbands in my survey admitted to having affairs during the second phase of marriage. Other research indicates that the infidelity rate may be considerably higher.

Husbands who did have affairs during the child-raising years offered me a variety of reasons. The major justification was that their wives were not interested in sex. Indeed, my survey showed that men want sex more than their wives during this phase by a wide margin. Only 16 percent of husbands married four to twenty years indicated that they and their wives had approximately equivalent desire for sex.

A few men I spoke with acknowledged that they were less attracted to their wife after childbirth because she gained weight and kept it on. More commonly, however, husbands said that sexual relations with their wives had dropped off because their wives showed no interest. Often, she was tired from taking care of the children, keeping up the household, or working a job outside the home. Even though husbands understood this—and many were tired as well—the lack of sex frustrated them.

A hospital chaplain who had a two-year-old daughter recalled the following exchange with his wife after she rejected his sexual advances a year into their daughter's life.

Him: I have the feeling that you don't want me anymore.
Her: I do want you.
Him: Well, act like it!

Such communication dynamics landed many couples in therapy. According to my survey, 25 percent of couples married four to twenty years had gone to a marriage counselor together. Encouragingly, more than three-quarters of the husbands said the therapy was helpful.

The hospital chaplain mentioned above did not seek therapy. But he soon realized that one reason his wife was less interested in sex after the birth of their child was that she didn't feel attractive anymore. She'd gained forty pounds during the pregnancy and acquired stretch marks on her belly and breasts. Only after she shed the extra pounds did her sexual interest reemerge. The husband, though tempted by other women, waited her out. "I love my wife and I love my marriage," he told me. "We spend so much time not having sex, I didn't want to blow it" by having an affair.

This was the sentiment of most of the husbands I surveyed in this phase of marriage. Sex outside the relationship was a temptation, and for some a moral taboo. But it was the fear of sabotaging their marriages that kept the majority of men in line.

If sex is a key issue in the child-raising phase, so too is the task of child-raising itself. In my survey, 13 percent of husbands married between four and twenty years reported that raising children caused the most disagreements in their marriages. For some of these couples, the disagreements revolved around the time—or lack of it—that husbands spent with the children. Several husbands told me that their wives wished they would involve themselves more in the children's daily lives, attending PTA meetings, ferrying the kids to various activities, and the like.

But even in some of these marriages, husbands said, wives sent mixed signals. One thirty-one-year-old husband, for example, said that he and his wife had decided before their baby was born a decade earlier that the husband would be equally involved in raising their daughter. Once the child arrived, however, the wife was loath to give up the diaper bag. "She'd always tell me, 'I've got it. I can handle it,' " the husband recalled. "It was like she didn't trust me."

A more common source of disagreement on the topic of child-raising was specifically how to guide and discipline the kids. As I spoke with men, it became increasingly clear to me that husbands and wives often have very different views of what constitutes appropriate parenting.

With infants, the differences tend to reveal themselves when the baby cries. One husband, a marriage counselor, told me: "My philosophy of raising an infant was to let him cry it out. My wife was very much against that. Her philosophy was to meet the child's need for security early on" by responding quickly to the child's cries. This husband said: "I had a hard time accepting that. My concern was: When does 'meeting needs' cross over into pampering?"

This man eventually acceded to his wife's approach and, fifteen years later, told me that he was glad he did. "We have a child who by three or four was really secure." Now a teenager, the son is thriving, this man said.

Gary Marks, a forty-year-old Atlanta police officer, described a similar early-childhood situation with his wife, Claudia. As Gary recalled, after putting their infant son in bed, the couple would typically relax in front of the TV. Then the boy would start to cry. Some variation on the following exchange took place:

> *Gary:* He just needs to cry it out. He'll relax and go to sleep.
> *Claudia:* He needs to know we're here.
> *Gary:* Then yell to him and let him know we're here.
> *Claudia:* I'm going in.

This couple's son is now nine years old; they also have a six-year-old son. Gary told me that he and Claudia have continued to disagree over a variety of child-raising strategies, including discipline. Claudia, whose own father was physically abusive when she was a child, does not support spanking of any kind. Gary, who does not recall his father ever hitting him, believes that when a child is willfully disobedient, "a crack on the butt" can change his behavior in the future.

Gary acknowledged that he accidentally sprained his older son's shoulder when the boy was two. The child had repeatedly ignored Gary's calls to leave a play area, so Gary grabbed the child's arm and yanked. The incident "showed me that I can't jerk him around like my criminals," Gary said.

Gary conceded that since this son started kindergarten, spanking has been mostly ineffective. As the boy moved through grade school, Gary found it more fruitful to take away video games or keep him from going to an event. "I just ask him what privilege he'd like me to take away this time."

In addition to discipline differences, Gary and Claudia don't see eye to eye on what to expect from the kids. "She's like the waitress at our house," Gary says. "We'll be sitting at the dinner table and one of the kids will say, 'I need some milk,' and she'll jump up [to get it]. I'll say, 'Sit down. They know where the milk is.' "

Gary contends that "she's not doing [the children] a service" by waiting on them. When Gary and Claudia discuss this issue in private, Claudia usually agrees. "I just can't help it," she'll acknowledge. However, she strongly disagrees with Gary about spanking the children. He said he rarely hits his six-year-old son. "I've started to spank [the younger child] and stopped myself. I never did that" with the older one. Because of the shoulder incident, he said, he realizes that if he hits the younger son, he might hurt him.

Differences between husbands and wives on child-rearing continue, of course, beyond grade school; in some families, they get worse as the children reach puberty. Again, the most important difference, from the husband's point of view, is the issue of "toughness," or lack of it. Husbands report that their wives are "too sympathetic," "let the kids off the hook," "don't follow through," or are "afraid of conflict."

A retired university administrator from Iowa told me that his two adult children "are basically decent people" but suffer from a lack of discipline in their lives. He relates this deficit to the way he and his wife raised them. They had few parenting differences early on. But after the kids hit grade school, and continuing through high school, the parents struggled persistently over what to expect of their children.

One typical example: When their son was in high school, the couple agreed that the adolescent should cook one dinner a week so he'd be able to cook for himself later on. But almost every week, the father told me twenty years later, the son had found a way to get out of it. He had too much homework, or an important event would come up. So Mom agreed to make the dinner. This infuriated the father, who felt that the boy must learn how to follow through on his commitments.

The couple's daughter also failed to learn personal discipline, according to this husband, because his wife commonly made excuses for the girl's poor performance in school and other activities. The result, the husband said, was that the daughter flunked out of college in the first semester, married the wrong man, had a child too early, and now, divorced, can't find a good-paying job. "If she had finished college," her father told me, "she would have had a very different life."

While this man said that his wife's permissive parenting style contributed to their children's problems, he acknowledged his own role. After his wife overruled or ignored his ideas, he said, "I ended up distancing myself from the kids' discipline. I sort of said: 'I'm not needed around here.' I felt that I couldn't battle both my wife and the kids."

During the children's teen years, this man considered leaving his wife and family. And he's not alone. According to a variety of studies, marital satisfaction reaches a low point at about the time that the oldest children reach adolescence.

Interestingly, research by John Gottman and Robert Wayne Levenson indicates that the problem is not primarily the children specifically, and it's not even the disagreements, criticism, and other negative interactions between a husband and wife during this period. More important, these researchers contend, is the *lack of positive interactions between husband and wife:* affection, humor, active listening. The implication is that if couples focus on the positive aspects of their own relationship during the teen-raising years, they can insulate themselves from at least some of the marital dangers of this phase.

Indeed, while child-raising differences arise in virtually all marriages, most husbands still enjoy this phase of their lives. Here's a sampling of what husbands had to say about the *positive* impact of children on their marriages:

Forty-one-year-old pastor, married eleven years, two sons, aged nine and eight: "I feel that somehow having children increases our depth of relationship. As husband and wife, you share this joint project of raising kids. . . . There *are* challenges. We can't have sex in the kitchen as often!"

Fifty-four-year-old salesman, married thirty-three years, one daughter, aged twenty-four: "I was disappointed when I found out my wife was pregnant because I thought I would lose her to our baby. However, I never told my wife. [But] the positives of being a dad far outweigh the negatives. We are very much a family, even though our daughter now lives on her own."

Forty-two-year-old industrial designer, married fifteen years, one nine-year-old son, one seven-year-old daughter: "They really are the focus of our relationship. The kids have given us an opportunity to come to agreement and speak with one voice. And that is good. I do wonder, though: When we engineer an evening or weekend without the kids, we are both uneasy and really wish for the getaway to be over."

Thirty-six-year-old psychologist, married five years, two daughters, aged three and one: "[Parenthood] has been a wonderful addition to our relationship and has only accentuated how similar and complementary our values and goals are. We coparent very well, not without some tensions, but mostly we agree on how to approach things. Parenting is an aspect of our relationship that has strengthened our connection to each other, even though we have less time with just the two of us."

While married men who were born before 1945—pre–Baby Boomers—tended to have more children than those born later, my survey indicated that older, middle-aged, and younger husbands were about equally likely to disagree with their wives over some aspect related to children. But one story indicates how generational issues can influence the *content* of the arguments.

A forty-four-year-old university professor told me that after his daughter was born six years ago, he loved coming home from work and focusing attention on the child. He played with her, fed her, changed her diapers, put her to bed. His wife appreciated this but also felt slighted. "She said I didn't pamper her like I used to, and it's true," this man said.

Nonetheless, the man took exception to his wife's attitude. "I'm thinking: Don't beat up the good guy. I could come home like a father of the fifties—eat, drink, and go to bed. Women say they don't want us to be the dads our fathers were. Now that I'm doing that, why doesn't she like it?"

About 10 percent of husbands spend their married lives without children, by choice or fate. For these men, the second phase of marriage is ushered in less dramatically than for those husbands who produce children, and the marital issues, naturally, are different.

For one thing, childless couples tend to be more in synch about sex. According to the VoiceMale Survey, a childless wife is more likely than a wife with children to have a sex drive equal to that of her husband. Perhaps because of this, men who have no children are less likely to have affairs, the survey suggests.

On the other hand, sex for couples with fertility problems can become perfunctory, or worse. One husband recalled how his wife would call out "It's time!" when her body temperature and other vital signs indicated that she was primed for conception. Even the style of intercourse—who's on top, for example—was sometimes dictated by a doctor, based on theories of how to increase the odds of conception. "I have to admit, [sex] became a chore," one man said.

Adoption proved to be an acceptable alternative for many infertile couples. These couples tended to have the same problems and pleasures as those who had biological children together. Other couples who could not have biological children, and did not adopt, sometimes found that being involved with other people's children could satisfy some of their parenting needs.

One sixty-one-year-old husband told me that about twenty years into his thirty-five-year marriage he and his wife saw a counselor because they were fighting a lot. They discovered that the anger was related to their grief over the loss of their dream of having children together. This husband said that he and his wife had since come to terms with childlessness. It's helped that he's a teacher in his church school.

Husbands I spoke with who *chose* childlessness generally seemed satisfied with the decision. During this second phase of marriage, they tended to focus their nonworking time on personal growth, friendships, and their marriages. "When we talked about children early on, neither of us wanted to have any," one engineer told me. "It was an issue with my parents, but not for us. We wanted to travel, to be free to take whatever road came up."

This man was forty-four and married eighteen years when I spoke with him. He said that, five years earlier, his wife had questioned their original decision to have no children. For a couple of months, they spent extra time with other people's kids to see how they liked it. Then they said no to children again. "As it turned out, she just needed to get in touch with the maternal side of herself."

More than a quarter of the husbands I interviewed had been previously divorced, and most had exited their earlier marriages during the second phase. What killed those marriages? The reasons were as varied as the personalities involved.

> Forty-eight-year-old librarian, first married in 1982, divorced after fifteen years: "Our worlds started separating. She was in construction and I was in school. My world was one of books and ideas, and hers was one of bookshelves and beer. We didn't have many shared interests anymore. . . . I met another woman. [The other woman and I] never had any physical relationship, but we sure had an emotional relationship. My emotional energy went to this other woman."
>
> Thirty-five-year-old mortgage broker, first married in 1990, divorced after eight years: "I think the last straw was children. I was in a band back then, and my thinking was that once musicians had children there was no time for the

band. For most of our twenties, she didn't care. But something happens to a woman when she gets about twenty-
eight or thirty. Her biological clock starts ticking. When I
told her to forget about kids for now, I think she fell in love
with someone else."

Fifty-nine-year-old photographer, first married in 1972, divorced after ten years: "She didn't get fat, but she didn't
take care of herself. And she never tried to be romantic
with me. She didn't initiate. There was no passion left.
We'd become really good friends, roommates."

The second phase of marriage is of course unique for every couple, influenced by, among other factors, the timing and number of children; the
health of the children; job circumstances; and the unique personalities of
the husband and wife involved. It's also the phase, as we've seen, in which
marital struggles often become intense. According to my survey, the percentage of couples who argue at least several times a week triples in this
phase, as compared to the honeymoon years.

If a couple makes it through this period, the chances of the marriage
surviving for life are greatly enhanced. And, at least from the husband's
point of view, marriages that survive the child-raising years also tend to become increasingly satisfying in the years ahead.

Chapter Six

THE EMPTY NEST: YEARS 21 TO 35

We're very compatible. Basically, we go through museums at the same rate.
— Fifty-four-year-old management consultant

H IS MUSCLES THROBBED and his joints creaked, but as Bert
Hooper, fifty-five, sped homeward toward New Orleans through
East Texas, the cruelest ache came from a deeper source.

For four years, Bert had counted himself a lucky dad. His only child
had left the nest at age eighteen but had moved just two blocks away. All
through college, the son had returned to launder his clothes, share meals,
and seek advice from the folks. Father and son had rarely gone a week
without seeing each other.

But college had ended. And now, sadly for the father, the son was moving away for good. The day before, Bert and his wife, Peggy, had driven the
U-Haul carrying their son's belongings to Houston, where the twenty-two-
year-old would begin his career at a local bank. In Houston, Bert and
Peggy had helped angle their son's sofa through apartment hallways and
doorways. They'd lugged box after burgeoning box. Their arms had ached
as they hugged their son good-bye.

But only as they pulled away from the apartment complex where the
young man now lived did they feel the stomach punch of loss. "We were
stunned," Bert recalled when I spoke with him two years later. "Neither of
us said a word for a hundred miles."

Not surprisingly, when words did start flowing between them again, they were not always friendly ones. The weeks after their son's departure began what Bert calls "the troubled times" of his marriage. Peggy regularly turned down Bert's sexual advances and didn't want to talk about it. When Bert told his wife he was lonely, she felt criticized and pulled further away. He was so hurt that at times he shut himself in his home office to avoid saying things he'd later regret.

And that's where Bert, a successful real-estate agent, spoke with me two years after the departure of his son. He was still depressed about his relationship with Peggy. "The last couple of years have been the hardest," he told me. "She's not very responsive to me. But I have good memories, and I'm hoping that we can recapture some of that. All I can do is hope for better days."

If Bert is like most husbands entering the third stage of marriage, better days *will* come. The transition to the empty nest—like the transitions to living together and having a first child—tests the strength and flexibility of a marriage. No longer are children present to buffer the relationship, to give couples a "joint project," to divert attention from their bond to each other. No longer are husbands and wives young, firm, and endlessly energetic. No longer is a couple's future undeniably more compelling than their past. The age of loss has begun.

The stereotype is that men don't deal with loss very well. Stung by the diminishment of body and future, it is said, men grasp for immortality through younger women, red sports cars, and other trophies. Indeed, the early empty-nest years, according to most studies, are a delicate time in a marriage.

But most couples make it through. And those who do tend to be richly rewarded. According to my survey, the empty-nest phase—which runs from about years twenty-one to thirty-five—is an era of gradual revival in many marriages. Two-thirds of husbands who are in this phase say they are "very happy" in their relationships, up from half during the child-raising years. While the frequency of sex tends not to rise after the children leave home, sexual *satisfaction* generally improves as husbands and wives converge in their level of desire. Meanwhile, couples argue less often as they gradually accept their differences.

Even Bert Hooper, alone in his study, remains optimistic. His wife has told him she has no interest in leaving the marriage, and they've set a date to retire and move to the town where they met nearly thirty years before. "I'm not even thinking about [affairs]. I don't even consider leaving her," Bert told me emphatically. "We need to create something new because our life situation has changed. But staying together is not one option. It's the *only* option."

It's important to remember that for this book, I surveyed only currently married men. Thus, husbands who split from their wives in the honeymoon or child-raising phases—the first twenty years of marriage—are not represented here (unless they're in long-term second marriages). The husbands described in this chapter are a select group within the population of American married males. They're among the battle-tested.

And it's a good thing. Because challenges are ahead in the empty-nest years. And negotiating the end of child-raising is usually the first.

The end of Stanley Cooper's child-raising life provided the biggest challenge of his marriage. Stanley is a fifty-six-year-old autoworker from a midsized city in Ohio. He met his wife, Lauren, in high school in the 1960s. They had an on-and-off relationship for a couple of years. Then he was drafted. While he was in Vietnam, she sent him packages of food and small gifts. He survived the war, got a job with General Motors, proposed to Lauren, and married her at age twenty-one.

Stanley particularly enjoyed the first few years of the marriage, before their children were born. Like most in their generation, Stanley and Lauren had neither lived together nor slept together before they took their vows. After the wedding, exploring these dimensions of life was a shared adventure, Stanley said, and both reveled in the freedom and fun.

Then they had two daughters, two years apart. Lauren, a secretary, kept working even after the children were born and, when she was home, focused most of her attention on the kids. Stanley's work life was struggle-filled; he went through a series of layoffs followed by periods of heavy overtime. Balancing work with family became a major marital issue. Stanley remembers several years of "a very, very hectic life. There wasn't much of a home life, and it hurt our marriage. We weren't communicating well."

Nonetheless, Stanley says, he remained committed. He tried to be a good father to his daughters. As the girls moved through adolescence, Stanley also kept his eye on the calendar, aware that in just a few years, he and Lauren would be on their own again. It would be a simpler time, he thought, and a happier one.

But then, at least from Stanley's point of view, tragedy struck. Their younger daughter, Naomi, in the midst of college a couple of hundred miles away, became pregnant. Abortion was not an option for religious reasons, and Stanley and Lauren's grandson was born when Stanley was forty-six. Stanley told me that he had expected his daughter to stay in college, find a job, and raise her child on her own. Instead, she and Lauren agreed that she would go back to school without the baby; Lauren would take care of the child's day-to-day needs until graduation.

The decision was a blow to Stanley. "Our marriage hit rock-bottom at that point," Stanley recalls. He didn't want a baby in the house, and he issued Lauren an ultimatum: Either their grandson went to live with Naomi, or Stanley went to live somewhere else.

Soon, Stanley was sleeping alone in a stark apartment. He came back to his marital home only when Lauren wasn't there, mostly to mow lawns, repair water leaks, and the like. They rarely talked. Stanley saw his grandson occasionally. He considered seeing other women, but sensed that doing so "might burn the bridge" to reconciliation with his wife. Despite his anger and disappointment, he was not ready to give up on their twenty-five-year marriage.

After two years of separation, their daughter graduated from college and found an apartment near the family home. Lauren still helped with the baby, but the boy's transition back to his real mother had begun. It was then that Lauren called Stanley one day to ask if he wanted to go to a boat show. They had a good time that day, joking and laughing together, Stanley recalled, and soon they planned a weekend trip to a casino. After two months of "dating," Stanley moved back home.

Seven years later, when I spoke with him, Stanley declared himself happy with the marriage. "It's not always exciting, but it's interesting. We do things together, go to out-of-the-way places to eat supper. We're traveling more. . . . I've always loved my wife and respected her and felt she was a very nice-looking lady." More than anything else, Stanley says, he enjoys "home life," the security of a comfortable place and a partner who knows him and cares about him.

His only significant frustration now is sex. Stanley said that Lauren has a "take-it-or-leave-it attitude" about lovemaking. "She doesn't make it a priority. She could go a long time with no sex, and she would be just as happy." He wishes she would initiate every now and then, but adds: "I don't think being [sexually] frustrated is a life-or-death issue." About their future, he says: "I think we're going to stay together. At least I hope we can. I have no desire to do anything else."

Stanley acknowledges that he and Lauren had problems even before the crisis over their daughter's pregnancy. Had the pregnancy not occurred, Stanley surmises that something else might have shaken up the marriage.

In addition to long-standing differences in their levels of sexual desire, they'd also had trouble solving disagreements. When differences arose, one or the other would blow up. "One of her comments was that we're always walking on eggshells," Stanley said. "The least thing, and she would get upset or I would get upset." To avoid angry exchanges, Stanley had a long-standing habit of withdrawing to his workshop in the basement. He said he went there to "regroup." Lauren thought he went to hide.

Stanley and Lauren didn't address these problems while the kids were in the house. And, not surprisingly, they reemerged as the empty-nest years began. Indeed, according to the husbands I interviewed, *the quality of the empty-nest years often depends on the personal investment a couple puts into the marriage during the child-raising phase.* When, during the child-raising years, couples give all of their passion to children, work, and day-to-day concerns, they tend to grow in different directions, or "exist on parallel tracks," as one husband put it. Then, when the children leave, "you can be sitting across the dinner table from someone you've hardly met."

Conversely, those couples who consciously nurtured their marriages while their children were still in the house fared best in the third and fourth decades of marriage. A fifty-four-year-old salesman told me he had made it a point to plan at least one night out each month throughout their child-raising years. Early on, when their daughter was young and they had little money, they called in Grandma to babysit for free. Later, they found sitters in their neighborhood and church. "Just because you're married doesn't mean you forget to date," advised this husband, now twenty-eight years into his marriage.

Another husband, sixty-one years old and the father of five grown children, told me: "I got married because I wanted to be with my wife. We're not like leeches on top of each other. But I've never needed a night out with the boys. And she doesn't need one out with the girls." This man said he had a tradition in his marriage that spanned nearly thirty years of raising kids: He and his wife went away overnight together every wedding anniversary.

While such attention to the marriage usually helps, it does not inoculate couples from pressures in the empty-nest period. And one of the particular pressures most commonly mentioned by husbands is their wives' menopause.

Most midlife and older husbands told me that they had known almost nothing about menopause before their wives went through it. At first glance, these husbands tended to see menopause as a good thing: Their wives would have fewer mood swings, while concerns about contraception would be eliminated. They often expected menopausal symptoms to last a year or less.

And for some wives, menopause did go smoothly. Several men told me that they noticed no difference in their menopausal wives, except that, eventually, their periods stopped. More commonly, men could sense that their wives were less patient, less lubricated during intercourse, and less likely to sleep soundly at night.

One husband told me of what he called "menopause parties" that his wife held, by herself, during her late forties. As the husband tells it, he would awaken in the middle of the night to discover his wife's side of the bed empty. The next morning, he'd go downstairs and find that "everything's clean and there's a new things-to-do list. I thought: Wow, she's just lived an extra day without me!"

These middle-of-the-night escapades caused no problem in the relationship. But occasionally, a woman's menopause—and her husband's reaction to it—creates significant disturbance in the marriage.

A sixty-year-old salesman, now retired, told me that after his children left the home fifteen years ago his wife "had a hard time of it. It was a real adjustment for her because she'd been home more with the kids." The couple made it through the early empty-nest period by focusing on their common interests—church and couple friendships, among them—and creating new dinnertime and evening rituals.

About five years into the empty-nest period, the wife started menopause. The husband had always noticed that his wife was "physically sensitive," and now her sensitivity became heightened. She complained almost daily of feeling hot, achy, and fatigued. She visited her doctor regularly.

The husband tried to be sympathetic but often felt powerless. During this period, his wife was short-tempered and pushed him away. She was rarely interested in sex. The husband acknowledged that he was attracted to other women but knew that it was "an illusion to think that life would be perfect" with a new woman. "In the marriage vows, we said there's going to be ups and downs. Bailing out is a cop-out. Sure, it would be exciting [to sleep with someone else]. But after the excitement wears off, it's a mess."

So he waited out his wife's changes. And his patience paid off. Since menopause ended for her about five years ago, she has expressed appreciation for her husband's support through it. She's also regained some of her libido. For the husband, meanwhile, menopause helped him learn to be more thick-skinned and attentive. "I grew up a bit," he told me. "I learned to listen to the subtle cues."

Female menopause is the result of hormonal changes, particularly decreases in the body's production of estrogen. Some researchers say that men go through their own version of menopause as production of the primary male hormone, testosterone, declines. Doctors at the Institute of Endocrinology and Reproductive Medicine in Atlanta have found that about 40 percent of men in their forties experience such menopause-like symptoms as fatigue, depression, irritability, reduced sex drive, and difficulty attaining or sustaining an erection.

Whether testosterone deficiency was the cause or not, many of the middle-aged and older men I interviewed had indeed experienced some or all of these symptoms. Particularly unsettling was sexual decline.

One fifty-six-year-old man told me that in the year after his last child moved out of the house, his mother and the family dog had both died. He was distraught, he told me, adding, "I didn't even know I liked the dog." Shortly thereafter, he started experiencing difficulty achieving an erection. He wanted to have sex but was unable to. After a few incidents of impotence, he said, he started putting extra pressure on himself, which led to even more problems.

His wife was generally accepting of his struggles. But the man was not. So he went to a doctor, who prescribed Viagra. The drug worked. To the man's surprise, however, his wife reacted negatively. She told him that his use of "an artificial enhancement" led her to think that he wasn't attracted to her anymore. Though he tried to reassure her, she said she didn't want to have sex with him if he used Viagra. When I last talked with this man, he and his wife were still trying to work this out.

Other men told me of similar bouts with erectile dysfunction in the empty-nest years. For many, it was the first time that their bodies did not respond sexually. Some feared they'd never regain their ability to have sex. In most cases, sexual potency returned, sometimes with the help of medication. But even for men who never experienced impotence, the intensity of their sexual drive and orgasms tended to diminish through the empty-nest years. As one fifty-eight-year-old husband told me: "My orgasms are still good, but they're nothing like they used to be." Perhaps as a result, this man found himself less interested in sex. For the first time in his long marriage, he occasionally declined his wife's sexual advances.

* * *

This touches on another issue regarding the changes that men and women go through in the middle and late-middle years. It has long been noted, by psychoanalyst Carl Jung and others, that the genders tend to evolve differently during adulthood. In young adulthood, men are generally more competitive and work-oriented than women. Women, meanwhile, are more family-oriented and openly emotional in their young adulthood.

In middle age, however, the genders converge—and sometimes pass by each other. Men tend to mellow, becoming increasingly emotional and home-centered; midlife women often become more independent, shifting their focus to activities outside the home, including their own careers.

While these male-female personality tendencies are by no means universal, they were true in the lives of many husbands I interviewed. Often, these personality changes were helpful to the marriage, bringing the partners into synch. Occasionally, however, they caused upheaval in the relationship.

For Marcus Goode, a retired city engineer from suburban Denver, the empty nest seemed to promise marital rejuvenation. Marcus had married his wife, Celia, in the early 1960s, when both were just out of college. Over the next two-plus decades, the couple focused on raising their four children. When the kids were young, Marcus worked fifty hours a week or more while Celia focused on the family and the PTA. Marcus enjoyed fatherhood. The family spent its vacations outdoors, camping, hiking, and exploring the Rockies.

When the children started heading off to college, Marcus put extra energy into his work. He performed consulting jobs on the side to help pay the children's education bills. Celia, meanwhile, trained for and became a real-estate agent.

By the time their last child was through college in the mid-1990s, Marcus was fifty-six and ready for a break. Above all, he wanted to travel with Celia, relax with her, get to know her again, and reenergize their marriage.

But Celia's focus was elsewhere. After decades of giving to her family, of putting her professional ambitions on hold, she was finally in a position to excel in her career. She rejected Marcus's urging to slow down. To add to Marcus's disappointment, she also rejected his sexual advances. She had always been less interested in sex than Marcus; now she told him one reason why: Sex was sometimes painful for her. She wanted to stay married but live as partners, not lovers.

At the time, Marcus told me, he had been hurt and angry. He considered leaving Celia but couldn't bring himself to do it. He imagined the pain such a split-up would cause his children. He also realized that he loved his wife for her steadiness, ambition, and intellectual strength. He added: "I just couldn't imagine getting into the same dating scene" as his now-grown kids.

He did give himself permission "to entertain sexual opportunities" outside his marriage, and on a business trip two years into his marital celibacy, he made love with a woman he'd known for several years. But he felt lousy about it and decided to "turn my energy toward other things," particularly his grandchildren. In his early sixties, Marcus cut his work hours and became child-care provider one day a week for his first granddaughter. "Nothing in my life compares" to the joy of that experience, he told me.

I spoke with Marcus when he was sixty-five. He had fully retired the year before. His wife was still working. Marcus said that he sometimes traveled on his own or with groups. He said he'd forgiven Celia for ending their sex life before he was ready. He accepted that she honestly loved him but simply didn't experience the pleasure of sexuality that he did. (In my survey, 13 percent of empty-nest husbands said they no longer had sex with their wives. Health issues and the side effects of medication were the top causes.)

Today, Marcus and Celia still sleep in the same bed. They kiss each other hello and good-bye, but Marcus is wary about other kinds of physical affection. Occasionally, when they're watching TV together, Celia will snuggle up next to him or take his hand. All that does is remind him of the sex he's not getting, Marcus says, and he feels disappointment. After a few minutes, he'll usually make an excuse to get up from the couch. When he sits down again, he'll put a little space between him and his wife.

* * *

Thus far, I've focused on the trouble spots in the empty-nest phase. But my interviews and survey reveal plenty of good news—sexual and otherwise—about this third phase of marriage.

On the sexual front, even in their fifties and sixties, 61 percent of empty-nest husbands reported having sex at least once a week, about the same as in the previous phase of marriage. And 83 percent of husbands in this phase considered themselves sexually satisfied, a significant increase from the child-raising phase. This rise was due in part to the increased number of couples whose sex drives had finally equalized. In the child-raising years, only 16 percent of husbands said that they and their wives had equivalent levels of sexual desire; in the empty-nest period, that figure jumped to 29 percent.

There was good news on the arguing front as well. According to our survey, the frequency of marital arguing drops dramatically in the third and fourth decades of marriage. Only 10 percent of empty-nest husbands said they argued with their wives at least once a week, compared to 26 percent of newlyweds and 29 percent of couples in the child-raising years. Meanwhile, nearly one-quarter of empty-nest husbands said they had argued with their wives *not at all* in the previous six months; among couples in the child-raising years, only 5 percent never argued.

The intensity of the marital arguments also seemed to diminish in midlife. Our survey showed that 54 percent of husbands in the empty-nest years said solutions to marital disagreements came "easily" for them. In the child-raising years, that figure was only 35 percent.

Most likely, this last comparison reflects, at least in part, the fact that some couples who argued regularly during the child-raising years never made it to the empty nest. Their marriages dissolved. But the numbers also indicate a general decrease in tension for marriages that last into midlife and beyond.

Looking over my many conversations with empty-nest husbands, I was struck by how intentional the happiest couples are about investing in their relationships. By the time couples reach the twenty-year mark, they know each other well and sense whether they want to stay in the relationship for good. But they also realize that resting on their laurels, allowing momentum to carry them, is not enough. If they want to remain happily married, they have to *continue* to invest in their relationship.

One man told me that after their son went away to college, he and his wife quit their jobs, flew to Europe, bought a VW camper, and drove around the continent, living together in the camper for a year. It was their way of recommitting to one another. Ten years later, the husband told me what he remembered most from the trip: "We're very compatible. Basically, we go through museums at the same rate." When this husband and wife returned to the United States, they were so confident in their compatibility that they launched a husband-wife consulting business.

Another husband, who didn't have the money to quit his job, was concerned that he and his wife would grow apart. He took up square dancing with her in order to stay connected. "Both of us were independent persons, and we appreciated that," this husband said. Eventually, they became dance instructors. "We were out together quite a few nights a week, calling dances and teaching classes," he recalled. Now ninety-two years old and married sixty-five years, this man said he and his wife still dance together occasionally at home.

Why do husbands expend the energy to keep their marriages vital after the children leave? What is so compelling about marriage for them? I was struck as well by men's answers to these questions.

A fifty-seven-year-old lawyer, who acknowledged having had a two-year affair early in his marriage, spoke for many men when he described the value of marriage for him during the empty-nest years. "Marriage gives me an automatic partner and best friend. It gives me an automatic home base. I know there's a place where I can go where there's someone who will accept me. I don't have to pretend to be somebody I'm not. I don't have to put on an act. I can be me. That's a great feeling. I don't know how you get that by having a different girlfriend every week. I don't think it's possible."

Chapter Seven

Mature Marriage: Years 36 and Beyond

If you ever leave me, I'm going with you.
—Seventy-five-year-old retired Army officer to his wife of fifty-five years

IT IS EIGHT O'CLOCK on a sunny morning at Thomas Kaufman's ranch-style house. Thomas, who is eighty-one years old and a retired New England university professor, is in his blue cotton pajamas at his kitchen table, sipping tea, hovering over the spread-out newspaper. A bowl with the remnants of oatmeal rests to the side. On the stove squats the half-filled pot of oatmeal he stirred up an hour before. On this morning, Thomas has already put in his hearing aids, so he's aware of Stella's footsteps in the hallway leading to the kitchen. He looks up from the paper at the bathrobed, brown-and-gray-haired woman framed in the doorway. A smile spreads across his face.

It has been fifty-nine years since Thomas met Stella at a mutual friend's Christmas party. World War II was reaching its climax, and the two were living in their parents' homes while attending college. Thomas remembers that they ate in a small downtown restaurant on their first date and, afterward, walked the two miles to her home. On the way, Thomas became enthralled with Stella: He found her intelligent, pretty, witty, and, like him, oriented toward public service. Thomas recalls that they were so consumed by their conversation that they walked right past Stella's home.

Twelve days later, Thomas proposed marriage. It was a simple wedding, and as in so many marriages of their era, the first child came quickly.

"In our generation, we saw it as an obligation" to have kids, Thomas says. Within six years, four more children filled the house. For the next two decades, Thomas focused on growing his reputation as one of the nation's premier scientists while Stella cared for the children and helped Thomas manage his career. She typed his papers, arranged the family's schedule around his work, and moved the household several times.

After the kids left home, Thomas continued to excel in his career while Stella became a highly respected middle-school teacher. She retired first, and they traveled together as he presented papers and took visiting professorships. After he left the university, Thomas and Stella visited the Middle East, the Far East, Europe, and virtually every region of their own country. They spent holidays with their children and a growing brood of grandchildren.

In his seventies, health problems slowed Thomas. He and Stella traveled less. Both got involved in local volunteer activities, from mentoring young children to raising money for charitable causes. In her late seventies, Stella had health problems too, forcing her to cut back her active schedule.

The morning mentioned above is a typical one in their home now. Thomas gets up first, cooks the oatmeal, and surveys the day's news. When Stella comes to the kitchen an hour or so later, he watches as she fills her bowl with oatmeal and reheats it in the microwave. Then, as the microwave hums, he will often get up from his chair, approach Stella, kiss her lightly on the lips, and wrap his arms around her for a long morning hug.

Later, clean-shaven and dressed in brown slacks and a shirt and tie, leaning back in a desk chair in his book-lined study, Thomas tells me about Stella: "I credit her with being the main reason I've reached eighty. Not just because she saw me through some critical times in my health. But because most people my age, though they might deny it, feel depressed sometimes. Depression is a natural part of aging. The relationship that she and I have is an antidote for that depression."

In a culture where youth is revered and sex worshiped, it is the oldest husbands who claim to be the happiest in their marriages, my survey shows. For these men, because of a shared space and history with their wives, marriage has deepened to a level of connection that they never imagined earlier in life.

While sex may no longer be a desire, or an option, for these couples, the level of intimacy between the partners can be extraordinary. They know each other's idiosyncrasies, routines, subtle tastes—and, for the most part, they've accepted them. According to the VoiceMale Survey, more than three-quarters of husbands married more than thirty-five years say they are "very happy" in their marriages. Moreover, 98 percent of husbands in long marriages say they'd marry the same woman if they had the chance to do it again.

"I've never regretted it," one husband, married fifty-five years, told me of his decision to wed his high-school sweetheart. "She's a lovely woman. . . . The best thing is knowing that whenever I walk through that door, she's going to be here. I've got somebody to come home to. I realize that one day, I may not have this. So I cherish every moment with her."

It's important to note that the husbands described in this chapter are of a distinctly different generation from the husbands married since 1970, and particularly compared with those married since the year 2000. Those of us in shorter marriages must be careful not to assume that the experiences of this older generation of husbands will predict our own futures.

In fact, the oldest group of husbands in my survey has a demographic profile that contrasts sharply with that of husbands married in recent years. Among other things, long-married husbands are:

Less likely to have been previously married. Among long-married husbands, only 4 percent were previously married, compared to 39 percent among men married since 2000.

Less likely to have lived with their wives before marriage. None of the forty-nine long-married men we surveyed had lived with their wives before marriage; 62 percent of husbands married since 2000 had lived with their wives.

Less likely to have had sex with their wives before marriage. Only 27 percent of long-married husbands had sex with their wives before marriage. That compares to 87 percent of husbands who married since 2000.

More likely to have married young. Fifty-five percent of long-married couples had married their wives by the age of twenty-four; among those married since 2000, just 11 percent married before age twenty-four.

Less likely to have married women who are older than they are. Only 4 percent of long-married husbands had wed women who were two years or more older than they were; among those married since 2000, 29 percent married women two years older or more.

Less likely to have married someone of a different race. None of those in our survey who married before 1968 married across racial lines, compared to less than 10 percent of those married since 2000.

Perhaps more important than any of these demographic differences are attitude contrasts between couples married before 1970 and those married later. In my interviews, I found two differences that seemed particularly noteworthy.

The first of these differences is that couples married before 1970 generally considered marriage to be *a merging of families,* not, as in more recent years, primarily a joining of two individuals. When Thomas Kaufman, the retired university professor mentioned at the beginning of this chapter, asked Stella to marry him, she didn't give him an answer immediately. Although Stella was legally an adult, she told Thomas that she needed time to talk it over with her parents. She did so and came back three days later with her yes.

Another man was required by his future wife to ask her parents for her hand in marriage. He went to them with a carnation. After the conversation with the parents, they still withheld their approval. Not until they had completed a thorough background check—consulting the local rabbi, among others—did they give their permission.

This respect for the bride's family cut across ethnicities in the pre-1970 period. I interviewed an eighty-two-year-old African-American man, married fifty-seven years, who'd lived his whole life in rural Tennessee. He recalled asking his girlfriend's mother for permission to marry. "We walked from [her home] to downtown. I told her, 'I would like to marry your daughter,'" this husband recalled. The mother asked about his work prospects and whether he planned to move away from the area. When he said he had a good local job and that he wanted to stay in town, she approved the marriage. This couple still lives within sight of the home in which the wife grew up.

Such situations are much rarer among married couples of today. While the phrase "traditional values" has made a political comeback, it's unusual for an American man of today to ask his girlfriend's parents for permission to marry her.

Another difference between couples married before 1970 and those married in more recent years is their expectations for the marriage. Longer-married husbands told me that when they were looking for a bride, they sought a "helpmate," not a "soul mate." A helpmate was someone on whom he could depend to handle duties in the home, to support him emotionally, and to care for their children. A deep, soulful connection was a bonus, and one that, when it occurred at all, grew only gradually over the many decades of the marriage. Younger men, on the other hand, tend to look less at the domestic skills of a wife-to-be and more at whether they perceive a powerful emotional, physical, and spiritual connection.

Because of the women's movement, one of the common experiences of couples married before 1970 has been the pressure to adapt, mid-marriage, to new cultural norms regarding marriage. As mentioned earlier, men who married in the 1940s through early 1960s expected that, for the duration of their marriage, they would make the money and rule the roost and that their wives would maintain the home. And in some cases, this expectation was fulfilled. Even as the feminist movement transformed cultural attitudes about marriage, some couples maintained their prefeminist marriage dynamics.

But in many cases, husbands told me, their marriages had to change as society did. Dale Carpenter was one of these men. When he and his wife, Lisa, wed in 1965, both seemed to know their role. "Our image of marriage was that the wife was supposed to do what the husband said," Dale recalled.

But several years into the marriage, following the birth of their two children, Lisa began to challenge Dale. Dale can't remember the first time Lisa disagreed with one of his decisions, but he recalls "a period of tension." Dale says: "It was a wake-up call. It made me stop and think that there is another opinion here and there's maybe some validity to it."

Now married thirty-nine years, with three grandchildren, Dale makes family decisions much differently than in the 1960s. He and Lisa talk about all major decisions before making them. If they can't agree, they keep trying. "It's been quite a profound change, and difficult at times," Dale told me. "But it's healthier. Some guys want to have mail-order brides, docile women. But then there's no equality. The person is your servant or something. I don't think that makes for a good, dynamic relationship. If you're going to have a dynamic relationship, you have to be uncomfortable at times."

Dale and other men I interviewed told me that they know many couples that did not make it through the changes of the 1960s and 1970s. Women who were suddenly freed from economic and cultural dependence on their husbands reevaluated their marriages; many left. Some husbands, meanwhile, challenged by the changing times, were unwilling to adapt to the changes in their wives. They divorced and found compliance in a second wife, or stayed unmarried.

Couples that do make it to later adulthood together still must negotiate some tricky transitions, not least of which is retirement. One retired banker said that his wife told him to "get off my elbow" after he crowded her in the weeks following the end of his work life three years ago. He went from working fifty hours a week to full-time retirement and was determined to start helping his wife around the house. "She'd been doing housework for our entire marriage," he told me. "I thought it was my time." But she resisted. "For her, having me around was more work, not less." This man eventually became active in SCORE, a government program in which retired executives mentor young businesspeople.

Another man, a seventy-year-old retired college professor, said he too had struggled with "role shifts" after he stopped working. He thought he would help his wife by doing some of the grocery shopping. But she complained that with both of them going to the supermarket, she couldn't keep track of what they needed. Sometimes she would say to him: "I'm feeling useless." He stopped shopping.

This couple also struggled around time spent together during the day. In the first weeks after his retirement, they had lunch together each day. But soon, he recalls, both felt pressure to show up in the kitchen at noon, even when doing so interrupted a project. So they cut out the daily lunch dates and met up for dinner only. "We had to say to each other: 'Let's not become Siamese twins here.' "

Now, five years into his retirement, this man has gone back to part-time teaching, and, he says, he's happier than ever. "I have the best of all worlds. I can say no when I want to. When you're working [before official retirement], someone can always tell you that you have to do it." The key to a successful retirement, he says, is "to keep busy with things you like, and stay flexible."

Not surprisingly, long-married couples have sex less often than shorter-married couples, in part because the sex drive naturally tends to drop after age 50. The VoiceMale Survey showed that only 28 percent of couples married more than thirty-five years have sex weekly, compared to more than half of empty-nest couples (those married twenty-one to thirty-five years). Thirty percent of couples married more than thirty-five years have no marital sex at all.

Given these statistics, it may seem odd that 88 percent of husbands in this long-married group say they are sexually satisfied in their marriages—

nearly as high a figure as in the honeymoon stage of marriage. It seems that for many husbands, sexual satisfaction is not directly related to the frequency of sexual intercourse.

Carl Cassidy, a ninety-two-year-old retired engineer, married sixty-five years, told me that he and his wife still kiss, hold hands, dance together at home, and touch each other genitally. But they no longer have marital sex in a traditional sense.

Here's how Carl described the course of his sexual relationship with his wife of more than six decades: Though both were in their mid-twenties when they married, neither had had sex previously. In the early years of marriage, Carl recalls, "I'm not bragging, but we [had sex] a lot." The frequency of sex held steady during their child-raising years, and through their late forties and fifties. At about age sixty, he recalls, "We didn't lose our attraction, but we started to lose our desire." Sexual frequency declined.

In his late seventies, Carl began having heart problems and took heart medication that left him unable to attain an erection. For several years, while he and his wife continued to be sensual with one another, they no longer had intercourse. Then, in his mid-eighties, the couple had a sexual revival. Viagra came on the market, and for the next four years, Carl used it. He and his wife made love once a month or so.

Finally, after suffering a heart attack at age ninety, Carl was warned away from Viagra by his doctor. Now Carl and his wife are back to hugging, kissing, and touching.

Carl says he's satisfied. And one way he and his wife continue to stimulate each other is by flirting with other people, Carl told me. He said that every week before or after church, he greets many of the older widows with a smile and a hug. About his wife, he says: "She knows they're just friends. She tells me that she likes it that her husband still has a way with the women."

Because relatively few long-married men slept with their wives before marriage, we might expect many of them to have had sexual problems due to incompatibility. But generally speaking, that didn't seem to be the case, according to the men I interviewed. Most older husbands told me that they tended to be the ones who initiated sex and that their wives were generally willing. They didn't expect "stand-on-your-head sex," as one man put it, and didn't get it.

There was, as is the case among shorter married couples, a disparity in desire between husbands and wives in long relationships. In my survey, I asked husbands who had been married for more than thirty-five years whether they wanted more sex than their wives or vice versa. The answer: 65 percent of husbands wanted more sex than their wives; only 2 percent of wives wanted more sex than their husbands. (In the rest of the cases, the level of desire was about equal, husbands said.)

A number of the men I spoke with said their wives appeared relieved, or at least readily accepting, when the husband's sexual desire or ability began to wane. One man became impotent in his early fifties after being diagnosed with diabetes. Twenty years later, when Viagra came on the market, he suggested to his wife that perhaps he should get a sample from the doctor. His wife, then seventy, offered a two-word response: "What for?" He got the point and let it go.

While most long-married couples have reached agreement on sexuality, it remains a point of contention in a small percentage of cases.

Tim Fuller was sixty-seven years old when I met with him in his suburban Cleveland, Ohio, home. He was a retired mechanic and foreman who now worked part-time delivering free local newspapers.

Tim told me that he had met his wife, Julia, in high school in 1953, just about the time that his parents were divorcing. Tim's father had been a tyrant and an alcoholic, Tim said, and his mother had finally bailed out. "Dinners were a disaster," Tim recalled of his childhood. "Dad had a thing about noisy eaters, and kids are noisy eaters. I still react to people at a theater who eat their popcorn loudly."

His father's idea of teaching Tim about sex was to whisper into Tim's ear the word "fuck" and ask Tim, who was a teenager at the time, if he knew what it meant. When Tim said yes, that was pretty much the end of his education.

When they first met, Tim was so attracted to Julia that it hurt, he told me. "There was this ache in my body. It was wonderfully painful." Julia and Tim necked a lot in high school, but sexually speaking, that was the extent of it. Upon graduation, Tim joined the Army. During one of Tim's weekends home, he asked Julia to marry him, and on his next leave from the military, they wed.

At first, the sex was fantastic, Tim told me. Before the wedding, he said, "I'd always had this moral mind-set that sex was bad. When I got married, I'm thinking: 'I'm getting away with murder here. I can't believe it's OK.' All the inhibition was gone."

For about four months, Tim and Julia had sex at least once a day. Then she got pregnant, and things were never the same. Suffering morning sickness, Julia lost fifteen pounds in the first weeks of the pregnancy; her body always seemed to be hurting. Later in the pregnancy, when Tim suggested sex, she said no. She told him she wanted to wait for the baby to come.

Tim was disappointed but figured things would get better once the baby was born. Instead, they got worse. Julia poured her energy into their child. In the second or third year of their marriage, they began arguing over sex. Tim recalls that at one point Julia told him: "I'm just frigid, and that's all there is to it." The only times she would have sex with Tim, he recalls, was just before he was scheduled to go away on business for a few days. "I think she did it to try to save the marriage."

The situation created a tension for Tim concerning his feelings for their son. He loved the boy, and, Tim says, "there was [also] a sense that he'd come between us. It was a battle to have sex once a month."

After one of their few sexual encounters, Julia became pregnant with a second child; a girl was born two years after the son. Tim made a conscious decision to focus on being an involved father. He and Julia made a good team, he said. Tim was a reliable provider, and Julia handled the house and children well. "We focused on being parents rather than lovers," Tim told me.

Tim stayed in parenting mode as his kids reached high school. Then he turned increasing energy toward church work. As the empty-nest period loomed, however, he became depressed. He sometimes imagined driving his car into an embankment. Once, he told a female coworker about his marital struggles. The coworker responded, "You need some TLC." If it was an invitation to an affair, he turned it down. He told me: "The biggest reason I've never cheated in forty-seven years of marriage is fear—fear of being an inadequate lover."

After the kids moved away, Tim hoped that his sex life with Julia would get better. But it didn't. He asked her what he could do to please her sexually, but she was unwilling to talk about sex openly. Tim noticed that while he referred to sex as "making love," she referred to it as "intercourse."

After about thirty-five years together, he began what he calls "a gradual confronting" of the situation. He talked about his frustration more directly with Julia. But there was little change. Finally, in their fortieth year of marriage, Tim moved out. For six months, he lived on his own in a small apartment, spending time mostly on volunteer work and with single male friends he'd met through his running and other sports activities. Then Julia was diagnosed with cancer, and Tim moved back home to help her through her treatment.

In addition to caring about Julia, Tim told me, he had returned because he'd found that single life was lonely. When I spoke with him, Julia was apparently cancer-free, and she and Tim continued to live together. He said his sex drive was diminishing and that he and his wife were making an effort to find mutually enjoyable activities such as working in their yard, eating out, and bird-watching.

Tim, however, remained torn about the future of the marriage. On the one hand, he told me, "I don't give up easily. I don't want to be the failure that my father was." But he also indicated that when he and Julia finally decide to downsize, he might get an apartment of his own.

Tim acknowledges that Julia is not completely to blame for their intimacy problems. Looking back, he recognizes that, because of his childhood, "I needed a lot of physical and emotional closeness. A lot of [our problems] stemmed from my insecurity." He thinks he put extra pressure on their marriage by expecting that "this relationship was going to be everything that my [childhood] life wasn't."

Nonetheless, he's still angry about Julia's lack of interest in physical intimacy and her way of thinking about sex. Tim recalled that Julia once entered the bedroom when he was masturbating. "Her attitude was that I was disgusting," Tim said. "She told me that she's never masturbated and never will."

While sex is still an issue for Tim, I found that it was a make-or-break issue for very few of the men I interviewed who were in long-term marriages. Previous research seems to support this finding as well.

A study of one hundred long-married couples in the 1980s found that sex was not among the top ten perceived reasons that husbands gave for their own successful long marriages. Rather, topping the husbands' list were the following: my wife is my best friend; I like my wife as a person; marriage is a long-term commitment; marriage is a sacred institution; we agree on aims and goals; and we laugh together frequently.

Another reason for successful long-term marriages is loyalty. A high percentage of long-married men performed military service, where loyalty to one's fellow soldiers and country was strongly reinforced. Many of the husbands I interviewed extended that sense of loyalty to their marriages as well. This was particularly noticeable in the cases where men were called upon to care for ill wives.

Previous studies have shown that women who must care for infirm husbands often feel somewhat resentful. After all, in most cases the women have been doing the bulk of the hands-on caring throughout their marriage. Now some feel sentenced to months or years of further care. Husbands, on the other hand, often see caring for a wife less as a burden than as an opportunity.

Why? First, husbands can give back to their wives in ways that their wives have given to them through their lifetimes—by nurturing, being patient, and meeting their needs. Second, by providing for the everyday needs of their wives, these men feel useful, a feeling that some men lose after leaving the working world. Finally, husbands tend to get kudos from families and friends for caring for their wives; wives caring for husbands falls more into the category of "expectation."

* * *

One of the most affecting stories I heard about a husband's late-life caring is that of Alberto Sanchez. Alberto was a second-generation Mexican-American who grew up near Detroit. Soon after joining the Army in 1948 as a skinny twenty-year-old, he met Juanita at a dance hall. It was a chance meeting. He and two military buddies had left the base on a weekend pass. A cabdriver drove them to his own favorite club, where Juanita happened to be dancing with a friend that night.

"The sparks started to fly," Alberto recalled. "She was a good-looking woman." Within a few weeks, they were dating regularly, and Alberto began thinking about marriage. "I was ready to settle down. I wanted a companion," Alberto told me. "She came along and hit all the right buttons." He was particularly impressed that she had acted as a surrogate mother to her four younger siblings after their mother had died. That experience, Alberto judged, would make her a mature, strong, and resilient partner.

The couple married in 1948, and Alberto decided to make a career out of the military. Within four years, three children were born. Economically, times were tough. "We used to go to the USO bingo night because the prizes were food," Alberto recalled. The winners got "six cans of pork and beans, a pound of pork chops."

Besides a lack of money, their major struggle in the child-raising years was Alberto's travel schedule. Often he'd be gone for two weeks at a time for training, and occasionally on even longer special assignments. On the phone during these separations, Alberto remembered Juanita telling him: "You've left me. Sometimes I feel like shipping [the kids] to you." Nonetheless, he always felt Juanita's support. "She's from the old school. She cooked all the meals, did all the washing. Anything that I wanted to do, she backed me—sometimes seventy-five percent, but she always backed me."

In appreciation for that support, Alberto tended to let the little disagreements go by. When Juanita had a strong opinion about something, he acceded to her. He does that to this day. "I try not to muddy the water. C'mon, most times it's not that big a deal."

The couple had very little time in an empty nest. By his fiftieth birthday, Alberto had four grandchildren. Having missed out on his own children's early years, he relished his time with his grandchildren, who lived nearby and stayed at Alberto's house often.

His fifties were a difficult time for Alberto healthwise, as he was diagnosed with diabetes and became impotent. Alberto said that both he and Juanita had accepted the loss of their sexual life. "I think probably for her, she was glad," Alberto said. He added: "Sometimes I still give her a pat on the ass and tell her, 'By god, you've got a good-looking body.' "

Alberto retired from the military at age sixty, set up an office at home, and began doing genealogical research and writing. Juanita continued to do the cooking, cleaning, and other household work. They had monthly gatherings of the clan, which included children, grandchildren, and eventually great-grandchildren.

Two years before I interviewed him, the couple had suffered a blow when Juanita was diagnosed with Alzheimer's disease. She had been forgetting names, telling the same stories repeatedly, and losing her way in the car. After the diagnosis was confirmed, Alberto decided he had to adapt creatively to the new circumstances.

Now, each morning, he writes out an hour-by-hour schedule for the day ahead and puts it on the kitchen table so Juanita can refer to it. He tries to make each day much like the last so Juanita doesn't get confused.

Juanita can still cook, so, according to the particular schedule Alberto showed me, she makes breakfast at 9 A.M. After some morning conversation, Alberto goes to his home office and stays until noon. At that point, Juanita makes lunch and they eat together. At 1 P.M., he returns to his office and works until 3 P.M. Then they sit side-by-side in easy chairs in their den and watch *Dr. Phil* and *Oprah*. At 5 P.M., Juanita starts fixing dinner and Alberto goes back to his office to close up for the day. They eat at 6 P.M., watch some TV together or read in the evening, and go to bed. A couple of nights a week, Alberto attends a civic or social meeting.

Alberto, who was seventy-five when I interviewed him, told me that he feels sadness about Juanita's illness but does not mind having to care for her. He is learning to cook for the first time so he can begin handling that responsibility as Juanita's illness progresses. He misses talking with her sometimes, but adds: "After fifty-five years, you're really kind of talked out." He still teases her by telling her: "If you ever leave me, I'm going with you."

He told me that despite Juanita's illness, he has a satisfying life. "I have no financial worries, no worry about food and shelter. Everything's paid for. We're gonna die in this house." He adds: "I've had a good marriage. Now it's about establishing memories for our children and grandchildren and great-grandkids. I'm living for the day that the youngest—the five-year-old twins—get married."

He does have one worry: life without Juanita. Even in her deteriorating state, he is comforted by her presence. "I know I'm going to react to the loss," he said. "When everything's over, when we put her in the grave, when everyone else goes home, you're alone. That's when it hits you. I'll be devastated. But I'll have no regrets."

Part Three

VoiceMale

Chapter Eight

~∞~

HOUSEWORK: THE LINK TO SEX

My wife has told me that she's never more turned on to me than when I'm doing housework, and she's proven it again and again.

—Thirty-nine-year-old guidance counselor

NOAH JAMES swears he never saw the grime. He had grown up "old-school traditional" in the 1980s, the second of five children in a midwestern family that strolled en masse to the neighborhood Catholic church each Sunday morning. Noah's parents, like so many of their contemporaries, divided the household responsibilities between inside and out. His father, an accountant, earned the family's income and kept the yard in shape; his mother cooked, cleaned, and tended the inside of the home. By the time Noah left this environment to get married, he was twenty-four years old—and he'd never seen a grown man dust.

Despite this, Noah expected to share in the housework with his new wife, Anne. Both were employed full-time as teachers when they married. And Noah had always wanted an equal relationship. Still, even as the couple settled into their first apartment after the wedding, they hadn't discussed who would be responsible for what around the house. Six years later, Noah told me in an interview: "I remember thinking at the time: 'When you get married, do you divide chores like you're little kids—one for you, one for me? Or do you do whatever needs to be done?' "

At first, they tried "whatever needs to be done." As Noah recalls it, Anne took the lead, buying the groceries, washing the clothes, and running the vacuum cleaner every few days. Anne also cooked meals because she was better at it. Apartment life meant no lawn to mow and few household items to repair. So Noah's main contribution to housework was taking out the garbage, clearing the table after meals, and handling the bills.

From Noah's perspective, all seemed well until about six months into the marriage. That's when Anne asked Noah a troubling question: Why, since she was doing most other chores, hadn't Noah picked up a rag and cleaned the dust and grime off the windowsills? Anne said she suspected that Noah simply expected her to do it all. Noah listened to the evidence and the charges. Then he issued what he contends was an honest defense: "I didn't even notice the dust."

Forty years ago, when it came to the division of household responsibility, both genders knew their roles. And as long as both partners accomplished their culturally assigned tasks, neither complained too much.

Today, the division of household work stands as a potent marital issue. In the VoiceMale Survey, household responsibilities ranked third on the list of topics most likely to cause marital discord (behind only money and balancing work and family). In most new marriages, deciding who does what around the house requires intense negotiations. And how those negotiations turn out has implications that go far beyond mere grit and grime. According to my survey, *those couples who work out a fair division of household duties have more frequent sex, are less likely to seek marriage counseling or consider a divorce, and are more happily married overall.*

The good news is that in two-thirds of the marriages I studied, the division of household responsibilities is perceived as generally fair. Men acknowledge that they are more likely than their wives to be satisfied with the housework split: 88 percent of husbands reported that they felt the division of housework was fair to them, while only 67 percent said their wife would say it was fair to her. Nonetheless, through confrontation, conversation, and compromise, most couples eventually settle on household-chore routines that they both can accept.

Here's what some men said about how they and their wives reached agreement on housework, which I defined as inside and outside responsibilities (not including paid work) that contribute to keeping up the home.

Fifty-year-old psychotherapist, married eighteen years: "It just kind of sorted itself out. She doesn't like to cook, so I cook. And we eat out a lot. I'm the shopper of the family, and she's the cleaner. I'm the vacuumer because she asked me. It probably helps that we don't have kids."

Forty-seven-year-old math teacher, married fourteen years: "Whatever needs to be done, we do it. I do the yard every week. I clean the cars every week. She doesn't allow me to do the washing, but I iron all the clothing. She's never complained that I don't do enough."

Forty-four-year-old computer technician, married twenty-one years: "I think we are about equally likely to dig in when it gets too messy and equally likely to be slow getting to it. We do have different chores, though. I don't like cooking, so my wife does that. I typically do daily kitchen cleanup, and I'm the one who most often takes care of the laundry. She does bathrooms, I do vacuuming."

Sixty-six-year-old retired engineer, married forty-one years: "She badgered me for a lot of years. I wasn't very cooperative. Finally, we wrote down everything on a piece of paper and divvied it up. Now I've got my chores and she's got hers, and we don't bother each other about it."

This last husband, like so many others, has gradually taken on a larger housework load over the course of his marriage. Since 1965, according to one study, the average husband has increased his contribution to housework more than threefold—from four to thirteen hours a week. That includes an increase in time spent cooking, cleaning, and doing other traditionally female tasks around the house.

Still, married women continue to spend about twice as much time as their husbands on household labor. A 2002 study found that wives do more than their husbands (on average) in preparing the meals, washing the dishes, cleaning the house, shopping for groceries, laundering the clothes, and paying the bills. Husbands, meanwhile, spend more time than their wives in only two areas: caring for the yard and keeping the cars in working order. This housework gender gap crosses all education levels and is especially stark when couples have two children or more. In those cases, women spend an average of thirty-two hours a week on household chores compared to thirteen hours for men.

These hourly inequities do not present a problem for some wives, particularly those whose husbands work long hours at a paying job. Most of these women have an agreement with their husbands: The man does more work at an office or other job site; the woman makes up the difference at home.

Some wives also will cut their husbands slack on housework if they agree to handle the dirty jobs—taking care of mowers, toilets, water heaters, cars, garbage, and spiders, for example. If there *still* remains a housework gap in terms of hours, wives will often overlook this if the husband is in an ongoing and fair-minded negotiation on the topic, if he's willing to give and take.

"Couples take turns," says University of Virginia sociology professor Steven Nock, who has conducted groundbreaking research on housework fairness. "Couples exchange present responsibilities for future benefits, past sacrifices for contemporary advantages." In other words, over the course of a marriage, what matters most is that each partner perceives the big picture to be fair.

Joseph Fields knows that if he wants to increase the odds of sex with his wife, he can bring her flowers or suggest a candlelit dinner at their favorite restaurant. But if he wants to be *sure* of a romantic evening, he goes for the vacuum cleaner. "My wife has told me that she's never more turned on to me than when I'm doing housework," says Joseph, a thirty-nine-year-old guidance counselor, "and she's proven it again and again."

For years, American women have hinted that seeing their husbands doing housework—or at least seeing the results of that work—is an aphrodisiac. Marriage researchers also have noticed anecdotally that housework and sex seem to be linked. Now, for the first time, a survey of men affirms the connection. According to the VoiceMale Survey, *the more satisfied a wife is with the division of household duties, the more satisfied a man is with his marital sex life.*

In addition to this rise in sexual satisfaction, the actual *frequency* of sex tends to be higher when a woman feels that the housework is divided fairly, our survey showed. Among wives who were satisfied with the division of housework, two-thirds had sex with their husbands at least once a week, according to the husbands. When the wife was *un*satisfied with the housework situation, the proportion having weekly sex dropped to 50 percent.

Joseph Fields, mentioned above, told me that he recognized early in his thirteen-year-long marriage that his wife was turned on when he did housework. And at first, he resented it. "It seemed that she was holding sex hostage," he told me, that she was punishing him for not doing housework. Eventually, he says, he realized that when he did housework, his wife felt loved and appreciated—and was subsequently more inspired to show love and appreciate him.

In addition to its implications for a couple's sex life, the fairness of housework appears to have other powerful influences on marriages. I compared couples in which the husband reported that both partners felt the housework was split fairly ("fair couples") to couples in which at least one partner felt it was divided unfairly ("unfair couples"). Here are three of the most compelling results:

• Unfair couples were more than twice as likely as fair couples to have considered separation or divorce.
• The husbands in unfair couples were more than twice as likely as those in fair couples to report that their wives had affairs.
• The husbands in unfair couples were more than ten times as likely as those in fair couples to say that their marriage was "not stable at all."

As indicated earlier, fairness in housework does not necessarily mean that each partner puts in the same amount of time on housework. When a husband, for example, works outside the home fifty hours a week while his wife holds an outside job for twenty hours a week, it will probably be deemed fair that she do most of the housework.

In some cases, fairness may actually involve *less* housework for both partners. When I mentioned the link between housework and marital quality to one husband of forty years, he told me: "It's funny. I always thought one of the best investments I ever made in my marriage was when I hired a Molly Maid to do the housework."

While the housecleaning service cost this couple money on a weekly basis, it may have saved them cash in the long run. According to our survey, couples in which both partners feel the housework is fairly divided are half as likely to seek counseling as those in unfair homes. Thus, in some instances at least, couples can either pay a housecleaner now or a marriage counselor down the road.

While wives are more likely than husbands to focus on housework, this dynamic is not universal. In almost a third of the marriages where housework was contentious, the survey showed, it was the husband who wished his wife would do more.

In some of these cases, husbands who worked more hours than their wives outside the home often expected—or even agreed specifically—that their wives would maintain a clean and efficient house. "I make the money. I work all day," one fifty-one-year-old steelworker told me. "I hate coming home to a mess." But even though he and his wife had agreed that she would do the cleaning and other housework, she rarely did it, he said—at least not to his standards.

In other cases, husbands simply had higher standards of cleanliness than did their wives. Their complaints were similar to those of many traditional wives—that the spouse was inadequate and inattentive when it came to housework.

Cliff Graham was one of three men I interviewed who were stay-at-home dads. After the first of their three children was born in 1996, Cliff and his wife recognized that her earning potential—she was a scientist working at a chemical plant, he was a billing clerk with a health insurance company—was much higher than his. Thus, they agreed that Cliff would quit his job and stay home with the newborn.

Cliff told me that even before their daughter came along he had done most of the housework. "I'm a firstborn, and maybe because of that, I tend to be a little anal about things—I want things a certain way," he said. "I'm certainly much neater than my wife. . . . I don't like clutter; she couldn't care less." As their family grew from one to three children through the late 1990s, Cliff said he had accepted that his share of the housework would grow too. He doesn't enjoy cleaning, he told me, but considers it part of his contribution to the family.

What *does* bother him is that even when his wife is not working she rarely helps out. "When she has a day off, she wants to relax," Cliff says. "But sometimes I find it frustrating that while I'm finishing up the load of laundry or putting [clothes] away, she's lounging on the couch, watching some movie or reading a book. So there certainly have been times that I resent the fact that I do so much of the cleaning." Cliff added: "I've been doing the stay-at-home-dad thing since 1996, and I've had only a handful of days off. Being on call twenty-four/seven, even on vacation, really drains your energy."

Cliff's disagreements with his wife over housework have never threatened their fourteen-year marriage, but he acknowledged wishing that she would occasionally surprise him on the housework front. "I appreciate all that she does to provide for the family," he said. "I wish she'd appreciate what I'm doing too."

Other husbands, even some who worked outside the home full-time while their wives stayed home, told me they also had trouble convincing their wives to share the housework load fairly. A thirty-nine-year-old corporate controller told me that he and his wife of eighteen years have at least one big argument a year over housework.

"I'm a high-energy person," this husband said. "I'll start by taking on half of the housework. But gradually, I'll do a little more here or a little more there. I'll see something that needs to be done and I'll do it." Over several months, this husband said, "the balance will tilt more and more to my side, and I'll start bitching about it." Finally, he'll initiate a conversation with his wife on the topic, and "we'll fight and claw our way back to a balance."

While longer-married couples tend to disagree somewhat less often than shorter-married ones about housework, my survey found that the issue flares up in all phases of marriage. Between 30 and 41 percent of husbands in each of the four phases reported that at least one partner thinks things are unfair on the housework front.

In my in-depth interviews, I noticed that housework problems tend to spike particularly during transition times: when a couple moves in together for the first time; when the first child is born; when the last child moves out of the house; and when one or both partners retire. These are times when couple dynamics are in flux, and negotiations are ongoing (explicitly or not) over what each partner will contribute to the operations of the home.

My survey also showed, contrary to what I expected, that having a stay-at-home parent did *not* reduce the likelihood that one partner will think things are unfair. As the stay-at-home husband, Cliff Graham, indicated just above, even men and women who acknowledge that housework is primarily their responsibility often feel underappreciated by their spouses.

Cliff Graham's case notwithstanding, wives do tend to focus more than their husbands on housework. And this remains a mystery to many men. The husbands I spoke with particularly wanted to know: Why, even when a woman is working full-time outside the home, would she spend the end of her day, or much of her weekend, vacuuming, mopping, and scrubbing the tub?

Michael Gurian, the author of several books about gender differences, believes biology plays a role in housework. He cited studies showing that women typically have more acute senses of smell, sight, and touch than do men, and thus notice details of their surroundings more readily. "Having just sat down on his couch," Gurian asserts, "it is more likely that a man will not . . . register the bit of paper, the dog hair, the children's toy shoved into the couch." Gurian emphasizes that this is not an excuse for men to refuse housework; rather, it explains in part why some men seem oblivious to the clutter or dust piling up around them.

Gurian believes that most wives probably are not conscious about withholding sex when their husbands are unfair about housework. Rather, wives feel the physical and emotional weight of the extra responsibility. "When her husband doesn't help, she feels a distance," Gurian told me. "She feels awkward in her own home. She also feels like she has to become a mom and dominate him to get him to help her out. Why would she want to have sex with someone who makes her feel like that?"

Interestingly, several men attributed their lack of interest and competence in housework to the way their mothers raised them. Noah James, the man at the beginning of this chapter whose wife was frustrated because he never noticed the grime, told me that in his childhood his mother had rarely called upon him to clean. Nor did she show him how to cook a meal, wash a load of clothing, scour a toilet, or do other routine housework.

Noah recalled that early in his own marriage his wife became ill and had to stay in bed for a couple of weeks. Noah's mother, who lived nearby, visited almost daily to help with the housekeeping. On those visits, "my mother even cleaned the cupboards," Noah recalled. "She dusted everywhere. She seems to thrive on cleaning."

Another husband I interviewed, Jean-Luc Gaillard, also cited his mother when we discussed his marital problems over housework. Jean-Luc was the thirty-three-year-old Haitian-American (introduced in Chapter Four) whose two-year-long marriage was suffering because he and his African-American wife could not agree on how to balance their work and family time. Intertwined with that issue were their expectations of who should do the household chores.

In his childhood home, Jean-Luc told me, his Haitian-born mother "was responsible for everything within the walls" of the house. "Life was beautiful," recalled Jean-Luc. He said that his mother "accepted her role with humility." When Jean-Luc married his wife, Victoria, in 2001, he was hoping for the same kind of setup. But Victoria was not cooperating. In fact, she wasn't much interested in housework at all.

Jean-Luc tried to be open-minded, he says, and agreed to do a good portion of the housework. But the more pressure he put on Victoria to help out, the more resistant she became. Jean-Luc told me, resignedly, "She may never clean as much, or cook as much, as I'd want. But she could at least cook and clean *some*."

While both Jean-Luc and Noah James noted their mothers' roles in leaving them unprepared for housework in married life, their fathers' influence should not go unmentioned. In both cases, the fathers neither asked their sons to do housework nor did it themselves. Thus, the sons had no model of a man performing day-to-day tasks in the home.

On the other hand, when a father made housework a personal priority, the son usually did the same. As a thirty-two-year-old construction worker, married eight years, explained: "My dad always pitched in. I learned that if you get up, you clean the plate. If there are dirty dishes, you just don't leave them until the 'little woman' shows up. My parents had high expectations, and we have the same expectations of our children."

So how can couples bring fairness to a home in which one partner isn't doing a fair share of the housework? Since women tend to do more housework, I asked husbands what their wives have done to try to encourage them to increase their share.

First, husbands cited strategies that *don't* work:

Nagging. Husbands told me overwhelmingly that they react negatively to nagging. When their wives made statements that began with such phrases as "I'm the only one who does anything around here . . ." and "I'm not your mother . . . ," the husbands were particularly apt to resist doing housework.

Criticism. A forty-three-year-old advertising copywriter told me: "When she is overly critical of the quality of my housework—when she tells me that I don't meet her standards of cleanliness—I am less motivated to clean. I think she's critical because I work fast. She feels that because I get things done quickly, I must not be cleaning thoroughly." A thirty-three-year-old husband added that his wife sometimes ridicules his housework as "half-assed." This husband told me: "Comments that are negative do not motivate me. When she approaches me reasonably, I think I respond reasonably."

Accusations. One husband, married seven years, said that he had made a variety of "housekeeping errors" in the first few months of their marriage. Once, for example, after loading and starting the dishwasher, he heard strange noises coming from the kitchen. He discovered suds pouring out of the dishwasher onto the floor; apparently, he'd used the wrong kind of detergent. He also shrank some of his wife's clothes in the dryer. What bothered him—and made him more resistant to doing housework, he said—was that his wife accused him of *trying* to screw up so he wouldn't have to do the work in the future. He denied that this was the case.

Here are three approaches that husbands said *did* work in motivating them:

Creating a master plan. Many husbands told me that things worked most smoothly when they and their wives created an overall plan for work in and around the house. Several couples listed all of the household responsibilities and divided them based on who wanted to do what. Both partners usually ended up doing most of what they preferred doing, along with some chores they didn't like at all. Every few months, the tasks could be divided again if one or the other partner was unhappy with the list.

Giving notice. One husband told me that he does housework at a different pace than his wife does. She likes to do all of her housework at once; he likes to distribute his over the course of the week. He said he's far more likely to accommodate his wife's housework desires when she recognizes this, accepts it, and, if she has specific cleaning wishes, makes them clear well in advance. This husband said: "When she says she wants it done *now*, it usually doesn't happen."

Changing expectations. Several husbands suggested that their wives put too much emphasis on cleaning. One man spoke of his wife's "vigilante attitude" about housework. This husband, and others, said they would be more interested in doing housework if their wives compromised on the thoroughness and frequency of the cleaning.

In a few cases among the men I interviewed, a husband said there was nothing his wife could do to enlist him in the housework. One fifty-two-year-old teacher told me: "Only when she is sick do I chip in, because I feel it is only fair. Other than that, the outside of the house is my responsibility; the dishes, laundry, and inside routine cleanliness is her deal. She's tried negotiating, pleading, begging, withholding sex—it doesn't make a real difference."

In my own marriage, housework was a major issue for most of our first ten years together. Eventually, in an effort to work our way through this divisive issue, we were inspired to try an experiment in switching.

As I mentioned in the introduction to this book, I spent my earliest years in a traditional household, where cooking, cleaning, and washing were women's work. I chose to marry a nontraditional woman, but I hadn't mastered the nuts and bolts of many household tasks. Thus, my wife and I quickly developed an unhealthy pattern: She initiated virtually all the housecleaning, assigning me various chores as if I were her offspring or handyman.

Not surprisingly, these housework dynamics created an atmosphere of resentment—in both directions—and they inspired many of our most intense arguments. Kelly often charged me with doing too little too late; I accused her of overestimating the value of cleanliness and underestimating my contribution.

After weary years of discord, we tried an experiment. Each of us made a list of all of the things we did around the house—and then we handed that list to the other person to carry out. For three months, I would do the cooking, cleaning, laundry, and Kelly's other duties; she would deal with the yard care, car care, bill-paying, and my other household-related tasks.

The experiment transformed us, and our relationship. Kelly realized that some of my tasks required attention on a level that she hadn't appreciated. For example, managing our family's finances was a job that required research, extended conversations (or waiting) on the phone, and ultimate responsibility for our solvency. Kelly found that she was averse to detailed numbers work and noted that it seemed to take her twice as long to complete the job as it had taken me. Meanwhile, I saw that in terms of time spent on the household, she had been outdistancing me by several hours a week.

After three months, we traded our chores back—with some adjustments. To even out the time commitment, I took on one new, significant task: the laundry. Of all the major tasks that Kelly originally did, laundry was the one that she disliked the most and the one I found to be least offensive. During our experiment, I had found that doing the laundry involved a lot of sitting, sorting, and folding, most of which I could do while watching sports on television.

Kelly had to compromise too. Specifically, she agreed to decrease from twice to once a month the frequency of our deep cleaning. And she agreed not to comment about how and when I did my part. She's a "burst cleaner," someone who likes to dedicate all of a Saturday afternoon to a major overhaul of the house. I'd much prefer to put in fifteen minutes each weeknight so I can lounge on the weekend.

Since we completed this experiment, Kelly and I have had to continually adjust the balance of our household responsibilities. Moving to a bigger home, changing job schedules, and having a child all required significant alterations. But for us, the positive impact of our switching experience can't be overstated. Looking back, both of us agree that the experiment coincided with the point in our marriage when we stopped doubting that it would last.

Chapter Nine

⌘

Sex: "Lubricant in the Gears"

To hear her laugh in bed—wow!

—Forty-eight-year-old management consultant

MEN HAVE ONLY ONE THING ON THEIR MINDS. For decades, this statement has echoed through American culture. The disapproving tone of voice with which it is usually uttered makes clear its implication: that men—even married men—care more about their sexual gratification than they do about their partners.

In fact, according to most research on this topic (including my own), men *do* want more sex than their wives, *do* initiate sex more often in their marriages, and *do* wish for more sexually interested partners. But my research reveals clearly that men have far more than one thing on their minds. When sex is a problem, most men are willing to wait it out, work it out, and, if required, live without. As one thirty-six-year-old husband told me after reporting that he hadn't had sex in three months: "When push comes to shove, no one is walking."

The good news, according to our survey, is that 82 percent of husbands say they are generally satisfied with their marital sex lives, including 36 percent who claim to be "very satisfied." Sex ranks a lowly fifth among the issues men say are most likely to cause arguments in their marriages. Managing money, balancing work and family, raising children, and dividing housework all rate higher. Only 5 percent of husbands report that sex is the number-one topic of disagreement in their marriages, and of the twenty or so men I interviewed in depth who had been previously divorced, just one said that the main reason was sexual incompatibility.

And yet, just as there remains a gender gap in housework (see previous chapter), an opposite gender gap exists in the arena of sexuality. The majority of men are *not* OK with a sexless marriage, or even a low-sex one. Men don't want to push their wives into bed. But just as modern women expect their husbands to negotiate over housework, today's men look for their wives to bargain in the bedroom. "What frustrates me is that my wife won't even discuss it," a fifty-six-year-old doctor says. "Basically, she's told me: 'Sex is no longer an ambition of mine. End of story.' "

It was not supposed to be this way. When feminism caught fire in the 1960s and the birth-control pill became widely available, one of the anticipated results was female sexual liberation. Convinced that women had long repressed their sexual desire in a male-dominated culture, social scientists predicted that women's sex drives would soon be fully unleashed and would prove to be as robust as those of men.

Two generations later, the trend is indeed in this direction. For what appears to be the first time in U.S. history, a majority of women are having sex before marriage—and not only with their future husbands. And according to my survey, husbands born after 1964 (post-Boomers) are more than twice as likely as their older brethren to be married to women who have larger sexual appetites than they do.

But overall, equality of sexual desire remains elusive. Even among these post-Boomers, it is still the husband who wants more sex in about three out of four marriages where a difference in sexual desire exists. And among middle-aged and older couples, the sexual appetite of women has been even slower to match that of men. In our survey, husbands born before 1946 report that they want sex more often than do their wives by a fifteen-to-one margin.

Frequency (or lack of it), in fact, is the top sexual concern among husbands.

Francisco Martinez is a forty-eight-year-old dentist whose parents emigrated from Cuba to Texas in the 1960s. When I spoke with him in his cluttered Houston office, he had been married sixteen years to Sandra. They had four children, aged six to fourteen. As we discussed various aspects of his marriage, Francisco mentioned that he wasn't satisfied with his sex life. To get a sense of the problem, I asked how long it had been since he and Sandra had had sex. His response: "Four years, seven months."

Sex had once been an important part of their relationship. Practicing Catholics, Francisco and Sandra did not sleep together before marriage. But after their wedding, they were as busy in the bedroom as most newlyweds, Francisco said. The death of one of Sandra's relatives, about six months into their marriage, changed things. Sandra and Francisco agreed to provide temporary shelter for three nieces, and the stresses of child care put sex to the side.

By the time the children moved out a year later, Sandra and Francisco were making love less than once a month. Nonetheless, their bond was strong enough that they decided to start their own family. Their preference was to provide homes for abandoned kids, and over the ensuing nine years, they adopted their four children. It was during this time that Francisco and Sandra's sex life atrophied. The final blow came about thirteen years into the marriage, when Sandra began a premature menopause and lost what little libido she had left.

Throughout their marriage, Francisco had sought to inspire sexual interest in his wife. He brought her flowers regularly; he took her on trips; he offered romantic gifts on her birthday and their anniversary. None of it changed the sexual dynamic. Finally, at Francisco's suggestion, Sandra agreed to join him for a visit to a marriage counselor. But in the week that followed their very first session, Sandra became so angry that Francisco decided to give up. "I know that sometimes things have to get worse before they get better," Francisco told me. "But I wasn't willing to go through the getting-worse part."

Today, he says, "I'm biding my time. I'm waiting for the day when it's just us." He hopes that once Sandra's menopause is over and the kids are out of the house, their sex life will return. Even if it doesn't, he has no intention of leaving. "We made a commitment to each other. When we got married in the church, we got married forever. We have lots of things in common: music, books, travel. . . . You have to accept the things you can't control."

Most husbands recognize that there will be sexual ebbs and flows in their marriages, and that over the decades of a long relationship, sexual frequency will probably decline gradually. My survey confirmed the findings of many others that, as couples age, the frequency of sex—notwithstanding occasional spikes—trends downward.

According to the VoiceMale Survey, newly married couples tend to have the most sex. Among couples married three years or less, 54 percent of husbands reported having sex at least three times a week, including 8 percent who said they have it every day. Only 8 percent of newlyweds had sex once a month or less. (Keep in mind that most surveys of men's sex lives report a slightly higher frequency than is the objective reality.)

Newly married husbands in the once-a-month-or-less category were often deeply frustrated. One told me he felt betrayed by his wife's sudden disinterest in sex after they married. They'd had great sex before tying the knot, he said, adding, "I think she saw her job as 'putting out' until she got her man." Another husband related his frustration in a joke: "What food kills a woman's sex drive?" he asked me, then answered quickly, "Wedding cake."

One thirty-two-year-old husband told me he found it especially upsetting that his wife regularly declined sex after they married—until they agreed to have their first child. "At that point," he said, "she could go every day." It turned out that these "fertility fucks" were less than satisfying for him. He recalled that his wife believed that the best chance for pregnancy was "missionary-style intercourse with no twists." So she "laid back and let me do the work." Her interest in sex vanished soon after the baby was conceived.

Couples in the second phase of marriage—years four to twenty—have sex considerably less frequently than in phase one. The percentage of those having sex three times a week or more drops from 54 to 24 percent in this phase, husbands reported, while those having sex once a month or less rises from 8 to 18 percent. These are generally the child-raising years, when both partners tend to work more hours (paying job, housework, plus child care) than ever before. Often, citing exhaustion, wives turn down sex at the end of the day, their husbands say.

Husbands also report that when their children are small, finding private time can be difficult. One man told me that even when he succeeds in initiating a sexual encounter with his wife, they are often interrupted by an infant's cry. When this happens, the husband added, "I want to keep going [with the sex]. She can't do it."

Husbands' sexual satisfaction tends to hold steady through the children's middle- and high-school years, according to my interviews. For some couples, however, the transformation of children into adolescents reinspires the parents, at least for a while. "When you see this pubescent flirting and dating, when you see the kids dancing, it's kind of heartwarming," one father of three teenagers told me. "You remember what it was like."

The third stage of marriage—years twenty-one to thirty-five—brings an increase in sex for many couples. A computer programmer from New Jersey told me that when his stepdaughter was an adolescent, he and she had battled almost daily, creating "hostility in the house." The anger spilled over into the marriage, he said, and sex with his wife was rare. After the girl graduated and moved out, however, the marriage tensions abated and sexual feelings reemerged. "It's like going back to being adults," the husband told me. "This empty-nest thing is cool."

In some marriages, however, the empty nest brings more sexual struggle. In part, this is because husbands and wives are contending with midlife hormonal changes. Most men experience at least some midlife reduction in their desire. One man described it this way: "The passion is there, but like an old Firebird, the thrust isn't quite the same." Meanwhile, women's sex drives, according to my interviews, can be particularly erratic during the empty-nest phase. Women often start menopause during this stage, and many suffer from a variety of related ailments, including insomnia and body pain. Middle-aged wives who say that they are too tired for sex, or have a headache, are not always making excuses.

When there's a difference in sex drive among empty-nest couples, it continues to be men who want more sex by a wide margin. At the same time, however, the odds are higher in this stage that both partners will want sex equally. According to our survey, only 16 percent of husbands in the child-rearing phase reported that they and their wives had an equal sex drive. In the empty-nest phase, that figure nearly doubles to 29 percent.

And many men speak of this phase of their sex lives as the sweetest. A forty-eight-year-old management consultant told me that he and his wife "always felt that a good sex life is part of a good relationship," so they made a priority of it. When sex threatened to get boring, they talked openly about how to spice things up. "The lovemaking sessions are longer now. We take our time more," this husband told me. "We're probably more focused on giving the other pleasure." He adds: "When the other person is enjoying it so much, you can't calculate how it increases your own pleasure. To hear her laugh in bed—wow!"

In the fourth and final stage of marriage—thirty-five years and beyond—the frequency of marital sex drops significantly. Less than a third of these long-married couples have sex once a week (compared to 61 percent in the previous phase), and 43 percent have sex once a month or less, our survey showed. Fully one-third of couples have no marital sex at all. In light of this, it's fascinating that men's sexual satisfaction actually rises during this phase (to 88 percent). This indicates that a husband's definition of sexual satisfaction may no longer be limited to intercourse or any kind of genital stimulation.

A retired biologist, who was eighty-four years old, told me that medication he takes had made him unable to achieve an erection. While he was sad about that, he said, "Hugging and kissing are still there, and feeling, and respect, and love."

* * *

When men marry, some believe that they'll have as much sex as they want for the rest of their lives. As we've seen, this is rarely so. According to my survey, only 23 percent of couples have equal sex drives. This seems consistent with a 2004 American Broadcasting Company survey of 1,500 men and women, which found that while 70 percent of men think about sex every day, only 34 percent of women do. Yet, even when they're denied sex by their wives, the vast majority of men do not leave their marriages. Rather, they adapt. They do this in one or more of the following ways:

Compromise. Many husbands told me that it was typical, particularly during the child-raising years, for them to want sex two or three times a week while their wives were happy with once or twice a month. "When I'm feeling stressed, I love to have sex—it relaxes me," one husband said. "When she's stressed, she won't even consider it." For these couples, one common solution is to split the difference in their desires. They agree, for example, to set aside the same night each week for lovemaking, or to take advantage of a spontaneous opportunity every weekend.

Masturbate. Most married men masturbate. "It's one of the basic rights," a fifty-year-old husband told me. "I'd have a problem if my wife said 'don't.'" Several husbands in their twenties told me that they feel the physical urge to have an orgasm almost daily. If their wives aren't interested in sex, they masturbate. Older husbands tend to masturbate less frequently, but I talked to men married forty years and longer who continue to masturbate regularly.

Nearly four in ten husbands in my survey reported that they'd used pornography—sexually explicit magazines, Web sites, videos, and the like—at some point since they got married. Some of those men used pornography with their wives, but many also used it for masturbation. Using pornography did not hurt their marital sex lives, most of these men said; they preferred to make love with their wives and used X-rated material when their wives weren't interested.

Two husbands acknowledged that they'd become addicted to pornography and that it was damaging their relationships. One thirty-year-old contractor said he put an extra password on his computer to "make me reconsider" before going online to find pornography. Why did it bother him? After looking at pornography, he said, "I start to think that my wife should be perfect. I start to ask myself, 'Why can't I have women like these?' I don't want to be that way."

Many men expressed surprise by the intensity of women's negative reaction to porn. And one man nearly lost his relationship over it. This man had spent most of his twenties, when he was unmarried, addicted to pornographic magazines. He had recovered from his addiction in his early thirties, about a year before meeting his future wife. As they became increasingly close, however, he felt it was important to tell her about his past interest in pornography. Her reaction was to stop seeing him.

After a few weeks, however, the couple reconciled and later married. The woman told him that she had been sexually abused in childhood and that his revelation had triggered a fear that he might be abusive. Five years later, when I interviewed him, this man said: "Pornography distorts a boy's world. It sends the message that a woman's worth is what she looks like, and that my worth is whether I can be with her."

This man added that he had experienced an epiphany while watching the birth of his daughter three years before. "I saw what a woman looks like giving birth. It's the other side of porn."

Rechannel the energy. Francisco Martinez, the dentist we met earlier in the chapter who hadn't had sex in more than four years, told me that he channeled his sexual energy into fathering, his work, and other creative outlets. Another husband I interviewed had become a long-distance runner. "Running sapped off the frustration," he told me. "I'd run at lunch, and the frustration just soaked into the pavement. It was a diversion."

Have affairs. Husbands who are not sexually satisfied in their marriages are more likely to have sex outside the marriage, my survey showed. About one in eight husbands (12 percent) reported that they'd had at least one affair during their current marriage, and of those husbands who strayed, 38 percent said they were dissatisfied with their marital sex lives. By comparison, among husbands who had *not* had affairs, only 15 percent said they were dissatisfied at home.

While sexual dissatisfaction—primarily with the quantity, not the quality, of sex—may be linked to infidelity, it is not the overriding factor in most cases, husbands told me. My survey showed that 62 percent of those who had affairs were generally satisfied with their marital sex lives. (In the next chapter, which focuses on affairs, I'll enumerate some of the other reasons that men choose to have affairs.)

One reason many women cite for not wanting sex with their husbands is that the men are not adept at arousing and satisfying them. And on this point, men tend to agree. Most husbands I interviewed said it had taken them a long time to figure out what their wives desired sexually, and many were still in the hunt.

At least in part, husbands blamed themselves. Several told me that especially early on in their relationships, they hadn't taken the time to understand how a woman's sexual response is different from a man's. Thus, they often figured that there was something wrong with their wives, themselves, or their relationship, because they couldn't get in synch on sex.

Men also attributed their lack of sexual understanding of their wives to the reluctance of their wives to talk about sex. When, husbands said, they brought up ideas for enhancing their sex lives—suggesting new kinds of foreplay or lovemaking positions, for example—wives often reacted with embarrassment or judged their husbands negatively.

One forty-one-year-old husband told me his wife accused him of "selfishness" when he said he wanted to try a new sexual position. The rebuff made him angry. "I've asked her a million times: 'What do you want?' All she says is 'I don't know.' Then I bring up what I want, and I'm selfish." Another husband, aged fifty, reported that his inability to satisfy his wife had taken a toll on his self-image: "I consider myself a below-average performer in bed."

When women do say what turns them on, most husbands seem determined to deliver. Many men told me that it had been a revelation to learn that arousing their wives sometimes had less to do with her body than with her mind and heart. But for the most part, men were game. "If I want sex on Thursday, I'll start romancing her on Monday," one forty-one-year-old husband told me. He said this might involve flirting through e-mails, giving a small gift, or cooking a meal. After several days of this, a gentle offer of a back rub often leads to lovemaking, he said.

Another husband, married twenty-five years, told me: "Before I even touch her, we sit in bed and talk for an hour. We'll talk about the kids, the plans for the house, a fantasy vacation, A to Z. It's verbal foreplay. . . . It works for her. I'm not against it." This man went on to acknowledge: "When I was twenty-two, I don't think I would have had the patience."

A major concern for many men is sexual initiation—that is, who gets sex going. While men generally are OK with being the primary initiator, most also would like their wives to reach out to them at least some of the time. They long for the enthusiasm that their wives often showed early in the relationship. "I wish she'd just *take* me," one husband said. Said another: "I like it when she growls." A few husbands told me that after being turned down by their wives repeatedly, they had decided to wait for their wives to initiate sex. Most of these men eventually gave up. "I found that she can hold out a lot longer than I can," one husband told me.

Other husbands accepted that their wives would never initiate directly. But they found that their wives sent positive signals in subtle ways. She might wear her sexiest clothes out to dinner, or nothing to bed. "When my wife takes a shower in the evening," one man told me, "I figure I've got a pretty good chance."

Most husbands say that they've been through at least one low-sex period in their marriage. I asked how they dealt with these periods, which tended to be the result of their wives' lack of interest. Here's what they said:

> Sixty-four-year-old retired lawyer, married forty years: "I try to find out what's causing her loss of interest, whether it's physical, emotional, or something else. If the cause can be identified, then hopefully we can jointly agree on a plan of action. Easier said than done sometimes."

Forty-four-year-old personnel director, married twenty-one years: "I oftentimes have waited [low-sex periods] out. Sometimes I have been forced to talk them out because they were *very* low periods. I guess what has happened after twenty-one years of marriage is that I have come to the realization that this part of our lives is more important to me, or I enjoy it more than she does, and that is probably never going to change, so I have come to terms with it. I have too much invested in the marriage at this point to go looking elsewhere for this release, so I just deal with it."

Thirty-six-year-old pastor, married eight years: "We generally talk about it. There is a double-edged sword to the situation because if she wants romance, then talking about it kills the mood. But unless we talk, we can't discuss what the problem is. . . . In some cases, I have taken action to consult a doctor about my drive or performance. I am realizing that stress is the biggest impediment."

Sixty-year-old movie producer, newly married: "With my ex-wife, the whole marriage was low-sex and part of a control issue on her part. We went to a sex therapist, who ended up telling us we should not be married. I finally got so tired of hearing 'Go find a whore for your oversexed sex drive' that I left her for another woman whose sex drive is just as strong as mine."

Thirty-year-old teacher, married six years: "Since having a child, the amount of sex has decreased, but perhaps it has become even better when we do have it. Good things come to those who wait. It's like savoring a good dessert!"

Because men live in a society drenched in sexual images of young, thin, smooth-skinned women (and not only in pornography), I wondered whether husbands found it difficult to remain attracted to their wives as they aged. Several men told me that they struggled with it. Weight gain was a particular issue. A few men said that both they and their wives had gained considerable weight, which coincided with lower sexual interest for both. In some cases, when they got on a program to lose weight together, their sex life improved.

But a majority of husbands reported that gradual weight gain, graying, wrinkling, and other symptoms of aging did not turn them off sexually. In some cases, it was just the opposite. Listen to the following men:

Forty-eight-year-old business consultant, married twenty-two years: "I may not see the same woman I married, but I see the woman I'm in love with. I know what she can do, and that's incredibly exciting. . . . No one's swinging from the chandelier, but the degree of safety in the relationship has more than made up for the thrill of discovery."

Seventy-six-year-old retired principal, married forty-six years: "Sometimes I stand back and marvel at how she's changed. But when I'm close to her, I see the same eyes, the same nose, the same smile."

Fifty-five-year-old professor, married twenty-nine years: "I used to look at other women a lot more, but as we've aged, I can't even fantasize about sex with anyone else. I am hopelessly attracted to my wife."

Fifty-two-year-old records clerk, married twenty-two years: "To me, she's the way I've always seen her. From the inside. She's aged. She's gained some pounds. She has some gray hair. But the way I look at it, I *put* some of those gray hairs on her head."

In more than a few cases in my study, a couple's sex life had been profoundly affected by an issue that's rarely addressed, particularly by men: previous sexual abuse. Studies indicate that as many as half of all females (and many males too) have been sexually abused or assaulted at some time in their lives. Such abuse, men told me, can be devastating to a marriage.

One husband said that he was shocked when, in the early months of his first marriage, his wife said to him: "You raped me last night." That's how he learned of her previous abuse. He tried to be compassionate and understanding, he said, but she never trusted him. "I thought I could save her, but I was wrong," this man told me. "Sex abuse destroys people; it destroyed an otherwise beautiful person." They divorced after four years.

Another man, Seth Anderson, a social worker who was thirty-six when I interviewed him, has managed to maintain his relationship. He told me that he was friends with his future wife, Jenny, for several months before they acknowledged a romantic interest in each other. On the day they decided to date, she told him she'd been raped ten years earlier, at age twenty. "We both cried. It was the first time she'd cried about it," Seth recalled.

Their early sexual relationship was a challenge. To build trust, Seth agreed to let Jenny lead in bed. "The trust had to come slowly, and it had to be on her pace," he said. Holding back was frustrating for Seth. "She had to be in control. But she wouldn't initiate." During their many sexual droughts, Seth told himself that the relationship was too valuable to give up simply because of the lack of lovemaking. "I'd had long periods of my life without sex," he told me. "I grew up Catholic, for crying out loud!"

At one point, about a year before their marriage, intercourse became so painful for Jenny that they had to stop. Doctors diagnosed a constriction of her vaginal muscles, probably due to her previous sexual trauma. The treatment required Jenny to use cylinders of increasing width to loosen the muscles.

As Jenny gradually opened to Seth, he began having sexual difficulties of his own. He could attain an erection, but his orgasms took an extraordinarily long time to arrive. "I started to have performance anxiety. I wanted so much for the sex to be good," he told me. After several months of struggle, his sexual function returned to normal. And over the ensuing years, Seth says, his sexual relationship with his wife has become increasingly relaxed and pleasurable.

Seth told me he'd had a range of feelings about Jenny's rape. "At one time, I wanted to be her savior. I wanted to meet the guy and beat him up." More recently, he felt some remorse about his sexual behavior with women he'd dated before Jenny. "I remembered times I was inappropriate or pushy and how that may have impacted those women," he said.

* * *

Seth's experience touches on another sexual issue for married men that is increasingly a topic of discussion: male sexual dysfunction. While Seth experienced delayed orgasm, the most common male sexual affliction is an inability to attain an erection.

The majority of men with this problem are older than fifty. As I mentioned earlier in the chapter, my survey showed that one-third of men married longer than thirty-five years no longer have sex with their wives. In a significant portion of these cases, the men have heart problems, diabetes, or other ailments that adversely affect their circulatory systems. Others take antidepressants or similar medications that suppress their sex drive.

Some of these older men simply accept their condition and remain intimate with their wives in nongenital ways. But many told me that they had chosen to use Viagra, Cialis, or other anti-impotence medications to extend their sex lives.

The erection-enhancing drugs are increasingly popular among midlife men too, some of whom have occasional difficulty achieving or sustaining an erection. In addition to health problems, other issues may contribute to impotence. One man told me that when he was forty-two his father died; in the months that followed, he couldn't get an erection. "It was the grief," he reported to me. "I felt that I shouldn't enjoy anything." Gradually, this feeling abated, but not before he used Viagra several times. Now he keeps a few tablets in his medicine cabinet just in case.

Several even younger men described incidents of erectile dysfunction. One man began having problems before he got married at age twenty-six. They intensified shortly after the marriage. When he couldn't become erect, his wife felt rejected, this man told me. The situation deteriorated as she became more hurt and angry, and he more insecure. "I started to associate sex with fear," he told me. Things hit bottom about two years into the marriage when his wife, desperate to jump-start his sex drive, invited another woman to join them in bed. Not only did the strategy fail, but the situation created distrust between the husband and wife.

Sixteen years later, when I spoke with this man, his marital sex life had improved, though he and his wife still went through phases when he didn't want sex. With the help of various counselors, he'd learned more about the causes of his struggles. His wife had always been the dominant partner, and his failure to achieve an erection might have been his unconscious way of asserting himself. Over time, as he found other ways to demonstrate assertiveness—expressing his everyday likes and dislikes openly, for example—his sexual interest and capabilities gradually improved.

Interestingly, several men told me that their wives did not want them to use Viagra or other similar medications. These women believed that a man who had to use medication probably was not that attracted to his wife. One husband said he had to reassure his wife that "my taking a pill has nothing to do with her attractiveness. I'm taking it because I want to be with her so much."

According to the VoiceMale Survey, in about a quarter of marriages where a disparity in sexual desire exists, it is the woman who wants more sex. Sometimes, this represents a change in the desire of each partner over the course of the marriage. "They say men hit their sexual peaks when they're eighteen, women when they're forty," one forty-four-year-old salesman said. "That's what we're dealing with now."

Most times, however, when the wife is more interested than her husband in sex, it's a dynamic that extends throughout the length of the marriage. The women in these marriages prefer to express love physically, through sexual contact, while the husband may be satisfied with other, less physical, forms of intimacy.

A forty-eight-year-old graphic artist, married sixteen years, told me that his wife had always wanted sex more often than he did, even when their children were young. He said he'd like sex once or twice a week, but his wife could have it every day. "Early on, I'd just say no. It hurt her feelings." More recently, he's learned that it helps if he says: "I love having sex with you, but not right now."

When he speaks of the sexual dynamics in his marriage, he echoes phrases that wives are often heard to say. "I just find that I have to mentally be in the right place" to have sex, he told me. "It's hard to switch gears." These days, he adds, sexual frequency is a topic he and his wife are comfortable talking about. "She has known for a long time that [her high interest in sex] is part of her emotional makeup. She's used sex at times to compensate for other things that are lacking in her life."

Occasionally, a husband is less interested in sex because he is gay or bisexual. Such men may choose to marry women in order to have children, enjoy the legal and social benefits of marriage, or hide their sexual orientation, even from themselves. I spoke with two married men who were bisexual. One, having raised a son with his wife, had recently decided to end his marriage after twenty-two years in order to explore relationships with men. He said he'd been honest with his wife (he told her of his bisexuality before they married) and had honored his vow not to sleep with anyone else while they were together.

The second man, a forty-nine-year-old public-relations executive, told me he had married at twenty-six. In his early forties, he noticed that he was having strong homosexual impulses. He realized that he was "afraid of my gay side, afraid of my own orientation." So without telling his wife, he had an affair with a man.

Since then, he has had several other sexual encounters with men. He continues to have sex occasionally with his wife, but told me that he is probably more attracted to men than to women. He does not tell his wife of his past extramarital encounters because he believes it would hurt her unnecessarily. Through internal questioning and therapy, he says, "I've really come to a state of peace with things as they are. I've done the struggle. I've done the guilt. It's enough already. Things just are."

Why not get a divorce? This husband says he loves his wife and children and does not want to disrupt that part of his life. He adds: "It's a matter of a trade-off. I look at what I have. It's so precious."

While it's clear that men have more than just sex on their minds, it's also clear that sex represents a major reason that men marry and stay married. I asked husbands if they could explain why sex is important to them.

Most mentioned, at least in passing, their enjoyment of the physical acts and release. "At the most basic level," one forty-four-year-old computer programmer said, "I want sex because I get horny. My wife's attractive to me and I want sex with her." A forty-year-old educator, married eighteen years, added: "It matters that we have sex because I think about it so often that if I didn't have it, at least once in a while, my life would be so disassociated from reality I'd belong in a home for the pathetically delusional." A stay-at-home father said that sex offers a respite: "Everything going on in our lives—kids, work, troubles, worries, busy schedules, messy house, whatever—is all put on hold for a while."

Many husbands also spoke of the emotional connection that comes with sex. One man said that sex "cements our feelings." Another reported that "the importance of sex is to feel close and to share the love we have for each other." Still another husband said sex "expresses one's desire to be close and personal with the one you love. It continues to indicate attraction and desire."

Several husbands said that sex distinguishes their relationships with their wives from all other connections. A forty-four-year-old management consultant put it this way: "It's nice that we share our life emotionally, philosophically, and even intellectually, but without the physical closeness, it's a different kind of relationship. What I like about our sex life is that it creates a physical warmth between us [that continues] even during those times when we are not making love. Like those times when we are walking down the street and she grabs my hand, or when we are talking after dinner and I reach across the table to take her hand. Those are special moments, and without the physical bond we have created in our sex life, they would not have the meaning that they do."

Finally, a thirty-nine-year-old corporate controller told me that the frequency and quality of sex serve as a barometer of the health of his marriage. He offered a fascinating analogy. "I think marriage is like a machine, a big, complicated thing with lots of little cogs that keep things turning. Taking out the garbage, making dinner, doing dishes, herding the kids to practice and school—all this practical, everyday stuff takes constant effort to keep things moving. My theory is that we all have little problems with the machine frequently—you accidentally say something inconsiderate, you forget to pick up a skirt from the cleaners, you laugh when you should have been serious, you don't listen well at the dinner table, and so on. It's sand in the machine.

"Sex is like lubricant in the gears. It makes you feel warm and loved and close to your spouse. Then you can think, well, they were thoughtless that once, but so what? You can step back, get a little perspective on the relationship. It gives you something to be positive about. Then you can overlook the sand. I mean, it doesn't make the problems go away, but it gives you a reason to put up with them."

Chapter Ten

AFFAIRS: DON'T ASK, DON'T TELL?

I look at it this way: If I go out and fool around, I can't love my wife one hundred percent.
—Forty-seven-year-old high-school teacher

IT WAS NOTHING that Paula did wrong. Edward Hill had met her at UCLA in 1968, dated her for two years, and told her over a romantic dinner: "I want to spend my entire life with you." She had cried and said she wanted the same. Both were smart and adventurous. It seemed a magnificent match.

After the wedding, they rented an apartment in suburban Los Angeles. For more than a year, Paula worked as a secretary while Edward spent his days as a mid-level bureaucrat in a large corporation. Then Paula started talking about having kids. Edward was surprised to find himself not only resistant to the idea but increasingly irritated by most anything his wife said or did.

That's when he met Jeannette. She was nineteen—five years younger than Edward—svelte, and buxom. They first shared glances at work. He approached her; she flirted. They found that they shared a love of jazz and made a date to go to a club when Paula would be out of town. After the date, Jeannette invited him to her apartment, where they made love. Suddenly, Edward's constant irritation at his wife began to make sense to him. "I'm too young to be married," he remembers thinking in the early weeks of his affair. "Look what I've been missing."

At home during the affair, Edward was plagued with guilt. He busied himself with take-home work. He feigned fatigue when Paula suggested sex. Meanwhile, he and Jeannette met regularly at her apartment.

Six months into the affair, Edward told Paula that he would be leaving for a weekend to attend a work-related conference. Instead, he and Jeannette drove together forty miles away and stayed at the home of one of Jeannette's friends. And that's where Edward says he finally came to his senses. As Jeannette and her friend prepared for a night out at the bars and clubs—primping and drinking—it sunk in to Edward that this was not really the life he wanted.

Returning from the weekend, he told Paula that he was ready for children. He stopped seeing Jeannette and, he says now, never strayed again. He also never confessed the affair to Paula. He told me: "I'm sure she knows. But there's no use bringing it up. For both of us, it's the past." About the affair, he feels that he betrayed his wife's trust but tries to look at the positive side of the ledger: "I learned that my wife was everything I wanted. . . . I'm lucky that I didn't lose her."

Infidelity—by both husbands and wives—is one of the major destroyers of American marriages. Among the husbands I interviewed who had been divorced previously, most cited an affair as at least one factor leading to their breakup. The breach of trust is usually so great, and the pain so primal, husbands say, that it can take years of work to repair it. Often, even when the marriage survives, it is never quite the same. As one husband told me after his wife discovered his affair: "Once you go over certain barriers, you can never go back."

According to the VoiceMale Survey, one in eight men have had at least one affair during their current marriage. As I reported in the last chapter, men who have affairs are often those who are unsatisfied in their marital sex lives. Jorge Cruz, whom I introduced in Chapter Five, told me that his wife stopped wanting sex after their children were born. After several years during which she resisted him sexually, Jorge told me, he found a lover on the side.

But a troublesome sex life at home is by no means a predictor of infidelity. In our survey, 73 percent of husbands who were dissatisfied with their sex lives reported that they had *not* had affairs. And 10 percent of those who were satisfied with their marital sex lives said that, despite this, they'd had at least one affair.

Edward Hill, the man profiled at the beginning of this chapter, was one of the latter. He admitted that his infidelity early in his marriage was a result of his own shortcomings and had nothing to do with actions his wife had or had not taken.

"I always loved her, but we met too early," Edward told me. As their college days were winding up, he didn't want to lose Paula, so he asked her to marry him. It was the late 1960s, and while male-female relationships were changing, it was still common for couples to marry as they graduated from college. Soon after they wed, however, as Edward heard tales of his male friends' sexual exploits, he began to feel that he'd missed out. "It seemed unfair" that he couldn't play the field too, he recalls thinking.

Looking back now, Edward says that he was coming to terms with what it means to be committed to someone for life. He praises his wife for "giving me space, letting me go through my paces." He says he'd probably be divorced today had it not been for an uncle. Edward confided in the older man about the affair and said that he was ready to leave the marriage. The uncle, who had been married for more than forty years, advised against that. He told Edward: "If you love [your wife], you just need to work through this. It's not an easy thing to be married. It takes dedication. Life is going to get tough sometimes. You can't just walk away and go onto the next subject."

This advice saw Edward through his infatuation with the other woman. When it ended, he chose not to tell Paula about the affair because he feared it would hurt her terribly and threaten the marriage. Edward says, "I had done my soul-searching" and was now committed to having no more affairs; he decided that confessing would do more harm than good.

Indeed, to tell or not to tell was a major point of contention among the men I spoke with who had had affairs. Edward was among a group who said that, at least in some circumstances, it was selfish and destructive to share such information after the infidelity was over. Other husbands said they felt it was important to be honest, even if it meant that the marriage might fall apart.

And fall apart they sometimes did.

Rick Young, a thirty-seven-year-old college professor, told me that his two-year marriage had ended not long after he admitted to his wife that he was having an affair. A self-confessed womanizer through his early adulthood, Rick had married hoping that his new wife would help settle him down. But, as he recalls it, even on his honeymoon, he felt "tethered, confined." He sensed his wife's "huge, jealous possessiveness," though he acknowledged that she hadn't said or done anything that was overtly possessive. "It's her presence, her watching. . . . I know that she's watching me."

Within a few months of the wedding, Rick met a new work colleague and began flirting with her. The colleague was aware that Rick was married and turned away his advances at first. But Rick persisted, even bringing her a single yellow rose on Valentine's Day. On the same day, Rick presented his wife with a dozen roses.

Rick eventually wrangled an invitation to his colleague's apartment, where, he says, "I pushed the limits. I wouldn't take no for an answer." I asked what he meant by that. "I just kept holding her, touching her, kissing her neck, and making her feel good." When it comes to women, Rick says, "I'm not going to do something against their will, but I'll try to bend their will."

Rick's wife traveled a lot, so it was easy for him to find time for the new woman in his life. He acknowledged being in a personal state of denial about the affair. "I never actually slept over" at the other woman's house, he told me, looking back. "So I could say to myself, in my twisted way, that I'm not sleeping with anybody."

At home, Rick and his wife argued increasingly over a variety of everyday issues. But Rick's biggest struggle was his own difficulty in commiting to one woman, he acknowledged. He told me that he "felt driven to enjoy the energy of different women. I didn't want to give that up." But at the same time, he cared about his wife and didn't want to hurt her, he said.

At one point, Rick agreed to go into marital therapy with his wife, and they made some progress on their differences. But he withheld the truth about his infidelity. Finally, torn inside, he confessed the affair to his wife.

Then he asked her: "Can you live with that?" Her response: "I can't live with it unless you're working to change it." To which he replied: "I don't want to work on it." Soon after, their marriage ended.

Even when a marriage doesn't end over an affair, the wreckage from infidelity can be considerable. Five years into his marriage, Carl Watson had his first affair. The year was 1971, and, Carl told me, "Everybody was doing everybody. It was almost stylish" to have affairs.

Carl, a tool-and-die maker, said he met a woman from the front office of his company and lied to his wife about his whereabouts one evening so he could go to the woman's house and have sex. He intended for it to be a one-night stand, soon forgotten. But a few days later, the woman called Carl's wife to tell her about the incident. "The worst thing I did," Carl told me, "was to fess up."

Carl and his wife, Rebecca, had two small children at the time, and splitting up did not seem like an option. Instead, Rebecca got even, and then some: She had an affair with one of Carl's friends. "How could I say anything?" Carl asked me. "I was guilty too." So he raised the stakes even more. He began sleeping around regularly and, as far as he knows, she did too. When it comes to affairs, he told me, "Our attitude is: Don't ask, don't tell."

When I spoke with Carl, he was sixty-one years old. Carl told me that at one point he and Rebecca had planned to split up when the children moved out of the house. But that time came and went. By then, they had created "a comfort zone," Carl said, and neither was interested in leaving it.

It's not the marriage Carl had once imagined. Both he and Rebecca have secret lives. They are careful what they ask each other and what they share with each other. They're suspicious. But of his wife, Carl says, "She's the mother of my kids. She's a fabulous cook. She gives me a long leash. I'd be stupid to walk."

Carl calls his sexual interest in other women "the weakness"—a condition that he is powerless to stop. Beyond that, he said, he could not explain why he seemed to need sex beyond his marriage.

Other men I interviewed did have theories as to why they had affairs. Several said that they'd learned that their fathers, uncles, and other male role models had had affairs, or heard men talking about women in sexually objectified terms. This "laid the groundwork" for their own infidelity, as one husband told me.

Another man, married twenty-five years, said he'd had an affair early in his marriage. He believes that virtually all married men battle internally over whether to stay monogamous. This man said that part of him has always wanted the stability of married life; another part "wants to be wild, like the five-year-old boy who's pulling things out of his pocket yelling: 'Look what I have here!' "

Rick Young, the college professor who brought Valentine's Day flowers to both his wife and his lover, told me that years of therapy and reflection have convinced him that his relationship with his mother was a factor in his womanizing. When he was a child, his mother was highly critical of him, he said, constantly pointing out his flaws and missteps. Her love toward him "was tied to my doing what pleased her," Rick recalled. His response, he says, was "to hide those things that did not please her, so that I could still have her love *and* get what I wanted."

As an adult, he reenacted this dynamic. Often, he sensed that his female partners were watching him as his mother had. His reaction was to again create a secret life, this time by having affairs. He recalls one exasperated exchange with his wife, who sensed that he was still mired in his "mother issues." Rick's wife finally said to him: "I'm not your mother!" To which Rick replied: "The whole world is my mother!"

When I last interviewed Rick, after his divorce, he told me that he was finally coming to terms with himself. "Basically, at heart, I'm a serial monogamist. I want the depth" of having one person to focus on, he said. "But I don't want the overlay of marriage that pushes it past its time."

Ironically, having affairs was a way for some men to try to protect themselves from being abandoned by their wives. One husband told me that having sex with other women "ensured that if my wife left me, I'd have a backup plan." This husband was addicted to cocaine during the early part of his marriage. When he finally got treatment to overcome his addiction, he also had the chance to sort through his childhood. He realized that he had felt abandoned by his parents: His father had died early in his son's childhood, and the boy's mother had become distant after that. The pain of the experience spurred him to create "backup plans" in his personal relationships.

Reexamining all of this helped the son understand the roots of his fears and eventually steered him away from infidelity. When I spoke with him, he and his wife had been married for eighteen years. She knew of his early affairs, but attributed them to the person he had been before he got off drugs.

The Atlanta psychiatrist and marriage counselor Frank Pittman, author of *Private Lies,* has counseled scores of men who have had affairs. He agrees that men's affairs usually originate with conflicts within the man. Often, the conflict is between a man's image of masculinity and the reality of his own life. After men marry, Pittman told me in an interview, "they begin to see themselves in a less-than-heroic light. They think of all the mountains they haven't climbed, all the supermodels they haven't screwed. There's something forbidding [to a man] about the very comfort of a good marriage."

Pittman believes that "most men are faithful most of the time" and that "most of those who screw around only do it once." Under these circumstances, he says, he understands why a man would be skittish about telling his wife of an affair. But he contends that a man is "not home free" if he manages to keep it secret. "Men who assume that what the little lady doesn't know won't hurt her are always going to be more distant" from their wives, Pittman says. "The fewer lies you have to tell, the closer you can be to your wife."

According to the VoiceMale Survey, 7 percent of husbands are aware that their current wives have had affairs. Men who learn specifically of a wife's affair speak of the blow in compelling terms: "a kick in the gut"; "a shattering experience"; "I was sick." It even drove some men to violence, they said. When I visited a jail to talk with inmates about their relationships, two of the fourteen men in the room said they were there for assaulting men whom they had caught sleeping with their wives.

One of these inmates filed for divorce after the incident (and had received the final papers on the day of my visit). But most men said their marriages had survived their wife's affair. According to the VoiceMale Survey, 5 percent of husbands who considered themselves "very happy" in their marriages knew that their wife had had an affair during the marriage. One husband even said that the turmoil of infidelity, though extraordinarily painful, had reinvigorated a struggling relationship.

Jason Pulaski and his wife, Cynthia, were married in the early 1960s, not long after they'd both graduated from college. Their marital problems began early on, Jason told me, when Cynthia had a miscarriage and became deeply depressed. She recovered, but a couple of years after that, her father died and she suffered a psychological breakdown. Jason decided that she needed to be involuntarily confined to a mental hospital.

She stayed there for eight weeks. "These were some of the scariest days of my life," Jason told me. He thought his marriage might end, as his wife resisted the confinement, accusing Jason of imprisoning her. In the years that followed, Cynthia reminded Jason again and again how angry she was about the lockup.

The couple pulled through, however, and eventually had two children. But as the children reached school age, Cynthia became depressed again. During this period, Jason told me, "She felt that she didn't love me anymore. She thought she would leave me. I didn't know whether it was coming from her healthy self or not."

At one point, Cynthia did leave Jason and the children for about ten days, but returned. The marriage calmed down again after that, but none of the fundamental issues were confronted, Jason said. Meanwhile, Cynthia, inspired by her personal experience, went back to graduate school to become a psychologist. Gradually, she gained confidence both as a person and as a professional.

Then one day, when the children were in high school, Jason noticed that Cynthia was writing a Valentine's Day card. When she wasn't looking, he examined the card and saw that it was addressed to a man she worked with. Riffling through her desk, he found cards that the man had sent to

Cynthia with the salutation "From someone who loves you." Jason says: "I lived with that for a couple of days. I spent hours thinking about it. I was nervous and afraid."

Finally, he confronted Cynthia.

> *Jason:* I know we've had our ups and downs. But I'm not going to be number two. So you can just leave now.
> *Cynthia:* Yes, [the affair] happened. But it's over now.
> *Jason:* Get out! Leave!

But Cynthia wouldn't leave. Jason decided to see a counselor alone. During his weekly sessions, he revisited his childhood and also made a balance sheet of sorts: he listed all the reasons to stay with Cynthia—kids together, intellectual connection, physical attraction—and all the reasons to leave, including her affair. He also focused on his own sexual conduct through the years, which had included many clandestine visits to sex clubs. Though he'd never actually had a sexual relationship with anyone else, he sensed that he too had violated his marriage vows.

And then an odd thing happened. "As I changed, I began to experience very positive feelings" for Cynthia, Jason told me. He recalls a "D-Day" of sorts, after he and Cynthia had dropped off their son at college. They hadn't had sex in a while and had not talked beyond superficialities.

In a hotel room that evening, Jason decided that things had to change. "I told her that I wasn't going to be in a marriage that didn't have sex and intimacy and love. I decided that no matter what happened with the marriage, I was going to be happy." Then he waited for Cynthia to respond. "The next thing I knew, we were in each other's arms," Jason said. "After that came five years of the best sex we've ever had."

When I spoke with Jason, it had been fifteen years since that day, and the marriage was solid, he said. "There are certain days I love her more, and I'm sure there are some days I don't love her at all." But he no longer stays for long on the emotional roller coaster. He has come to see love not as out of his control, but as "a conscious act. We've chosen to stay married and look for the gold."

* * *

Despite the temptations, most husbands and wives do not have affairs. And even spouses who are prone to cheating do not take all of the opportunities that present themselves. I asked husbands what stopped them from having affairs, how they resisted the temptations. Here are some of their responses:

Retired military officer, married twenty-nine years: "Once or twice I had to say no. I wouldn't want to hurt my wife. Had I done it, and my kids had found out, they would have been destroyed."

Teacher, married twenty-one years: "I look at it this way: If I go out and fool around, I can't love my wife one hundred percent. My father was a womanizer, and I did that for a number of years [in previous relationships]. But this woman made me respect her. I don't allow myself to be tempted. It would destroy my family and children."

Doctor, married twenty-two years: "It's against my religion. It would be easy to rationally justify [extramarital] sex, but logic is where the devil lurks."

Salesman, married thirty-three years: "I have had two opportunities, but I never considered either one. I think there are two reasons: I feel that I could not do better than my wife, and I am a Christian and believe affairs are wrong."

College administrator, married thirty years: "I see girls on campus all the time. Last year, cleavage was the in thing. This year, it's the midriff. I can't say I don't look. But I'm not really interested. Besides, what would they want with a bald, potbellied old man?"

> Salesman, married thirty-six years: "Sure, I look at other women. But I'm only seeing the best part of them. I know they've got their problems. I've got my problems too. Everyone has to work out their problems with somebody, sometime. You might as well do it with your wife."

Often, when I interviewed men about affairs, they asked me to define the word. It wasn't easy, so I turned the question back to them. What was an affair in their eyes? The range of answers was broad.

On one end of the continuum, a few husbands told me they considered themselves to have been unfaithful to their wives even though they'd never touched another woman. One such man, a forty-eight-year-old publicist, had been married for twenty years. He'd married in part because his wife "was a lot less complicated" than other women in his life at the time, and "I was wanting a less complicated life." Their early relationship revolved around their two children, and they didn't see eye to eye on issues ranging from child-rearing to politics. "It got to the point where we didn't fight all the time, but there was a distance."

When their kids left home, this husband planned to stay married—he believed that marriage was for life—and pour his passion into writing music and performing. After playing at a club one evening, he met a woman (also married) who was equally passionate about music. They were drawn to each other. They began meeting secretly at the public library and various coffee shops. They talked about their love of the arts, and also about the lack of intimacy they experienced in their marriages. "I would count the days, the hours" until the next meeting, this man said. "I was overtaken by this incredible closeness."

Though they met perhaps a dozen times, this man said, they never held hands or kissed. But he told me that their relationship was "a form of an affair." He says he crossed the line when he failed to tell his wife about their meetings and when he shared with the other woman intimate details of his marriage.

Most husbands I interviewed didn't accept this definition. They tended to define infidelity as physical involvement: kissing, sexual touching, oral sex, intercourse. Some also included phone sex and cybersex (in which two people share sexual fantasies at a distance, often accompanied by masturbation). Men tended to agree that secret meetings with another woman were dangerous, and perhaps dishonest, but not really infidelity unless they involved sex.

Of course, all dishonesty may be hazardous to a marriage. Frank Pittman, the psychiatrist and author mentioned earlier in this chapter, suggests a simple way for partners to determine whether something they are doing constitutes infidelity: If you're not sure, Pittman says, "Go ask your spouse."

The Women They Didn't Marry

Autoworker, age fifty-eight, married thirty-six years: *"At times I wonder what my life would have been like if I'd married another woman. I sometimes think about old girlfriends and know of some of their life stories over the years. One of them has been married several times and seems very demanding of those that she dates or marries. I look at that situation and am so happy to be with whom I'm with. Others, I have not seen for many years and sometimes just wonder about. There are, of course, the thoughts about sexual relationships and what this other person may have liked or not liked in a sexual way."*

Human resources officer, forty-three, married twenty years: *"There is really no one special woman from the past that I think about. If I happen to be watching a University of Texas football game, I will probably think about a girl or two that I dated while I was there. If I hear a certain song from the seventies or eighties, I will probably think of a girl whom I shared a special moment with. This in no way means that I don't love my wife. It's sort of like a stroll down memory lane or a retrospective in my mind."*

Police officer, thirty-eight, married thirteen years: *"Once in a great while, we will get into some frustrating argument that causes me to wonder what I've gotten myself into. But this passes quickly, and then I wonder why I ever wondered that to begin with. Until the next time."*

Computer programmer, fifty-three, married thirteen years: *"Sure, I think about several old girlfriends, old almost-girlfriends, old could-have-been-lovers-but-was-too-stupid-to-realize-it. Ask if I ever think about other women from my present. [The answer is] sure—my fantasy life is active, sometimes achingly so. And in what way do I think of them? Mostly explicitly sexually. Fantasies, real memories, or fantasies based on memories."*

Engineer, aged fifty-nine, married thirty-two years: *"I recall, now and then, most of my old girlfriends. One was a high-school girlfriend that I dated some when she and I were in college. I see her at our reunions. She has met my wife. I do have fond memories of her. Certainly, there has been nothing between us since she and I broke up. But deep inside, I do carry a bit of a charge for her. She was my first serious love."*

Chapter Eleven

———— ❧ ————

MONEY AND WORK: SCRIMPERS AND SQUANDERERS

Necessities are our priority. Wants are secondary to needs.
Our happiness together is more valuable than money.
—Fifty-two-year-old records clerk

To ANDREW PALMER, it was just a jar of green olives with pimientos. To his wife, Glenna, however, it was a symbol of his fiscal recklessness.

Steering his cart down the supermarket's condiments aisle, he had spied the olives, recalled their succulent saltiness, and—though they weren't on the grocery list—placed a medium-sized jar of them among his other provisions. It wasn't until he got home that he learned of their controversial nature.

"What'd you buy *these* for?" Glenna asked as she unearthed the jar from the grocery bag.

"I don't know," Andrew replied. "They looked good."

"Well, we don't need them."

"I know we don't *need* them. But I *like* them."

Though they had been married just a few months, this wasn't the first, or last, time that Andrew and Glenna would argue over spending. But even a decade later, Andrew would recall the incident as emblematic of their early-marriage tensions. Like so many young couples, he and Glenna were poor and in debt. And like so many, they had wildly different ideas of how to manage this reality. As Andrew would later say of the jar of olives: "For her, it was a luxury she wouldn't even have thought of. For me, it was a dollar and a half."

* * *

Over the past thirty years, women's incomes in the United States have risen dramatically. Today, three in ten wives earn more money than their husbands. And even when husbands earn more, the difference between their income and their wives' tends to be much smaller than in the past. For new reasons and old, money—how to earn it and how to spend it—has solidified its ranking as the number-one topic of contention among married couples.

According to the VoiceMale Survey, 43 percent of couples have argued over money in their marriages, and one in five husbands listed money as the issue most likely to cause disagreement between them and their wives. That puts it well above the second-most-argued-about topic—how to balance work and family, which, in many cases, also is fueled by money insecurities. In our survey, one-third of husbands said they had argued with their wives about balancing work and family; 16 percent put it at the top of the list of their sources of marital discord.

In this chapter, I'll focus on these top two marital issues, particularly why they so often prompt disagreements and how husbands believe disputes over them can be most effectively resolved.

As with sex and housework, changes in the larger culture have influenced the dynamics of marital arguments over finances.

In the 1940s and 1950s, disagreement over who controlled the money was relatively rare. Men from that era told me that they earned the money in their families, and they decided how to spend it. Some had chosen to cede a portion of their financial authority to their wives. But most said they felt not only entitled to control the family money, but obligated to do so.

One husband, now a retired engineer, offered me a perspective on how things worked in the prefeminist era. As this man came of age in the late 1950s, he did not even consider marriage until he had a good job. "Every man knew that marrying meant supporting a family," he told me forty-five years later.

After settling into a job in his mid-twenties, he fell in love with a woman who worked at the same company. Then, as they planned their wedding, they faced their first money decisions together. Since both had secure jobs, they decided to pay for the wedding themselves. The dynamic around spending money on the wedding quickly became clear: She proposed ideas; he disposed of them.

One example: Having come from a Polish-Catholic family, she wanted a polka band at the reception. She had never been to a Polish wedding that didn't feature one. But there was a problem: The band would cost an extra $200. Since they had just $1,000 to spend on the wedding—and he'd never seen a band at a reception he'd attended—he nixed the idea. As he recalled years later: "She didn't pursue it. Her image of marriage was the wife was supposed to do what the husband said. She grew up that way. She figured if I said we couldn't afford it, that's it."

Within a few years, in this marriage and many others, the he's-in-charge dynamic would be thoroughly challenged. This husband recalled that gradually his wife "started having more of her own ideas and stopped deferring all the time." But in most marriages that began before 1970, men continued to believe that it was their responsibility to ensure the family's financial health.

Among most younger couples, these dynamics no longer hold. For good or ill, men don't necessarily believe they need a secure job before marrying; few jobs seem secure anymore anyway. In addition, increasing numbers of men no longer expect to be the primary breadwinner in their families. The number of stay-at-home husbands has skyrocketed in the past decade.

Their growing economic power gives women greater leverage in their marriages—leverage not only to decide how to spend family money, but to decide nonfinancial issues as well. It should come as no surprise that wives who are economically independent of their husbands are more likely to initiate separations and divorces.

Usually, over finances, it doesn't come to that. Although money is the number-one topic of marital arguments, most husbands and wives find ways to come to an understanding on it. Here's how some men said they did it:

Management consultant, married twenty-four years: "My wife is more likely than I am to be concerned with physical and financial security, so I defer in her direction by being more cautious than I might be if I were on my own. It's not a big deal, because if she's feeling safe and secure, I'm happier too."

Records clerk, married twenty-two years: "Both of our paychecks are automatically deposited. The bills, our tithe, and church budget offerings are paid from that. Personal items like underwear, gifts for anniversaries and birthdays, are done on an as-needed basis. As far as Christmas goes, we decide what the limit is that we will spend for each other. . . . I think the key to getting along without money arguments is to trust and be trustworthy. There are no secrets about money in our relationship. Necessities are our priority. Wants are secondary to needs. Our happiness together is more valuable than money."

Technical writer, married sixteen years: "We check in with each other periodically to see what's going on financially, what's needed, what might be coming up, that sort of thing. We occasionally reset goals. Maybe a vacation is coming and we need to save a certain amount, so we'll talk about it. The key is realizing a trust level. She trusts me to take care of the bills, and I trust her to take care of her spending."

What these three couples have in common is trust and openness. But for many couples, such confidence in a spouse comes slowly, if ever.

The chasm between Will Greenberg and his wife, Mary, became apparent with their first major joint purchase: their bed. It was the mid-1980s, and Will remembers driving through the mattress district of Chicago. At their first stop, they sampled a variety of mattresses and found one they both liked. Mary was ready to buy it and get on with a relaxing weekend. Will thought the mattress was overpriced and wanted to keep looking.

Several hours later, both could claim victory, sort of. They had bought the original mattress, as Mary had wanted. But because they'd visited other mattress stores, they had been able to negotiate a 20 percent discount. Score one for Will.

Unfortunately, the experience felt to both of them like a defeat. They were irritated with each other that day. And their irritation over money would grow.

When the Greenbergs moved away from Chicago a few months later for a job that Will had landed, they decided to close the last of their separate accounts and pool their money. It didn't occur to Will at first how bothered he'd be watching Mary spend his paychecks in her "lavish" style. Will took to criticizing Mary and examining their credit-card statements for unnecessary purchases. Mary retaliated by hiding her spending. Only years later did she tell Will that she sometimes wrote checks for groceries— and pocketed $20 or $30 in cash that she added on.

What disturbed Will more than the spending was Mary's lack of interest in their long-term financial future. In the first years of their marriage, Mary didn't know at any moment whether she and Will had $1,000 in the bank or $10,000. She didn't know whether they were on target with their retirement savings or hopelessly behind. She wasn't even able to quote her own salary, he says.

Will acknowledges that he was on the opposite end of the continuum. He perused their finances regularly, anxious about stock-market dips and inflationary trends. He saved secretly, stashing money in various accounts. He resisted spending on himself. And, though he knew that receiving flowers pleased Mary, he could rarely bring himself to spend the cash.

Eighteen years into their marriage, when I heard their story, they had reached an accommodation on money. Will admitted that it was a tenuous agreement, based largely on the fact that Mary was earning a high salary. But at the same time, Will said, both he and Mary had matured. Most importantly, each had accepted the reality that their way of looking at money was not necessarily the only right way.

How did they get there? Mary, for her part, agreed to sit down with Will for semiannual assessments of their retirement savings. In these sessions, Will laid out details of their portfolio. He had the chance to point out, in a nonconfrontational moment, that if they wanted to retire by a certain date and have an adequate retirement income, they would have to save a certain amount each month. That meant keeping spending under control.

Seeing this picture helped Mary rein in her spending, Will said. And sharing the burden of their financial future allowed Will to relax too: He would not be (solely) to blame if their savings came up short. This freed Will to spend money on himself occasionally, and on Mary. Still, Will tends to be the spending damper in the family. If he suggests that they go out for dinner, Will said, it's not likely that Mary will ask, "Are you sure we can afford it?"

In this case, having more money helped alleviate some of the conflicts. Indeed, while wealth did not inoculate couples from disagreements about money, it seemed to lessen the frequency of such arguments. But perhaps more important to a relationship than the amount of money a couple earned was how each partner shared in the overall responsibility on financial matters.

In our survey, I asked husbands whether they felt financial responsibility was fairly divided in their household. Nearly 80 percent of husbands said there was fairness all around. But when one or both partners considered the financial responsibility to be divided unfairly, the marriage tended not to be as strong. The survey showed that husbands in these "financially unfair marriages" had less sex and were less happy in their marriages overall.

These tensions around money generally have their roots in the childhoods of the partners involved. Will and Mary Greenberg, who struggled over the bed purchase, emerged from very different family systems in this regard.

Will told me that he'd learned the "art of thrift" from his mother. She had collected Green Stamps and coupons, and was a garage-sale enthusiast, buying many household items in other people's yards. Will's family gradually became well off during his childhood, but those early lessons about frugality stuck with him.

Will also worked a paper route, starting at the age of eleven. He found security and self-confidence in having his own money. He saved most of his paper-route money until college, he said, when he spent it on a trip to Europe. He admits that he leans toward "a scarcity model" of money, never sure that it will be there when he needs it.

Mary, on the other hand, embraces "an abundance model" of money, Will said. She learned that from her father, who once brought home a motorboat he'd bought without telling Mary's mother. Mary's family had less money than Will's, but they tended to spend what they had. Will says that particularly early in their marriage, Mary's attitude was "spend now or risk having some left over."

Will said that to him, the value of money is the security it offers. "If one of us loses our job, I want some backup," he said. "Material things don't bring me peace of mind." Mary, on the other hand, sees money "as contributing to the quality of life," Will says. Good food, nice clothes, and a beautiful home cost money, Mary says—and they're worth it.

Gradually, over several years of negotiation, including numerous flare-ups, each partner has come to accept the other's attitude toward money. Will said that Mary openly admits that she'd be deeply in debt if she weren't married to him. And Will admits that Mary's money philosophy has brought pleasure into their lives.

While Mary was the spender in the Greenberg family, my in-depth interviews found no pattern indicating that women are more likely than men to take on this role. Women do seem to spend more than men on daily-use items such as food, clothes, and supplies for the kids. But men make up for this by buying the big-ticket items. Several men acknowledged that they had spent hundreds of dollars on stereo equipment, computers, tools, and other items without consulting their wives.

I did find that men are often frustrated with their wives for not aggressively negotiating prices. One man said his wife "caved in" to salespeople when buying appliances, cars, furniture, and other items. Psychologists say that the differences in the way boys and girls are raised may contribute to these attitudes toward negotiating. In the boy culture, competition is embraced, and negotiating prices is one accepted form of it. Girl culture emphasizes cooperation and avoiding conflict.

One way to avoid conflict, for some couples, is for each partner to have his or her own money. Among those in our survey, 32 percent of husbands said they and their wives had at least some of their money in separate accounts. Typically, in these situations, a husband and wife contributed monthly to a joint account that was used for the mortgage, utilities, insurance, retirement funds, tithes, and other recurring expenses. Their contributions often depended on what percentage of the family income each earned. The rest of their income stayed separate and was theirs to spend as they chose.

Interestingly, at least three out of four husbands I interviewed in depth said they had a marriage in which one partner leaned toward saving while the other tilted toward spending. This kind of setup was probably not an accident. It had the result of encouraging each partner to moderate his or her more extreme tendencies over time. Besides, marriages in which both partners are spenders (or both are savers) often produce their own set of difficulties.

One husband told me that he and his wife had had to declare bankruptcy after being married for two years. Each had come into the marriage with consumer debt, and both had lost their jobs in the first year of marriage. (They'd worked at the same company, which itself declared bankruptcy.) Even without steady paychecks, they had continued to spend impulsively, the husband said. Neither was able to be the spending brake in the family. By the time they acknowledged their problem, they were $60,000 in debt. They have since been through marital counseling on the issue and have cut up their credit cards.

Among younger couples, a new subject of disagreement has emerged on the money front. A generation ago, it was common for husbands to discourage or even "forbid" their wives from working outside the home. These men wanted someone to keep the house and care for the kids full-time.

Among young and midlife husbands, however, I found that this was rarely the case. Far more common were husbands who expressed frustration because their wives *didn't* work outside the home.

One husband in his early forties told me that several years earlier, he had threatened to leave his wife if she did not reenter the workforce after their two children reached school age. This husband said that he wanted the extra money for the family, but more importantly, "I knew women who stayed at home, and they became bitter over time. I really didn't want to be with her if she wouldn't tackle the real world. So I pushed."

This man reports that his wife is much happier now that she's working as a preschool teacher. "She tells me that she's more confident, that she feels better about herself, that she feels like she's got a place in the universe."

Then there's Buford Harvey, a crane operator in his mid-forties. He told me that he and his wife were currently arguing more about money than ever before in their twelve years of marriage. That's because three years ago, his wife quit her post-office job to start up a pottery business.

At first, Buford had given his blessing. But when I spoke with him, his wife hadn't come close to replacing her previous income, Buford said. He's especially frustrated when he sees his wife watching daytime TV; in his mind, "she should be building the business." Meanwhile, he contends, she's still spending money as if she had her old job. When I spoke with him, Buford said he was so frustrated with his wife's approach to money and work that he'd recently given himself a nickname: the Bank of Buford.

One way that Buford is dealing with his financial situation is to work as much overtime as he can. And this leads us to another key issue that often involves finances: balancing work and family.

In Buford's case, he often has the opportunity to work extra hours. But he usually doesn't learn about such opportunities until a few hours in advance. On numerous occasions, he has decided to cancel plans that he made with his wife in order to take the overtime hours. He recalls a major outburst from his wife on one occasion when he canceled a long-planned night on the town so he could take overtime. "She went red on me," Buford remembers. She yelled. She cursed. She threw a mug in his direction. Buford says he was equally dramatic in his response.

* * *

Buford earns considerably more than his wife, but he says he'd be happy if she earned more than him. Indeed, contrary to some stereotypes, the majority of men I interviewed said they weren't bothered when their wives earned more than they did.

The primary exception to this was when the husband had a salary that couldn't sustain the family. A twenty-nine-year-old freelance photographer told me he earned $15,000 a year, on average, while his wife made $55,000 as a magazine editor. The husband told me that he was happy with his wife's salary but wondered sometimes "whether I'm doing all I should be. Even though my wife says she's OK with [the financial arrangement], I feel guilty that I'm not pulling my weight."

The husband said he was particularly bothered that under the current circumstances, his wife would not have the option to quit working after they have a child. Yet the husband remained so uncomfortable with the creative and time compromises that came with taking a full-time job that he had few thoughts of ending his freelance life.

I did sense from some husbands of high-earning wives that they were more uncomfortable than even they would admit. A middle-school teacher who made $28,000 a year told me that his wife, a corporate lawyer, earned more than $80,000 annually. "There's something wrong with America" that these two jobs should have such a wide salary disparity, this man told me. When he sees his wife's paycheck, he said, "it sometimes pisses me off." On the other hand, he added, he's enormously grateful to her. Because of that paycheck, he's able to pursue his chosen career without the financial worries that so many of his colleagues face.

Like the spending of money, the issue of balancing work and family has gradually changed over the past three decades, due largely to the major shifts in who is working and how much.

Before 1965, when men were the major breadwinners in virtually all American families, wives expected (if not always accepted) their husbands' absence from the house. An eighty-two-year-old retired professor told me that in the first fifteen years of his marriage, when his career was developing, he considered it normal to be away from his wife and three children on two- or three-day trips several times a month. Early in his career, he recalled, "I drew all the [traveling] assignments that no one else wanted. I was low man on the totem pole."

Soon this man became well known in his field and received requests from all over the world to serve on committees and speak at conferences—on top of heavy responsibilities at his home university. By his mid-thirties, he recalls, he was working about eighty hours a week and spending much of his free time on plane flights.

Then he had a "comeuppance," as he put it. While waiting at an airport for a "red-eye" flight home, he started to feel pain in his chest and arm. Fearing a heart attack, he called a physician friend, who directed him to a local hospital. There, he was diagnosed with exhaustion. He spent two weeks in a hospital bed. He said the experience was "jolting" to both him and his wife. "From that point on, she was not so accommodating" about his traveling, he said, nor was he so eager to go "whenever the fire bell rang."

A few years later this man was waiting at his hometown airport for a flight to a business meeting. It was just before the winter holidays, and two of his grown children had come to visit him and his wife. He felt conflicted. Then an airline employee announced that the flight was full and one person had been unable to secure a seat. The professor gave up his ticket so the man could take the flight. Then he went home. "I decided that my family came first," he told me.

In recent years, a new wrinkle has emerged in the discussion of balancing work and family; it involves mostly men in their fifties and sixties.

Men in this age group generally began married life as the primary breadwinner in their homes; their wives tended to be stay-at-home moms when their kids were young. As the husbands reached midlife and the children left the nest, the men looked forward to winding down their careers and focusing their attention on travel and leisure. The problem for many:

Their wives were just hitting their stride in their own careers and had no interest in slowing down.

Aaron Godfrey was fifty-eight when I interviewed him. Not long before, his two children had finished college and he had retired early from his job as an engineer for an aerospace company. Even though his wife, Martha, had been the primary parent in the early years, Aaron said that he too had spent a lot of time with the children. His own father had not liked sports, and Aaron had made up for that by coaching his kids in Little League. Of his children, he said: "[Martha] and I were a presence in their lives. We stood behind them, beside them, and in front of them as a couple."

Martha had been a substitute teacher when the kids were small and, after they reached school age, took a full-time teaching position. That was OK with Aaron—until he retired. "If there was ever a time I felt deprived of my wife, it was then," he told me. "I figured that since the kids are out of here, we can live it up. But she's coming home tired." Aaron says he recognizes that his wife "derives a lot of satisfaction from her students and colleagues," and he wants her to decide when to retire. But he does sometimes urge her to consider it.

Recently, Aaron told me, Martha had hinted that she might retire soon. But even if she does, she's not interested in the rocking chair. She has suggested that they do missionary work, traveling the world for their church. Aaron says: "I wouldn't have thought of that on my own, but maybe it would bring us together." He adds, "My orientation is more toward home and workshop projects. My father always had a well-stocked workshop. I can see myself surrounded by tools, just making things."

While this case highlights a new twist on the home-family balance issue, it is still younger, two-income couples who continue to feel the greatest work-family balance pressures. And it's no longer unusual for husbands to be the ones complaining about a spouse who works too much.

A thirty-year-old city-government employee told me he's frustrated that his lawyer wife works until 8 P.M. on most weeknights. She earns $70,000 a year (compared to his $35,000). Nonetheless, this husband insists that he'd rather have less money and more time with his wife. "She tells me that she's putting in the hours now so we won't have to worry [about money] later. I'm worried that . . . there won't be a later."

This couple does not have children. Husbands with children at home say balancing work and family often becomes even more of a struggle. That's because they've got more reason than ever to be home—and more reason to do the best at their jobs.

Nick Gabler, a thirty-six-year-old investment banker with two children under five, said his wife stopped working outside the home when their three-year-old child was diagnosed with a chronic disease. Nick makes up for his wife's "retirement," putting in as many as eighty hours a week. Now the couple has a second child. "I come home at ten or eleven at night, give a bottle, change a diaper, and go to sleep," Nick told me. Less than eight hours later, at 6:30 A.M., he leaves the house to go back to work.

Nick spoke for many when he said: "I'm always feeling pulled in all directions at once. I need to work. But I still want to be a good husband and father." At his job, where he operates in a fast-paced, open-office environment, he says, "I rarely have time even to call my wife. I have to . . . stick my head under the desk."

Nick said he feels particularly stressed because he's been laid off once before, following a corporate merger. "I know this [job] could go away at any moment," he told me. "That keeps the pressure on. I can't slack off." Even when he's sick or exhausted, he says, he shows up.

Nick and his wife had recently begun discussing how to strengthen their marriage under the various pressures. When I spoke with him, they were about to leave for an overnight trip away from the kids. I asked how long it had been since the last time they'd spent focused, one-on-one time without any children around. He figured it had been at least six months.

My statistical survey picked up some of the struggles that couples face when one or both partners work long hours. According to the survey, the more hours a man works, the more frequently he argues with his wife. When women worked long hours, the frequency of arguments did not go up as much.

There was one other noteworthy finding about women who work long hours, and it had to do with sex. Some husbands with high-powered working wives fear that their spouses will meet men at their workplace and have affairs. But, according to our survey, this did not appear to be a problem. Instead, these women seemed to bring home an increased appetite for sex. The survey showed that the more hours a woman works at her job, the more sex she has at home.

Chapter Twelve

ARGUING: DEALING WITH ANGER

Winning isn't always the most desirable outcome. Sometimes you win by losing.
—Eighty-two-year-old retired biologist

BECKY SMITH was accustomed to docile men. Throughout her childhood, Becky's father had been the guy in the easy chair, reserved and compliant, deferring to his wife on most family decisions. In her twenty years of living at home, Becky never witnessed her dad expressing anger in any obvious way.

When Christopher Smith married Becky in the early 1980s, he didn't know this. If he had, he might have been less surprised at Becky's reaction when, a couple of months into their marriage, he raised his voice during an argument. As Christopher tells it, Becky's lower lip started quivering, tears welled in her eyes, and she fled to the bedroom. "My father was a take-charge kind of guy," Christopher told me. "So it was natural for me to be forceful. But when she reacted the way she did, I started holding back. I didn't bring up [difficult issues]. The last thing I wanted was to make my wife cry."

Wives often grumble that their husbands are unwilling to handle marital conflict. When faced with discord, men will give up, shut down, or walk out, many women contend. Indeed, most research indicates that husbands are less likely than their wives to bring up marital issues and less interested in working them through. But a good many of the men I interviewed said there's a compelling reason for their reticence: Their wives

174

don't fight fair. They don't value logic. And although a wife can show her fury, any significant expression of a man's anger is off limits. As one husband told me: "My wife wants me to share my feelings, but she only accepts certain ones."

Before we fully address this anger issue, it's important to note that arguing is a normal and generally healthy aspect of any marriage. While unhappily married couples tend to argue more than happily married ones, even many of the most satisfied couples disagree on a regular basis. According to the VoiceMale Survey, 31 percent of those men who said they were very happy in their marriages also said they argued with their wives at least twice a month. The key issue is not *whether* a couple argues, but *how*.

Though arguing occurs in every stage of marriage, its frequency changes noticeably through the years. In the honeymoon phase (the first three years), arguing is routine. My survey showed that among newlyweds, 59 percent argue once a month or more, including 26 percent who argue at least once a week. Those numbers are virtually unchanged for couples in the child-raising phase (years four to twenty), when the demands of children keep pressure on the relationship.

After the twenty-year point in a marriage, the number of arguments tends to drop dramatically. Among husbands married twenty-one to thirty-five years, 72 percent said they argued with their wives once a month or less. And that number crept upward to 79 percent among couples married more than thirty-five years. By then, it seems, hard-arguing couples had either gone their separate ways or made peace with their different ways.

Surviving into these later stages of marriage generally requires that a couple know how to argue effectively. And most husbands I interviewed admitted that they played a large role in mishandling disagreements with their wives, mostly because they lacked arguing skills. They hadn't witnessed effective arguing in their childhoods, so they often hoped to simply avoid marital discord. When it inevitably occurred, they tended to be artless or worse in their approach.

Here are some unpleasant arguing strategies that men admitted to employing:

Defensiveness. "When she questioned me, I reacted with a blocking response," one husband told me of his early-marriage arguing style. "Basically, whatever she's angry about, I didn't do it."

One man said his wife told him one morning that she was upset with him for speaking about their sex life at a dinner party the night before. His initial response: "I hardly said a thing." When she quoted him verbatim, he continued to deny that he'd done anything wrong. When she suggested they call another partygoer to get an outside opinion, the husband altered his position: "Oh, you're too sensitive."

Most husbands acknowledge that they've used this defensive tactic in reaction to criticism. Over time, however, they said they'd come to recognize that their wives' complaints were less about facts than about feelings. The wife mentioned above, for example, *felt* exposed and uncomfortable at the dinner party; what she wanted from her husband, he later learned, was an acknowledgment of that and a promise to be more aware in the future.

Intellectualizing. "When she's emotional, she doesn't think straight. I can tie her into knots," one twenty-five-year-old husband said of his arguing style. "I use logic. She gets confused. I win."

This husband was boasting to me about his intellectual prowess. But there's a realistic chance that he won't be boasting for long. Though his wife gives up on each specific disagreement, she may not accept in the long run his strategy of intellectually analyzing her concerns and turning them back on her.

Several experienced husbands told me that early in their marriages, they had tried to outmaneuver their wives intellectually to win arguments. Eventually, they gave up this practice. Like defensive arguers, they came to see that their wives wanted most to be heard and understood.

Disappearing. This strategy can manifest itself both literally and figuratively. Some husbands acknowledge that they will shut out their wife by walking out when she gets angry or combative. More often, they'll stay around but disappear emotionally.

One forty-three-year-old engineer told me that his parents had never argued openly when he was living in their home. His wife, on the other hand, had grown up in a large family where disagreements were commonplace and at times high-pitched. After they married, she voiced her complaints regularly; her main concern was his lack of responsibility in taking care of the household.

His strategy was to shut down internally, nod incessantly, and agree readily with everything she said. Yes, she was right. Yes, he was screwing up. Yes, he would do things differently. Then—and this is what *really* infuriated his wife—he wouldn't follow through on what he agreed to do. It wasn't until years later, in marital therapy, that he learned "that I was being passive-aggressive. I couldn't stand up to her directly."

Understanding his arguing style helped him change it. He told me that in recent years he has learned to argue back when he feels he is being unfairly criticized. Interestingly, he adds, the passion he and his wife generate in their occasionally heated arguments often spills over into, and invigorates, their sex life.

Verbal or physical abuse. According to my survey, 8 percent of husbands say they've hit their wives in anger at some point in their marriages. In my face-to-face interviews with men, several acknowledged that physical or verbal abuse played a part in their relationships. One was a forty-seven-year-old businessman, Albert Kennedy, who told me that he had been verbally abusive in both of his marriages. His first marriage ended after seven years, when his wife began seeing another man. His second marriage was ongoing when I spoke with him, and he said he was no longer abusive.

Getting beyond abuse hadn't been easy. Albert met his second wife, Cindy, on a blind date in the mid-1980s and was initially attracted by her beauty and brains. He liked the fact the "she was smart enough that I couldn't get away" with manipulating her. It didn't take long, however, for an unhealthy pattern to take hold in their relationship.

Typically, Cindy would complain about Albert working too much. He'd become angry and respond that she didn't appreciate him. Eventually, the argument would escalate into name-calling, cursing, and vicious accusations. On some occasions, Albert might smash a plate on the floor for emphasis. None of this scared Cindy away. "She could match me in verbal abuse, word for word, shout for shout," Albert told me.

These episodes were cyclical, Albert said. After an argument, he and Cindy might "be pissed off at each other for weeks at a time," Albert said. "Sometimes I'd go stay in a motel." Eventually, they'd forgive each other and reconnect primarily through sex. Things would be good for another few weeks; then the cycle would begin again.

Despite their arguing (or maybe because they mistook it for passion), the couple married after two years of dating. Three years later, their first child was born. That's when they decided that they'd better get help. They'd already tried marital therapy, which Albert called "worse than useless, and expensive." So this time, they agreed that each would enter a local diversion program that mostly served couples in physically violent relationships.

Cindy joined a group of women; Albert attached himself to a separate group of men. The program, which involved sixteen weekly meetings, transformed their marriage. Albert recalls that most of the men in his group had hit their wives or girlfriends and had been arrested. They were attending the program to avoid jail time. "Nothing gets your attention more than sitting with a roomful of convicted felons," Albert said.

By listening and telling his story, Albert learned that his abusiveness was a response to a childhood full of threats. His mother had yelled derisive criticism at him for years; then, before Albert reached full adulthood, she died. His anger and grief came out in a form he had learned from her: verbal violence. "I remember thinking that I know what *not* to do [when arguing], but what *do* I do?"

In the diversion program, he developed the ability to step away from arguments before they escalate. He also learned to ask both himself and his wife, "What's going on inside?" More than a decade later, still married to Cindy, Albert told me that he will occasionally say something to his wife that he regrets. But when they faced the problem directly, their all-out verbal warfare ended.

Albert never hit Cindy, he told me. But several men I interviewed acknowledged that they had struck their wives. In retrospect, most of these men were appalled at their behavior; they felt guilty and small, they told me. Several explained their hitting by contending that their wives had hit them first. In fact, in my survey, husbands were twice as likely to report that their wives had hit them in anger than that they hit their wives. For obvious reasons, the accuracy of this finding is suspect. But other studies do suggest that marital violence is often a two-way street.

Not that this in any way justifies a man hitting, shoving, slapping, or otherwise physically manhandling his wife. Husbands tend to be larger, stronger, and more experienced in physical fighting than their wives. Thus, in most cases, men can cause more damage than the women can inflict on them.

Most men who had hit their wives struggled when explaining why. "I'm a redhead," one man told me, "and I tend to act like one." Another said: "I just lash out. I get so upset. I act in an aggressive, juvenile way."

Some level of denial is common among these men. One told me he had hit his wife one time; later, in the same conversation, he reported that he'd hit her "a couple or several times" over the course of the marriage. He couldn't remember what arguments had led to the violence. "Usually, it's a disagreement over something stupid," he said. "If there's a genesis, it's usually my fault as opposed to hers. I feel slighted. Maybe she's not taking my feelings into account, or she's making decisions without me. I overreact."

Shortly before I spoke with this man, his wife had pressured him to get help. Skeptical of psychological therapy, he went to a medical doctor, who prescribed antidepression medication. Since then, he said, the medicine had "begun mellowing me out. I relax a bit more."

Interestingly, this man said that his parents hadn't argued at all in front of him when he was young. Then, when he was a teenager, they divorced. As a result, he said, he decided that "keeping it all inside was the wrong way to go." He admitted to me, however, that "I've overcompensated. I need to harness it. I need to regulate it. I want to get to the point where our life is not determined by whatever mood I'm in."

Going to the doctor had been very difficult for this man, he told me. "I don't like to ask for help. I always think I can do everything on my own. But I finally realized that doing it by myself is not working."

* * *

Given the potentially dangerous consequences of physical violence, it's understandable that many women become anxious when their husbands express anger. Nonetheless, the majority of husbands I interviewed said they'd never hit another person, let alone their wives, and they were confused and frustrated when their wives feared them. Frank Pittman, author of *Man Enough,* writes: "[Men] know that what we say when we're angry should be ignored, and our [male] friends do us the favor of ignoring it. We often wish women would do the same."

But women don't. And for that reason, Pittman, along with virtually all of the marriage researchers and therapists I interviewed, said that husbands should be very cautious about how they express anger in their marriages.

Terrence Real, a marriage counselor and author of *How Can I Get Through to You?,* told me that men can be most effective in expressing anger with their wives by using words. He suggests that men start sentences this way when they're mad: "I'm angry because . . ." Real acknowledges that such a phrase may seem foreign to many men, but he contends that yelling—whether done by a husband or wife—"is offensive behavior. It's a boundary violation."

Real said that too many husbands, when arguing, are "interested in getting the woman to shut up." He emphasizes that men's tendency to express anger loudly "is not a personal failing, but a cultural teaching. We can do better."

Linguists such as Deborah Tannen have studied the different ways in which men and women express themselves. In her book *You Just Don't Understand,* Tannen suggests that most men are probably not trying to intimidate their wives when they raise their voices—at least not consciously. Tannen points out that in male culture, "being able to fight with someone is evidence of intimacy."

In light of this, it's fascinating to note the results of the VoiceMale Survey on the question of anger. In the survey, I asked men: Who expresses anger more in your marriage, you or your wife? Forty-two percent said their wives were most likely to express anger, compared to only 29 percent who said they expressed anger more often. In 24 percent of cases, men said, both partners expressed equal amounts of anger, and in 5 percent of marriages, neither expressed anger.

In interviews, I also asked husbands what they feared most about their wives. The most common answer was *her anger*. A few husbands, who had been hit by their wives or had been the target of thrown objects, were physically afraid. But most were afraid of the emotional impact of their wives' anger.

Why are men so sensitive on this topic? Because for many men, a wife's anger carries a painful echo. These men recall that when they were children, their mothers tended to withdraw their love, at least temporarily, when they got angry. Thus, in men's experience, a woman's anger is linked with emotional abandonment. Just as women fear angry husbands because they've witnessed the damage caused by angry men, husbands fear their wives' anger because they've felt the wrath of women.

Given men's disinclination to face women's anger, it's no surprise that a common way husbands deal with marital disagreement is by attempting to steer clear of it.

"Happy wife, happy life," one man said in describing his approach to marital discord. Said another: "I agree with her and don't muddy the water." Still another husband told me: "I'm always asking myself: Is it worth winning this one? Winning isn't always the most desirable outcome. Sometimes you win by losing."

Some wives are happy with this approach. For others, it only adds to their frustration. One husband told me that when he feels the tension rising in an argument with his wife, he often goes to his workshop in the basement. His wife expresses exasperation over this. The husband told me that he goes downstairs "to avoid saying things I will regret. She thinks I'm hiding."

This man admits that if his wife doesn't reengage the argument, he probably won't either. But other husbands who exit the room during an argument told me they come back later and pick up the conversation when emotions have cooled. One husband describes how he makes up with his wife: "I apologize, ask her how she's doing, and tell her I love her. It doesn't matter who is right or wrong. You have to reach."

You have to reach. This may be the most valuable piece of advice I heard for dealing with disagreements. It fits with the findings of my research too. My survey found that husbands who solve their disagreements "easily" are far more likely to be in happy marriages than those for whom solutions to arguments come with extreme difficulty. Conversely, among husbands who described themselves as "not too happy," just 13 percent reached agreement easily; 33 percent said their marital arguments tended to result in no agreement at all.

The groundbreaking research of University of Washington psychologist John Gottman suggests that some conflict is probably good for a marriage because it helps couples "weed out actions and ways of dealing with each other that can harm the marriage in the long run." Marital problems tend to occur, Gottman contends, when negative interactions become the norm.

Gottman's research indicates that healthy couples have about a five-to-one ratio of positive to negative interactions. Positive contact includes physical affection, expressions of gratitude, gifts. Negative interactions include criticism, contempt, defensiveness, and stonewalling; Gottman calls these "The Four Horsemen of the Apocalypse" for marriages. Given that negative interactions will occur in every marriage, Gottman suggests that couples interrupt their arguments at times to make "repair attempts," each expressing concern for the welfare of the other.

Chapter Thirteen

⎯⎯⎯ ❧ ⎯⎯⎯

How to Change a Man

I married her for certain qualities, but I only wanted them in certain quantities.
—Fifty-year-old executive coach

I t's one of the first warnings that women hear when they begin dating a man: Don't try to change him. Not only is trying to change a man disrespectful, the admonition goes, it's fruitless too. A man is who he is. If you try to change him, he'll probably only resist, and resent your attempts.

It's time to reassess this warning. According to the VoiceMale Survey, nearly six out of ten husbands said that their wives had changed them in a significant way since they had married, and a whopping 93 percent of those men reported that the change had been for the better. "She saved my life. I probably wouldn't be here without her," said a taxi driver who had been married twenty-five years. He credits his wife with helping him overcome an alcohol problem fifteen years ago. Another husband, who'd lost sixty-five pounds in the previous two years, said of his wife: "She was my motivation."

While these comments may be inspirational to some women, it's important to note that not all men are ripe for change—nor in need of it. In some cases, trying to change a man can be as hazardous to a relationship as it may be helpful. Several husbands I interviewed recalled that pressure from their first wives to alter their behavior had created distrust and frustration, and ultimately contributed to the death of the relationship. "She married me, but she wanted a different man," a thirty-eight-year-old store manager said of his first wife.

Indeed, one of the traits men said they cherished most about their wives—and often tried to emulate—was women's capacity for acceptance. Acceptance did not mean becoming a doormat; rather, it meant allowing the spouse to be who he is even if it was sometimes irritating. Before trying to change a man, husbands suggested, a wife should consider whether she can live with, or adapt to, behavior of his that may be irritating or even infuriating, but not harmful. She also might consider whether the traits that bother her now are the same ones to which she was originally attracted.

One husband told me that he had tried to change his wife for years before realizing that it was disrespectful. He said he'd been initially attracted to his wife's exuberance and emotionalism. Only after he married her did he become overwhelmed at times by these aspects of her personality. As he put it: "I married her for certain qualities, but I only wanted them in certain quantities."

Years later, when I spoke with this husband, he'd come to the following conclusion: He doesn't get to decide how emotional his wife is. He added: "The question is not: Why is she acting this way? It's: Why am I *reacting* this way? I've realized that trying to control another person's actions is the antithesis of love."

As the writer Tim Hudson tells it, he and his wife, Sheila, had just celebrated their thirtieth wedding anniversary when somebody asked Sheila why she thought her marriage had lasted so long. She answered, "On my wedding day, I decided to make a list of ten of Tim's faults which, for the sake of our marriage, I would always overlook. I figured I could live with at least ten."

When she was asked which faults she had listed, Sheila replied, "I never did get around to listing them. Instead, every time he does something that makes me mad, I simply say to myself, 'Lucky for him, it's one of the ten!' "

Still, some men adopt (or continue) unhealthy behaviors after they marry, and at some point, their spouses may want changes. In such cases, a wife may not want to ratchet up the pressure too quickly. That's because many husbands will change on their own. Steven Nock, the University of Virginia professor introduced earlier and author of *Marriage in Men's Lives,* says that men naturally evolve in the years after they marry. "A marriage license is not just a piece of paper," Nock told me in an interview. "Other people treat you differently when you're married. They expect you to behave differently, you expect yourself to behave differently, and then you become a different person."

Judging by my interviews, this is true. Dozens of men told me that as they became aware of unhealthy aspects of themselves in adulthood, they decided to do something about them. They usually didn't need their wives to tell them—at least not repeatedly—what was wrong with them.

One example: An employee-benefits manager, now sixty-two years old, told me that when his two daughters were teenagers, he was highly critical of their activities and friendships. On many evenings, he would yell at the girls, and they would argue back or walk out of the room. Eventually, he came to "the gnawing realization that I was not the parent I wanted to be. I began to sense that I didn't play much of a role in my daughters' lives." This man finally realized that his use of alcohol was fueling the problem, and he decided to stop. "The future without change was not workable," he said.

Fifteen years later, when I interviewed him, he said that his relationship with his daughters had improved almost immediately after he quit drinking. In the years since, he has apologized directly to them for the way he treated them as adolescents. He's even spent some time in counseling. There, he says, he learned that he'd been trying to control his family. His biggest insight: "It's possible for me to have my reality and for someone else to view the same thing very differently. There's no right or wrong, just a different look." He now carries a quotation in his wallet: "If you want peace of mind, do not find fault with others."

This man's changes were spurred by his conscience and sensibilities. Other husbands I interviewed described similar changes, undertaken because they sensed something was wrong in their lives. But some men do not—or cannot—change by themselves. These are the men who may benefit from a wife's help.

Helping does not begin with threats, husbands say, or even suggestions for change. Males are raised to see the world hierarchically, and when someone tells them what to do, they tend to feel "one down." Their reaction is often to ignore the substance of the other person's request, even if it's reasonable. "Attempts to nag or directly modify my behavior don't work," one husband told me. "It only brings out the stubbornness in me." Rather than intense pressure, husbands say, *one of the most effective ways that a woman can change a man is to model healthy behavior herself.*

The taxi driver mentioned at the beginning of this chapter is a good example. He had grown up in a religious community in the South but told me that few people had taken the teachings of the church seriously. He was aware, even as a small child, of the drinking, drugging, and extramarital sex that went on among church members, including members of his own family. Not surprisingly, in his early adulthood, he followed their lead, spending much of his free time at local bars and clubs.

In his mid-twenties, he met his future wife. He was attracted to her beauty, he says, but also to "her moral standards. She was the type of girl that's clean on the inside and out. She's the type you don't find every day."

The first ten years of the marriage were stressful. The husband continued his regular drinking, even as three children were born. His wife's occasional complaints made no difference. But over time, something else did impress him, he told me: how spiritually grounded his wife, a Jehovah's Witness, appeared after worship each Sunday.

Up to that point, he rarely attended services with her. But as his children grew and his tolerance for alcohol diminished, he began looking for a new center to his life. He eventually found it, at his wife's side, in "the Kingdom Hall." His new religion not only offered firm guidelines on alcohol use, it provided clear principles for how to make a marriage work. Since he had little extra money, it was also helpful that the church provided elders who could counsel him and his wife at low cost.

When I interviewed this man, it had been twelve years since he'd been baptized. "I've developed a conscience," he told me. Tapping his fingers on a black, soft-cover Bible on the table in front of him, he said: "This is much smarter than me." He said he'd recently asked his wife why she had married him. He remembers her exact reply: "I was hoping and praying that you'd someday change."

Another husband I interviewed remembers his wife nagging him for years to stop drinking. But it was not the nagging that actually changed him.

This husband, an electrician, had begun his alcohol use in the military in the early 1960s, shortly before he met his future wife. In the first years of their marriage, he could control how much he drank. But by his mid-thirties, he said, "It got to the point where if I have one [drink], I'm going to finish the bottle. . . . I'd have a fifth [of liquor] a day on weekdays. On weekends, I'd *really* get down to some drinking."

His wife, a nurse, implored him to quit. Ashamed of him, she stopped inviting people to the house. Afraid of losing his income, she covered his tracks with his employer when he was too hung over to work. None of this helped.

Then she made the move that would change him: She started attending Al-Anon meetings. There, she learned to stop making excuses for her husband, to stop "enabling" his alcohol abuse. The husband recalls that at this point his wife began inviting friends over again—friends who witnessed him in a drunken stupor. When guests would arrive, he remembers, "They'd just step over the body."

Such experiences were humiliating to him. "Until that point, I didn't know alcohol was the problem. I only suspicioned that it was so." No longer protected by his wife from the impact of his drinking, this husband sought treatment at the employee-assistance program where he worked. When I spoke with him, he had been sober for sixteen years. "I'm grateful that my wife didn't run me off," he says.

Several husbands told me how their wives had helped them lose weight, not by begging them to eat less or exercise more, but by eating less and exercising more themselves. Another husband said that his wife, who used marijuana only occasionally, stopped using it altogether in hopes that it would help him fight his marijuana addiction. The strategy worked. And still another husband said that when his wife started taking classes at a local college, he became inspired to get his own degree—something his wife had urged him, unsuccessfully, to do for years.

These women learned that their own behavior could "rub off" on their spouses. At the same time, their husbands reported, most of these women also seemed to know, and accept, that there were no guarantees. They may have wanted their man to change; they may have worked for him to change; but if they were smart, they didn't *expect* him to change.

What happens when a woman can no longer live with the unhealthy aspects of a man, but no amount of praying, begging, and modeling works? Some wives go for threats and recriminations at this point. But husbands indicate that there may be one more step before pulling out the big guns: Invite him to marital counseling.

It's not easy for men to go for counseling. Seeking help is against the masculine code. But even men acknowledge that counseling is a tool that often works. In my survey, 22 percent of husbands said they'd been to a marriage counselor with their current wife. And more than two-thirds of those men said the counseling had been helpful.

One husband recounted to me how his wife had started suggesting the idea of counseling a couple of years into their marriage. The husband was aware that he and his wife weren't on the same wavelength when it came to sex, styles of arguing, and other issues. But he resisted therapy. He thought it was an admission that the marriage was in serious trouble. He also didn't believe it was important to "work on issues." His strategy was to "play through" the difficulties and hope that things got better over time.

When this man resisted counseling, his wife didn't push, implore, or threaten. Instead, she began seeing a therapist on her own. She kept her husband apprised of the details of the therapy, particularly when she and the therapist spoke about him. In this indirect way, the husband began to gain some insights about the marriage and to lose some of his fear of counseling.

She left open her invitation for him to join her in counseling, and finally, as the marriage continued to falter, he took up her invitation. At the first session, he told me, he expected to learn that "she was right and I needed to change." But it didn't happen. Rather, over three years of sessions, the man "got an education" in the dynamics of relationships. He also learned how different he and his wife were—and that both he and his wife wanted the relationship to last.

One dynamic that this couple addressed in counseling was how they argued with each other. Like sports analysts examining an instant replay, they probed the moment-to-moment dynamics of a typical argument between them. They realized that unless the argument reached an emotional climax, it was incomplete for her. On the other hand, if it got emotionally passionate, it was too much for him. He liked logic. "Just knowing this allowed us both to move to the middle," the husband told me.

Several years later, when I interviewed this man, he said he appreciated the way his wife had introduced him to therapy: gently. He still thinks, however, that most counseling is unfriendly to men. Feelings are overemphasized, he told me, while rationality and action are undervalued. He thinks more men would try counseling, and benefit from it, if they saw it not as "getting help," but as "learning a subject—relationships."

If all other strategies fail to change a man and the wife is prepared to put her marriage on the line, threatening a split-up may in some circumstances be an effective way to change a man. Even some husbands admit that this is true.

One husband told me that his wife of four years left him after he refused to stop using cocaine. He had used the drug even before they married, but she believed he'd stop afterward. When he didn't, she urged him, threatened him, and finally left him. She said she'd consider returning only after he completed a thirty-day drug-treatment program. He went into treatment. "My priorities finally got right," this husband told me. Twenty years later, this man helps other men overcome drug addiction. He's still married to the same woman.

Another man told me that about five years into their marriage he had slapped his wife during an argument. She left the room and didn't talk with him for a day. Then, she told him, "If you ever do that again, I'm gone." She added, "I'm serious about that." It's been twenty years, the man said, and he's never hit her again.

Any woman who is considering trying to change her husband should know that when she tinkers with a man, she risks altering more than just the single behavior she doesn't like. People are intricate and complex, and when a man changes one aspect of himself, he's likely to reevaluate—consciously or not—other aspects as well.

One forty-eight-year-old businessman told me that his first wife thought he became too angry too often. She suggested that he seek therapy. At first, he resisted, but eventually he agreed. Twenty years later, this man reported that the marriage had failed. He recalled that his wife had married him in large part because he was strong and successful, an "alpha male." In two years of therapy, he recalls, he became gentler and more sensitive. "I sort of became Alan Alda before her eyes. I talked about depression, feelings. It was foreign to her." And in the end, he was not the man she wanted. The marriage broke up.

Ultimately, most husbands are open to changing. And some actually look to their wives as agents of change. One man told me: "I have a sense of respect and integrity. It's something I learned from my wife." But like everyone, men also want to be accepted, appreciated for who they are, even if they don't always meet the highest standards. One challenge for a wife is to decide what aspects of her husband's personality she can live with and what she absolutely *must* try to change.

Chapter Fourteen

PARENTS AND IN-LAWS: THE VALUE OF FATHERS

[My father] is a constant gauge for me as far as my own behaviors are concerned,
something I can measure myself against.
—Thirty-year-old middle-school teacher

PAY ATTENTION TO HOW HE TREATS HIS MOTHER. It's a statement women often hear when they wonder aloud how a boyfriend or husband might behave toward them in the long run. And there's apparent logic in this comparison. A man's mother and his wife are both women; thus, it might seem, a man's attitude toward each should be similar. But, according to the VoiceMale Survey, a man's relationship with his mother does not influence his marriage as much as we may think. It is, more importantly, a man's relationship with his *father* that shapes him into the husband he will become.

"My dad had a high kindness quotient," a forty-three-year-old public-relations specialist tells me. "In that way, at least, I try to be every inch my father's son."

This husband says he often remembers a statement his father made more than thirty years ago, when the son was a grade-schooler. The father said: "Before my foot hits the floor each morning, I ask myself: 'What can I do for my family today?'" As a kid, the son didn't really understand. Now married for three years, those words inspire him. His father died four years before our conversation, but the son says: "A passion for family is something we'll always share."

This husband was one of many who saw the enormous influence

191

their fathers had on their married lives. Another man, a thirty-year-old middle-school teacher, credits his dad with teaching him most of what he knows about being a husband. Married six years, with one daughter, this husband says: "I think about how my dad handled various situations all the time. I think about how he reacted to things, how he spoke, how he managed when he was angry. He is a constant gauge for me as far as my own behaviors are concerned, something I can measure myself against."

Asking a man to explain how his parents shaped him is surely an incomplete method of discerning the parents' actual influence. Most parental influence is subtle, even preconscious. That's why, in addition to asking direct questions about such influence, I used my statistical survey to test for more subtle links. In the survey, I asked men, first, whether they had positive or negative relationships with their mothers and fathers in childhood. Later, I asked how happy they were in their current marriages.

One significant surprise: *Men who had very positive relationships with their mothers in childhood were no more or less likely to be happy in their relationships with their wives.* This does not mean that mothers are superfluous in shaping their sons; I'll report later in the chapter what men said about the importance of their mothers' influence. But the finding does challenge the conventional wisdom that a man's bond with his mother can predict his bond with his wife.

Particularly in light of this finding, our survey offered a second surprise on this topic: *Men who had very positive relationships with their fathers in childhood were considerably more likely than others to be happily married to their wives.* Specifically, a man who had a very positive bond with his father was, in his marriage, more likely to report fairness in housework, less likely to hit his wife during arguments, less likely to consider separation or divorce, and more likely be happily married overall.

Frank Pittman, in his book *Man Enough,* says that when working with male clients, he zeroes in on the relationship between the client and his father. "The impact of the father is so much more powerful than anything the mother can do or not do, short of dropping him on his head," Pittman told me in an interview. When a father is available and affirming of his son, the son generally feels strong and secure, Pittman said. If a father is not physically or emotionally present, the son will often "go through life feeling like an imposter."

In the course of my research, I had an opportunity to meet with a group of fourteen inmates while they were incarcerated for crimes ranging from drug-dealing to assault to child abuse. Tellingly, twelve of these men reported little or no interaction with their fathers in childhood: "He was never there when I was growing up." "He left when I was two." "I didn't meet my father until I was ten." "My grandmother raised me." "I was a foster child." "We were bounced around."

Such neglect had a devastating impact on their lives, most of them acknowledged, including on their relationships with women. Several admitted that they had treated women shabbily and had cheated on their wives and girlfriends. One never-married inmate, who was twenty-seven years old, reported having eight children, most of whom he rarely saw even before his jailing.

Most men with ineffectual fathering do not end up in jail. But their adult relationships often suffer. A fifty-four-year-old computer programmer told me he had a double dose of bad fathering. His biological dad abandoned him and his mother when he was an infant. After that, he saw his father once a year, for about an hour each time, until his early teens; the father died when the son was eighteen. For most of his growing-up years, the son also had a stepfather. But this man was intimidated by children, the son recalls, and rarely involved himself in the son's life. The son told me that he had learned from these two father figures that a man's posture toward the world should be one of "reserved distance."

Adopting this posture has haunted the man through three marriages, he told me. He said he has tended to be overly intellectual and analytical. He can be impatient with, and even dismissive of, the emotionalism his wife shows. "As you can imagine, [this attitude] gets me in trouble," he says.

* * *

Porter Williams was another man I interviewed whose father relationship was problematic. Porter's father abandoned the family when Porter was eight. Nearly forty years later, Porter told me: "Even to this day, I can tell you exactly the words that were said and where we were when my mother said, 'Daddy isn't coming home anymore.'" Porter and his sister cried. "We couldn't understand why [he had left]. I knew my father was a womanizer, even back then. I was old enough to see things but not totally understand."

In the years that followed, Porter remembers being teased by other kids who said he was a bad kid and "that's why your daddy don't stay home with you." He says of his mother: "She was a wonderful woman, and strong. She instilled in me a lot of good values. But that father image was what was missing. I didn't see a stern, family type of setting." After the divorce, Porter's father moved several states away. "There was a lot of anger in me toward him. I couldn't understand why he wasn't there. A lot of times, you carry that guilt. Maybe I did something wrong."

Without the monitoring and mentoring of an adult man, Porter acknowledges that he started treating girls and young women badly. "I would never allow them to get too [emotionally] close to me," he said. As a junior in high school, he got his girlfriend pregnant. She had the baby, and over the subsequent decade, he had another child out of wedlock. Because he remembered his own pain of abandonment, Porter could not neglect his own children. He saw them regularly and supported them financially. But he maintained only a distant relationship with the women.

Porter told me that he might never have emerged from his pattern of failed relationships had it not been for his high-school football coach. Porter, you'll recall, is an African-American man who grew up in a big city; the football coach, he said, was "a stone redneck" from Tennessee. Nonetheless, Porter says, the coach treated everyone fairly and eventually took an interest in Porter in particular. He helped Porter get into college and advised him in his personal and professional life through Porter's twenties. "He was the best thing that happened to me," Porter said. "He took me under his wing. When he retired, I got up and spoke on his behalf. I told everybody that he was more of a father to me than my own biological father."

With the older man's help, Porter gradually learned how to treat women, and how to treat himself. When I spoke with Porter, he was forty-seven and had been married almost fifteen years. He and his wife had a twelve-year-old daughter.

Porter, now a teacher at an inner-city middle school, said that among his students are dozens of fatherless teens. Like his old football coach, he tries to guide and advise them, particularly in the area of relationships. He occasionally will be in front of a class, call his wife on his cell phone, tell her that he loves her, and ask her if she needs anything. "The kids will make fun of me, but for some, it's all the modeling [about healthy marriage] that they'll ever get."

Why are fathers so important? One obvious value of a good father is someone to show a son how marriage is done. Sons notice how their fathers treat their mothers. They observe how their fathers balance work and family. They see how their dads solve family problems. From these observations, they create an internal template for what it means to be a family man. Sam Osherson, the author of *Finding Our Fathers* and other books on men, told me that sons who grow up with happily married fathers have a great advantage in life. "They realize that women are nothing to be afraid of," Osherson said. "They're able to identify with their fathers and come into marriage with a sense of confidence. It's not a conflictual role for them."

On a more subtle level, fathers also impact their sons' future relationships by affirming them as men. A son who has no father, or has a dysfunctional one, finds no one to welcome him into the world of mature men. Such fatherless sons often find their models of manhood in famous athletes and movie stars, whose sexual and financial conquests have the aura of success. But the traits they pick up are unlikely to support close, ongoing relationships.

In addition, men without good fathering tend to be angry. Like Porter, they were often hurt and teased as youngsters. They feel deprived of a birthright: an involved dad. In their early lives, sons tend to bury their anger, but it can reemerge to haunt them in their later relationships.

In highlighting the influence of fathers, I don't want to minimize the impact of mothers. For decades, research in the field of "attachment studies" has indicated that mothers play a powerful role in developing the ability of their sons to create healthy relationships.

Even today, most children are raised primarily by their mothers in their early years. At a certain point, children must break away, or individuate, from the mother and develop their own personalities. Girls tend to do this gradually, with little trauma; they can stay closer to their mothers, both psychologically and physically, for a longer time. Boys, however, learn that remaining closely connected to their mothers can stigmatize them as a "mama's boy." Thus, they tend to break more abruptly, with more ambivalence, often before they're ready.

Many boys struggle in this detachment scenario. To effect the separation from Mother, they find it necessary to demonize her; only then can they justify pulling away. The research indicates that those who struggle the most to differentiate are the most likely to struggle in their later love relationships. The legacy of the early difficulties in attaching and detaching is felt by these men's future wives and girlfriends.

It should be noted that sons tend to have a higher opinion of their mothers than they do of their fathers. According to our survey, men were more than twice as likely to say they had a negative relationship with their fathers in childhood than with their mothers.

In describing their positive feelings about mothers, men used words like "warm," "nurturing," "caring," "understanding," and "compassionate." Interestingly, this perception had the potential of cutting both ways when it came to the son's marriage. On the positive side, having warm and caring mothers sometimes encouraged them to enter into relationships with women who had generally good interpersonal skills.

Occasionally, though, men told me that they struggled in marriages where their wives didn't live up to the standard set by their mothers. One man said that his mother had been so generous about housework—she did all cooking, cleaning, and laundry during the man's childhood—that he came to expect his wife to be the same way. When he married and his wife resisted taking over his mother's role, this man said, he felt cheated.

In about 8 percent of cases, according to our survey, men report having had negative relationships with their mothers in childhood. While complaints about fathers tend to emphasize fathers' lack of involvement in their sons' lives, the complaints about mothers focus primarily on their *over*involvement. One psychiatrist describes this as "a mother collapsing on her son." In some instances, men said, this had contributed to their own subsequent relationship problems.

A forty-year-old mortgage broker recalls his mother telling him at age twelve that she was going to divorce his father. She hadn't told the father, however—and didn't tell him for the next six years. "I had an ongoing sense of impending doom," the son said. During those years, this man's mother repeatedly sought solace and support from her teenaged son.

As a result of his mother's inappropriate "invasion," this son said, he came to distrust women. Perhaps not coincidentally, he married a woman who had two affairs before leaving him. Only after years of counseling was he able to connect his struggles with women to its source: his ambivalent relationship with his mother. Eventually, he forgave his mother, he says, thus opening himself to a positive, trusting bond with a woman. When I spoke with him, he'd been happily married for eleven years.

As we've heard several times in the above stories, men's marriages are affected both individually by their mothers and fathers, and also by the relationship between the two. Sons (and daughters) learn about marriage largely by watching their parents in action. And it's clear that men from homes in which a marriage fractures are at higher risk for marital problems themselves.

According to my survey, about one in five current American husbands came from a home in which his parents divorced; nearly one in three are now in marriages to women in which one or both sets of their parents have divorced. Not surprisingly, men in these marriages tended to report more struggle than those in marriages in which neither partner has divorced parents. In their marriages, my survey showed, these men argued more often; perceived less fairness in housework, child care, and family finances; and more often considered separation or divorce.

Clearly, the impact of a man's parents on his marriage can be huge. But we shouldn't overlook the impact of *his wife's* parents. The ability of a couple to stay positively connected for the long haul has as much to do with her upbringing as it does with his.

The influence of in-laws becomes most apparent to men after the engagement, husbands told me. At this point, the mother-in-law often takes an active role in the wedding planning. This can cause tension as mother-in-law and husband-to-be tussle over access to, and influence over, the bride.

One husband recalled that he and his wife had bought a condominium a few months before their marriage twenty-five years earlier. He moved into it while his fiancée continued to live at her parents' home in the period leading up to the wedding. Then, at her bridal shower, she received a host of home-oriented gifts. The husband-to-be wanted to start using the gifts at the condo. But his fiancée's mother felt the gifts should not be used until the couple was officially married. This husband said the specific point of contention—whether to bring the gifts to the condo—was not nearly as important to him as who made the decision about it. "I told [my fiancée] that decisions that affect us are between us. We had an argument about that. Eventually, the gifts came my way."

While this couple resolved their disagreement, in-laws continue to remain a potent source of discord even after the wedding. According to the VoiceMale Survey, in-laws rank fifth on the list of most common topics of marital disagreement; in 9 percent of marriages, in-laws stand as the number-one topic of arguments.

Several husbands told me that their mothers-in-law had tried to sabotage their marriage. "Her mother didn't like me because I was poor," one husband recalled of his first mother-in-law. "She had upper-class values. I was driving this beat-up 1978 Aspen. She wanted a guy with more money, more class."

This man argued openly with his mother-in-law. At first, his wife sided with him. But as difficulties arose in the marriage relationship, she began to question her marital choice. Eventually, with moral support from her mother, she left her husband.

Cultural, religious, and ethnic differences are another potential flash-point with in-laws. About 5 percent of American marriages today involve partners from different races, and perhaps more than half cross religious and/or ethnic lines.

In some cases, in-laws rebel against such line-crossing. A forty-one-year-old Korean-American man I interviewed said he believes his first wife, who was European-American, left him in part because her parents would not accept him. This man and his wife were married for fifteen years and had three children together. From the very start of the couple's relationship, the wife's parents would neither visit their daughter and son-in-law nor welcome the son-in-law into their home. For several years, the daughter chose to stay away from her family too. But as the children grew, she felt it was important for them to know their grand-parents.

The husband told me: "I could see [my wife] gradually reattach to her family. It was distressing. I'm still angry about it. I try to keep in mind that we all need our parents." As with the previous couple, this woman turned to her parents when her marriage was struggling, and they gladly welcomed her back without her husband.

Another man, who is Asian Indian, recalls that when he called his mother in the early 1990s to tell her that he and his German-Irish girl-friend had decided to get married, the first words from his mother's mouth were "She's never cooked an Indian meal, and you're marrying her!"

Marriages between black and white partners were especially likely to cause rumblings among the in-laws, according to my interviews. One hus-band recalls his embarrassment when his mother asked his African-American wife what "colored folks" thought of a particular politician of the time. The husband said his wife was "understanding" about such incidents, and over time, his wife and mother have forged a loving relationship.

Their relationship was helped by the fact that both of their families were upper-middle-class. Indeed, class differences between a husband and wife sometimes created more friction than racial or religious differences. One husband, a university professor, told me that his parents-in-law are suspicious of him because of his job. The father-in-law had worked in a coal mine "and doesn't have much use for people who don't work with their hands."

The good news is that major tension between husbands and their parents-in-law is relatively rare. Nearly 90 percent of the men in our survey said they had a positive relationship with their mothers-in-law. Fathers-in-law were also highly esteemed.

I was particularly struck by how some in-laws went out of their way to support their children's marriages. Peter Kahana, the fifty-two-year-old hospital records clerk we met in Chapter Two, told me that he and his wife had almost no money when they married more than two decades earlier. To help the couple get on its feet financially, Peter's in-laws not only invited their daughter and Peter to live in their farmhouse after the wedding, but moved out for a year themselves. Peter told me: "They thought it was important that we live alone so our relationship could grow without being under a parent."

The honeymoon year helped the marriage and bonded Peter and his father-in-law too. The father-in-law was a farmer and still tended fruit trees on his property. He asked Peter to look after the trees while he was away. Peter made sure he did a good job. And before turning the house back over to his parents-in-law, he planted potatoes, strawberries, corn, squash, and other crops that the older man could harvest. "That meant points for me," Peter recalled.

Another husband also told me a touching story about his in-laws, who "kind of adopted me as their son." The man got along so well with his in-laws that, after the wedding, he and his wife decided to buy the house directly behind her parents' home. "Then we tore down the fence between us," the husband told me, creating a large shared yard. The young couple eventually had two children, and the in-laws were the primary day-care providers.

When this husband got a new job and was called upon to move fifty miles away, the in-laws decided to move as well. Fifteen years into their marriage, this man, his wife, and their kids live around the corner from his in-laws.

Chapter Fifteen

SECOND MARRIAGES: RISKS AND REWARDS

I felt like a permanent assistant coach. I was there on the sidelines, there at halftime,
but ultimately, I made none of the decisions.
—Forty-four-year-old social worker on being a stepfather

FOR GREG QUARLES, the first marriage was a wrongheaded disaster. It was the early 1970s, and he'd fallen for a college classmate who was pretty, intelligent, and available. Only after he married her did he discover their utter incompatibility. He saw life as something to enjoy, he recalls. She saw it as a forum for accomplishment—specifically, *his* accomplishment. "She had a lot of expectations of me," Greg told me thirty years later. "I needed to complete my graduate work, get a job, make a living, and get on with supporting her. . . . I was a perpetual disappointment."

Within two years of the wedding, resentment on both their parts crushed the marriage. Divorce was a relief for Greg but rendered him cautious. He lay low for three years. Then he met Amanda, a social worker and once-married mother of a little girl. Like Greg's first wife, Amanda was smart and pretty. But she was also funny and fun-loving. Greg fell for her. He envisioned a long and gratifying relationship.

But he overlooked one hazard: Amanda's five-year-old daughter. The girl wasn't shy, even when Amanda and Greg were first dating. Greg recalled that early in their relationship, he and his new love often held hands as they walked together. It was the daughter's habit to suddenly, quietly, "sneak up behind us and break us apart."

202

Like any concerned couple, Greg and Amanda tried to understand the child's fears and assure her that Greg was not an enemy. They wrote a part for her in the wedding and promised that she would always maintain her ties with her biological dad. Nonetheless, Greg recalls that he and his stepdaughter "went at each other" through the rest of her childhood. He admits to being "pigheaded" at times, an easy target for his stepdaughter's provocations.

The tension between Greg and his stepdaughter inevitably spilled over into his marriage. Amanda tried to play referee, which Greg resented; he wanted his wife to be firmer with her daughter. Months went by when Greg and Amanda's primary interactions focused on how to manage the child's defiance. "It never really occurred to me that a child could have such a huge impact" on a marriage, Greg, an admissions officer at a small midwestern college, told me. Staying together during the daughter's childhood, he said, "took everything we had."

One might expect that a man's previous experience with marriage would be helpful in his later relationships. And in some ways, it is. Most of the remarried husbands I interviewed confirmed that they'd learned enormous lessons from their earlier marriages, particularly about how to choose a compatible partner and communicate effectively. Later in this chapter, I'll address some of the positive differences between first and subsequent marriages.

But, as Greg Quarles's case demonstrates, when stepchildren are in the home, all bets are off. Few men are able to fully prepare for the role of stepfather, and even when they do, outside forces can roil the situation, damaging a man's bond with both his stepchildren and his wife.

One difficulty in preparing for stepfathering is the lack of consistent advice about how to do it effectively. Stepfamilies have been, until recently, a rare phenomenon. According to the VoiceMale Survey, only 4 percent of husbands who married before 1968 had been previously married, and a mere 2 percent of their wives had been married before. By contrast, among modern marriages, about 50 percent involve at least one partner who has a former spouse.

Most research indicates that when one or both partners have been married previously, a couple is less likely to be happy, as compared to first-time married couples. But my research found few statistical differences in happiness between these two kinds of couples. *Neither previously married couples nor first-time married couples were more likely to argue with each other, to have a satisfying sex life, or to be happy overall, the research showed.*

In at least one realm of marriage, having been previously married actually proved helpful. According to our survey, a previously married husband was more than three times *less* likely to have an affair than a husband who'd never been married before. It's quite possible that many men learn the hard way, in their first marriages, how damaging infidelity can be.

But as noted above, there is one area where first-time married couples have it easier than remarried couples: dealing with their children. Among first-time married couples in our survey, raising children ranked fifth on the list of issues most likely to cause disagreement in the marriage. By contrast, when both partners have been married before, raising children soars to the top of this list of most-divisive issues. In fully one-third of couples involving two previously married partners, raising children is the number-one cause of arguments.

It's difficult to discern why some men and their stepchildren clash so intensely while others do not. Surely, each child's temperament, mental and physical health, and relationship with the biological father are crucial factors. But among the stepfathers I interviewed, there seemed to be a pattern among those who struggled the most. In these cases, the stepfathers had generally tried to assert themselves quickly and authoritatively into the child's life.

One man, who at age thirty-three married a woman with three children under age ten, shared with me his trying experiences in fifteen years of hands-on stepfathering. He said that at the very beginning of his marriage he had "strong thoughts on how to raise young kids." This man was a middle-school teacher, so he felt particularly confident about his approach to children. He believed his three stepchildren needed more discipline than their mother was offering, and he set out to accomplish this. He used his position as man of the house to set rules and enforce them.

His assertiveness backfired, he now admits nearly twenty years later. For one thing, it drove a wedge between him and his wife. He estimates that about three-quarters of their arguments during those years focused on how to raise the children. And ultimately, his forcefulness with the kids pushed them away too. "The oldest child—we didn't do well together," he acknowledged. "He left and lived with relatives when he was sixteen." His stepdaughter, meanwhile, after dealing with him and her biological father, "decided that all men were bad." Now in an empty nest, this man says: "I worked really hard to be a good father. I probably should have just relaxed."

Stepfathering can be a particular struggle when a stepchild's biological father is stirring the pot. Harvey Lauer, a forty-four-year-old social worker, told me that it had been ten years since he married a woman with two middle-school children, a daughter and a son. In his wife's first marriage, Harvey said, she'd been verbally and emotionally abused. Her first husband had berated her, withheld money, and prevented her from seeing family and friends. "She had everything but the bruises," Harvey said.

It had taken a "heroic effort" for her to leave her husband, Harvey said, and not surprisingly, the jilted ex-husband continued to create problems afterward. Harvey told me that in his first several years of marriage, he and his wife "ran an emotional emergency room." The stepfather would require perfect behavior from the children while they were in his house. When they returned to their mother and Harvey, they were "like cats needing to scratch, but they had nowhere to scratch but on each other or us."

Harvey said that the closer he tried to get to his stepchildren, the more conflicted their relationship became. "It was double jeopardy. If I began to bond with them, they'd feel disloyal" to their biological father, he said. Around his own home, Harvey began to feel "like a permanent assistant coach. I was there on the sidelines, there at halftime, but ultimately, I made none of the decisions."

In the end, Harvey said, he had to accept that "they weren't my children, they were God's children. I had to focus on stewardship and service, not ownership. I just happen to be the guy who's here for this part" of their lives. He also had to accept that "I didn't have a fan club. The kids would never run to greet me: 'Daddy's here!' "

In the early years together, the relentless focus on stepchildren pushed the marriage to the side, Harvey said, and contributed to its near demise. Harvey recalled: "Given all the time needed to manage the children, there wasn't a whole lot of time for us." He remembers feeling a profound helplessness when it came to performing his role as a husband: "My instinct was to protect my wife" from her ex-husband's continuing manipulations. "But I was not able to do anything except hold her when she cried. It's like the enemy was in your house and you can't do anything about it."

At its worst, his emotions ranged from "rage to forlorn despair." But now, nearly twenty years into the marriage, Harvey says that he and his wife became stronger because of the struggle. "There's not much that we can imagine that could defeat us," Harvey said. "From an emotional-spiritual standpoint, the worst is over."

A few husbands reported that their transition to stepfatherhood went smoothly. And there were commonalities among these men too, including a self-confidence that steered them away from direct confrontation with the children. Luck also helped.

Terence Boone, a training consultant, told me he had been twenty-nine years old when he became stepfather to two boys, ages eleven and thirteen. (Terence's wife is five years older than he is.) Terence said his strategy, especially early on, was to defer to his wife on most decisions involving the kids. "I tried to handle things with a light touch," Terence told me twenty-four years into the marriage.

In addition, Terence asked his stepchildren to address him by his first name. He said that he and the children had been most comfortable with that before the marriage, "and I saw no reason to demand otherwise based on my own ego needs." As Terence put it: "I was just basically aware that I had a different role."

Terence also told me that he was lucky that his stepsons' biological father was emotionally healthy, remarried, and unthreatened by Terence. Terence said that the two parents and two stepparents often communicated with each other, in person or over the phone, about limits and discipline. That way, the kids got the same messages in both homes. Of his wife's ex-husband, Terence said: "We weren't bosom buddies, but even after all of these years, we're still cordial."

Both of Terence's stepsons are now in their thirties. Terence says the older stepson identifies more with Terence than with the biological father, and the younger son identifies more with his biological dad. Terence says he's just relieved that both sons, having experienced the split-up and remarriages of their biological parents, are doing well.

Another man, Jason Bailey, told me about his successful stepfathering strategy. Jason, a public-relations specialist, was thirty-six years old when he met his future wife. He says he fell in love with her and her seven-year-old son. Jason had lost a six-month-old baby in his first marriage. He still had "a burning desire to be a dad."

Like Terence Boone above, Jason let his wife handle the discipline early on; only as he and his stepson spent more time together and became more trusting of each other did Jason begin to assert some parentlike authority. Also, like Terence, Jason asked his stepson to call him by his first name. The boy's biological father lived locally and had custody on weekends; the boy already had a father.

What particularly struck me about Jason was how supportive he was of his stepson's relationship with the biological father. Jason often reminded his stepson to phone his biodad, write to him when on vacation, and buy him gifts for his birthday. Jason said he did this because it was good for his stepson. "With two men like us in his life," Jason said, "he's got the best of both worlds."

The stepfathers I've written about above married women who already had children. What about situations in which the *man* is the one with children from a previous relationship? For the most part, I discovered, this arrangement tends to cause less trouble in a remarriage. That's because in most cases, the man's ex-wife has physical custody of their children. Thus, his children are not in the home on a daily basis to inspire discord between the father and stepmother.

But these families still face difficulties. Several husbands told me they miss their biological children when they don't live with them; sometimes this makes them irritable or angry in the home, and they take out their frustration on their new wives and stepfamilies. Also, men in this situation are often torn between spending their free time with their new families or with their noncustodial children. "It helps to have a very understanding wife," one such husband told me.

Of course, even if a child is visiting only on weekends, tensions can arise. A pastoral counselor, aged forty-nine, reported that his daughter "will always see my [second] wife as someone who contributed to the breakup of her parents' marriage." This man's daughter was fifteen years old at the time of her father's second marriage. In the early months, on weekend visits, the girl clashed angrily with her stepmother over seemingly minor issues. Later, the daughter "went cold," the father said, uttering not a word to his new wife. Only in adulthood did she become civil to her stepmother.

Another husband had a seventeen-year-old son from his previous marriage. The boy chose to live with his dad and new stepmother when they married. The father said his son's presence caused no serious problems in this second marriage. He attributes this in part to a "pep talk" he gave his son shortly before the wedding. In this talk, the father said that his new wife "was not going to be a butler or maid for you. You're expected to do as she requests, as though it had come from me."

A handful of men I interviewed had both stepchildren and children of their own living in the house together. In these fully blended families, jealousy and divided loyalties were frequent issues.

A forty-year-old public-relations specialist told me that he and his stepdaughter, now eighteen, got along well when he first married her mother six years ago. He even legally adopted the girl, and she took his last name.

Then, three years into the marriage, this man and the girl's biological mother had a daughter together.

The husband told me that since then, his adopted daughter has kept him at arm's length. "My older daughter was in the prime of her mid-teen emotional growth" when her half sister was born, this man said. "I think it hit her pretty hard." The father acknowledges that he has found it easier to express his love toward the baby than to the teenager and that this seems to hurt the older daughter. He notices, with regret, that his older daughter hasn't warmed up to the younger one. "[The older daughter] just looks like she feels shut down by all the neediness of a three-year-old."

This husband said that his marriage had been affected too. "I think the hardest part on the marriage is that my wife and I see each child differently. I love them both, but differently. That has been a strain on my wife. She always wanted a good father for" the older daughter. "I am a good father, but I don't have the [same] connection with each child. . . . Blending the two children and our family has been a real joy and real heartache. I struggle with it most every day."

Most men in these blended families said that the various family members do eventually learn to get along with each other. But there are in-house disputes to be settled over space, noise, chores, bedtimes, neatness, and other issues. When the children live in different homes most of the time, the discord tends to be over different topics: time spent with the various children and money spent on them. "My [biological] kids are always comparing what I buy for them with what I buy for their stepsisters," one husband told me. "I try to be fair."

Fairness in treating kids should not be confused with *sameness* in treating them, this man added. He went to baseball games with one stepchild and visited museums with another. It was crucial, he and others said, to spend one-on-one time with each child, learning about the child's individual needs, frustrations, and sensitivities. He added: "We let the children form their own relationships" with each other. "We do things as a family, we try to create bonds. But we don't force it."

*   *   *

When couples remarry beyond middle age, they usually have no children at home. But even adult children can complicate their parents' remarriages. Personality clashes were commonplace between men's new wives and the adult children. One widower who had remarried told me that on holiday visits, his adult children at first "wanted it to be like the old days, when their mother was alive." They objected to new rituals and recipes that the new wife contributed.

Money also arose as a concern for the adult children. Would the new wife spend their inheritance or delay their receiving it? Recognizing this concern, the widower mentioned above created a prenuptial agreement with his second wife that protected his children and grandchildren. This older husband spoke for remarried men of all ages when he said: "Each of my children reacted differently. Each of my [new] wife's children reacted differently. The best thing I did was to talk openly with everyone."

If remarried couples can get beyond the stress of child-raising, they are usually much happier than they were in their own first marriages. That's partly because most previously married people tend to make better spousal choices the second time around. In addition, many of the remarried men I interviewed had been through marital or individual counseling. They'd learned about their own faults and frailties and what they wanted in a wife and a marriage.

Jason Bailey, the public-relations specialist mentioned earlier in this chapter, said his first marriage fell apart after five years because he didn't stand up for himself. "I was passive, willing to do whatever she wanted to make her happy," Jason told me. "But I could never do enough." After the divorce, he expected never to remarry.

That changed when the woman who would become his second wife encouraged him from the beginning of their relationship to be clear about his needs. "She encouraged me to be selfish," he told me. Jason, now married for three years, still tends to be a giver, but said he knows it's OK to receive as well. One example: Having lived alone for so many years, he needs at least fifteen minutes a day at home by himself. His wife helps make sure he gets it.

Other men said that compared to how they had chosen their first wives, they were more "thoughtful," "discerning," "wary," and "not as impulsive," and otherwise took greater care in choosing a second wife. These husbands said that their first wives' physical beauty, or sexual availability, had played a particularly large role in their decision to marry her. The second time around, they looked more at compatibility, generosity, and other personality traits.

In addition to choosing their second wives more carefully, husbands who were previously married tended to understand themselves, and relationships, better than first-time married men. A thirty-two-year-old ad salesman told me that he had entered therapy when his first wife left him for another man after an eight-year marriage. He discovered in retrospect that he had "stonewalled" during his first marriage. Whenever his wife wanted to talk about how the relationship was going, or about having a child together, he clammed up. He was also loath to compromise about sex and other issues.

With his second wife, whom he'd just married when I interviewed him, this man says, "I'm open to talking about everything. I don't hide. I don't hold back." A Catholic, this husband said that when he went to confession after his first marriage, he sought forgiveness for having "killed my [first] wife's dream of having a family." Even though he says he's still not ready to have children, when his second wife wants to discuss it, he does.

Several men said they had also learned the importance of sexual compatibility after living through a first marriage in which sex was awkward, nonexistent, or turned into a weapon. A fifty-six-year-old musician, now in his third marriage, recalled that his first wife had "cut me off" sexually when she was unhappy with something he said or did. His second wife simply wasn't much interested in sex after they married. After ending that relationship, he spoke openly to his subsequent girlfriends about the importance of sex to him—not only as a pleasurable activity but as a way of connecting spiritually. He eventually found a partner who shared an interest in "tantric sex," a spiritual-sexual practice that focuses more on touching, exploring, and safety than on achieving orgasms.

In addition to children, other common problems for remarried couples involve money and ex-wives. Often, these two topics are intertwined. Several men said that their ex-wives regularly requested money from them above and beyond their child-support payments. One man acknowledged that he sometimes had to decide whether to pay child support to his ex-wife or pay bills in his new life. If he's late on child support, he said, his ex-wife starts leaving angry messages.

For a few men I interviewed, it took more than two marriages to learn the lessons of a long-term relationship. One of these men was Jeff Hochman, a California movie producer who had been divorced five times when I spoke with him. He was sixty years old at the time and engaged to be married again.

Jeff told me that "as far as seeing a healthy relationship, I had no models" as a child. His mother physically abused him; his father ignored him. Jeff said he "didn't understand what passion was until I started getting laid." In his young adulthood, he recalls, sex and love had little to do with one another.

He married for the first time at age twenty-two. His first wife was an actress, "innocent and sweet with an awesome body. She was a ten," he recalls. But after they'd married, her looks could not hide their clear differences in values and ambitions. She also stopped being interested in sex within months of the wedding; Jeff eventually learned that she had been a rape victim in her teens.

The second marriage came three years later, soon after the first divorce. Again, sex was a key motivation. "She was nonstop, two or three times a day, every day," Jeff recalled. But her intense interest in sex may have been the result of a wound: Like his first wife, she had experienced sexual abuse in her past, having been molested by her father. After a few months, Jeff says, "I realized we couldn't have a conversation about anything. The only two things we had in common were pot and sex."

After this second divorce, Jeff says, "I took a deep breath and asked: 'What the fuck is going on?'" But he couldn't stay away from women who were unhealthy for him. He got married again two years later, this time to the eighteen-year-old daughter of one of his bosses. She even converted to Judaism, his religion. But within a year, she was having an affair. "I couldn't live with that," Jeff said.

By this time, Jeff was nearing thirty, and he decided to go into therapy. "I needed to learn more about me," he recalled, "to get to the point where I liked me." The counseling helped. He learned why he was choosing damaged women—he was a "rescuer"—and why he felt damaged as well. When he married for the fourth time several years later, it was primarily for compatibility, not sex. His new wife shared a love of sports and music, and was successful in her own career.

They stayed married for ten years, but by year six, Jeff recalls, things were deteriorating. One bothersome truth about his wife, Jeff told me: "She never tried to be romantic with me." He felt more like a "roommate" than a husband.

After the divorce, he dated around for four years before marrying for a fifth time. This marriage lasted twelve years, and when I interviewed Jeff, he said he still had fond feelings for this woman. "We went through the deaths of our parents together," he recalled. Differences about money and sex hampered them, however, and ten years into the marriage, he began to mentally check out of the relationship.

When I interviewed Jeff, he was engaged to marry again. He and his fiancée had been dating for four years. About tying the knot for the sixth time, he admitted, "I have a lot of fear." He said that he was doing it in part so that his new wife would be eligible to receive his Social Security benefits when he died.

I asked him to describe the woman who would be his sixth wife. He said: "She's beautiful inside and out. A friend once told me that if you're dating someone, and you unlock the [passenger-side] door to let her in, and then she reaches across and unlocks your side, you've got a winner. She does that. She also gives great foot massages."

When he marries, he'll be living not only with his new wife but with her three teenaged children. He admits that when it comes to kids, he lacks patience at times. But, he says, his future wife isn't worried about his patience, nor about his history of failed relationships. Is he sure he's chosen well this time? "I'm convinced," he told me. "I am. But there's a small part of me that wonders."

Chapter Sixteen

———⚜———

HUSBANDLY ADVICE: 8,000 YEARS OF EXPERIENCE

If you want to be treated like a king, you have to treat her like a queen.
—Fifty-two-year-old database manager

THE MEN IN MY STUDY had a combined eight thousand years as husbands. I determined that this qualified them, collectively, as "experienced," if not necessarily experts. So in the course of my research, I asked each husband to tell me *what advice he would give a younger man who was thinking of marrying*. Here's the gist of what they had to say.

Take Your Time

The foremost piece of advice from experienced husbands about marriage was this: *Don't rush into it.* Several husbands told me that they had married young because they felt pressured by friends or family, didn't like living alone, or mistook momentary passion for enduring love. Only after the wedding was over—and too often, after children were born—did they realize their mistake. By then, it was too late to avoid a painful upheaval in their family lives.

The husbands I spoke with generally thought that marrying before age twenty-five was risky. A few suggested that men wait until at least age thirty. (A recent study indicated that those who wait until age twenty-five have a 24 percent lower chance of divorcing in the first ten years of marriage.) One reason for waiting, the husbands said, was to give a man time to gain a sense of himself as a viable, independent person. "A balanced marriage comes when you don't *need* the relationship, when you can function on your own," a forty-eight-year-old shop owner, married fifteen years, told me. "When you're secure with yourself, you're not pulling at each other. You're free to give."

Several husbands said it was a good idea, for both psychological and practical reasons, for men to live alone for a while before marrying. Men who move directly from their childhood homes to their marital homes often expect their wives to act like their mothers. "The sooner a man separates his wife from his mother, the sooner he can get on with life," a fifty-two-year-old husband advised. Also, since the 1970s, women have expected their husbands to be able to cook, clean, and perform other household tasks. Men who live alone before marriage have an opportunity to get experience at such skills.

Another risk of marrying early is that a husband will not have the emotional maturity to make a long-lasting relationship work. At age eighteen or twenty, most men haven't learned, for example, how to argue lovingly, how to balance work and family, and how to listen to a woman. They also may not have learned how to focus their sexual energy on just one person. It comes as no surprise that, according to our survey, the younger a man is when he marries, the more likely he is to have an affair later on.

Keep Expectations Reasonable

There's nothing wrong with high hopes. But unrealistic expectations can kill a marriage.

Husbands told me that one of the key lessons of marriage is how important it is to adjust expectations to meet reality. One man said: "Your wife may be your soul mate, but not every minute of every day. There are going to be hard times, down times." Expecting an unfailingly positive connection with one's spouse will surely lead to disappointment.

According to husbands, here are some other common, unrealistic expectations men have in their early relationships:

- "Things will be easier if we get married."
- "Once we marry, I'll feel more secure."

- "Having children will solve our relationship problems."
- "Sex will always be this good (or bad)."

Long-married husbands suggested that men should see marriage not so much as the primary source of their happiness, but as a foundation upon which they can build a satisfying life. The closeness with their wives can be enormously fulfilling, husbands say, but only if the partners continue to have other outside interests, including friendships and meaningful work. Husbands contend that the most dangerous expectation a man can have about marriage is that his wife will fulfill all of his needs.

Make Your Marriage Your Top Priority

While a man's marriage shouldn't be the only priority in his life, it should be the most important one, husbands advised. "If you lose your job, you can always find another one," said a fifty-nine-year-old data manager. "But there's only one of her." Another man said: "She has to be more important than the issues between you."

Several husbands spoke of failed first marriages in which they had taken their wives for granted. Early in his marriage, one man remembered, he spent most nights practicing or performing with a garage band. When his wife asked him to cut back on his music to spend more time with her, he was dismissive. In retrospect, he says, he feared leaving his high-school friends and growing up. His wife eventually found a lover who *would* spend time with her, and the marriage broke up. "It died of my neglect," the man said a decade later.

Making marriage your top priority does not mean giving up outside interests, husbands said. What it does mean is taking the relationship seriously; when either partner decides that something is wrong, both must address the situation. "Marriage is a job, a hard job, and a low-paying one too," one fifty-four-year-old machinist commented. "You've got to constantly be asking if you're doing all you can" to keep it strong. Another man echoed: "A commitment is not a vacation. It's serious, and you have to work at it and be committed to work through good times and bad." Still another man advised: "Brace yourself. There's going to be stormy seas out there. Marriage is more about commitment than about love."

Marry a Friend

A woman's physical beauty is highly valued among men, but husbands tell me that men should seek friendship first in a wife.

Here's a sampling of how they made this point:

- "Find a woman you trust and feel comfortable with. Find someone with a compatible attitude."
- "Be sure she's your best friend."
- "Marry your friend. Treat her like a friend. Keep her your friend."
- "Make sure you not only love her but like her as well."
- "You have to be compatible in your personalities."
- "Make sure you have a mental attraction to the person."
- "Look into her eyes and see if there is love in there. Don't look for a woman who is sexy. Sex is skin deep."
- "Look for somebody with whom you can share your goals and ambitions and values."

One man acknowledged to me that he had married primarily because he wanted a good-looking wife. He got one, but the results have been troublesome. Not only has he struggled to accept the physical changes that aging has had on his wife, he has been unsuccessful in changing her personality to his liking. He's one of the 7 percent of men in my survey who told me that if they had to do it again, they wouldn't marry the same woman.

Learn to Give and Take

"Marriage isn't about getting what you want," advises a forty-seven-year-old pastor. "It's about creating something where both of you feel loved, appreciated, and made greater." This man crystallizes one of the most frequent pieces of advice I heard from married men: Learn to negotiate, compromise, and create win-win situations.

In the words of experienced husbands:

- "Marriage is not 50-50, it's 100-100."
- "Give more than you expect to get and you will get back much more than you give."
- "Always listen and be prepared to compromise."
- "Marriage is a lifelong relationship. Nobody is right all the time, and nobody is wrong all the time. So give and take."
- "Make yourself available to give, and you will receive a lot."
- "Try to give more than you take from the relationship."
- "If you want to be treated like a king, you have to treat her like a queen."

Stay Connected

Talking about feelings and emotions is a struggle for many husbands. But for a man who wants to keep his marriage healthy, it's a skill worth honing, husbands say. "Be sure you can talk about anything," a forty-three-year-old paralegal advised, "especially when things aren't going well." Another husband added, "Try not to hide."

Staying connected also means keeping romance alive. This can be particularly difficult in the child-raising years, husbands said. One father of two young children told me that he worried about his marriage because "every time we go out alone, we're wondering what's happening at home. Both of us seem anxious for [the date] to be over."

This is not unusual, but he's right to be concerned, husbands said. Unless a couple works to maintain a close relationship through all stages of marriage, there's a risk that the partners will grow apart. It's not surprising that one of the ripest times for divorce is at the beginning of the empty-nest phase.

Here's some other husbandly advice about staying connected with one's wife in a positive way:

- "Talk about things before they become an issue."
- "Enjoy each other; do things that are fun."
- "Don't offer advice unless asked."

- "God gave you two ears and one mouth. Listen more and talk less."
- "Keep a sense of humor."
- "Tell her you love her every day. Hold hands while discussing difficult topics."
- "Say what you mean and mean what you say."
- "Lose your ego and don't be selfish."
- "Treat her as an equal."
- "Don't try to manipulate."
- "Treat her like a lady. Never curse her, and never wave nothing but a loving hand to her."
- "Be charitable."

Nurture Your Partner's Dreams

One way couples stay connected for life is by developing and working toward common, long-term goals. One husband advised: "Talk to your spouse; understand her hopes and dreams and desires." Several husbands said they had bought retirement property with their wives decades before they planned to move onto it. Other couples who were raising children designed elaborate vacations for after the kids were out of the house. In these ways, the couples maintained a shared excitement about their futures; they invested emotionally (and sometimes financially) in staying together.

One husband, married nineteen years, said that he and his wife had attended a marriage-enrichment weekend at which the leaders asked each partner to write down what he or she believed were the *other person's* greatest fears, joys, griefs, and dreams. They also wrote down how they envisioned their own old age. Then each spouse shared this with the other. "I was shocked how much I didn't know about my wife," this man said.

Nurturing a partner's dreams is often difficult, husbands said. One man related how his wife had told him of her dream of changing careers: leaving her high-paying work as a corporate executive to become a schoolteacher. The husband feared the loss of money and status. But he decided to back her by rearranging his own work life and agreeing to downscale. "My wife would have resented me if I stood in her way," this husband said.

Keep the Faith

Husbands offered this advice both figuratively and literally. Many suggested that sharing a religious or spiritual affiliation with one's spouse helped keep them together. It gave them something to do together, a community of support, a clergyperson to consult, and potential mentors among their fellow members. Several men told me that they felt closest to their wives while sitting together in church, praying together at home, or doing some kind of missionary work together.

Other husbands spoke of the importance of maintaining faith in their marriage, particularly during the inevitable periods when it wasn't going smoothly. One man, married eleven years, advised: "Hold on tight. Like a roller-coaster ride, it's the whole ride that's fun, not every up and down."

222

What Surprises Them Most About Marriage

Management consultant, forty-eight, married twenty-two years: *"I'm surprised that [marriage] has been so fulfilling. I always wanted a partner, an equal. I am constantly amazed that I found one. I had very poor role models in my parents, as a couple. They seemed bored with each other. I'm surprised that my marriage never gets boring."*

Middle-school teacher, thirty, married six years: *"I'm surprised how much an independent person such as myself can grow to feel dependent upon someone else. In the very beginning, it would be fun to just get out and hang out with friends for a while. Now, I hardly drive over to visit my mom without feeling separation anxiety. The need to feel close to [my wife] and my daughter is extremely important."*

Investment manager, forty-one, married eight years: *"The amount of work surprised the hell out of me. I never noticed my parents working so hard [on their marriage]. They just seemed to go along without a hitch. If I try to just go along, something always goes wrong. I have to stay focused."*

Stay-at-home dad, thirty-five, married fourteen years: *"[I'm surprised] how after fourteen years, she still turns me on. My experience had been that I lost my attraction for a woman in a few weeks or months."*

Janitor, forty-seven, married twenty-one years: *"The biggest surprise to me is that we made it this far. The way we started out, I wouldn't have taken that bet."*

Pastor, forty-one, married eleven years: *"I'm surprised by the hard work!"*

Christian missionary, forty, married sixteen years: *"What surprises me is how easy marriage can be when everything is open and talked about."*

Travel agent, forty-two, married nine years: *"What surprises me? The lack of sex."*

Waiter, twenty-seven, married five years: *"I'm surprised by how fast things can change. A few weeks ago, my wife told me that she was feeling good about the way things were going in the marriage. Last week, she asked for a divorce."*

Copy editor, fifty-nine, married eight years: *"I'm surprised at how much depth marriage can add to a relationship."*

Psychologist, thirty-six, married five years: *"I'm surprised just how much I like marriage. I was worried that I would feel trapped in a gender-role play that would feel empty and routinized. I feared a loss of autonomy. I no longer fear it. I have learned to be my own person while being in an intimate relationship. Prior to married life, I thought that I had to sacrifice one for the other."*

Part Four

HOW MEN *DO* MARRIAGE

Chapter Seventeen

The Male Style of Loving

What men *do* is often very deep, and reflects a devotion that they can't express in words.
— Sixty-three-year-old retired editor

It's winter vacation at the Morrisons' house, and the dust is swirling. For months, Jake and Diane Morrison have been rehabbing their three-story, nineteenth-century "New Englander" home. This week, with their eleven-year-old son away at camp, they're preparing to attack the hideous textured wallpaper in the living room. In ratty jeans and a paint-splattered shirt, Jake ascends the stepladder, wallpaper steamer in hand. He presses the power tool against the gray wall. The motor whirrs and, moments later, glue scents waft. But instead of the paper peeling, the wall itself starts crumbling. Chunks of plaster drop to the floor. Jake shuts off the steamer. He stares at Diane in disbelief. Then both of them burst into laughter.

It's 7 A.M., and, for approximately the 3,700th time since their wedding, Roger Warden prepares to make his marital bed. Roger's wife, Janet, is already awake, dressed, and in the kitchen. First, Roger smoothes the wrinkles out of the blue fitted sheet on the queen-sized mattress. Next, he floats a second sheet atop the first, folding it down once near the wooden headboard. He lays a blanket over this sheet. Then, because Janet gets colder at night than he does, Roger spreads a second blanket on her side. Fluffing, flattening, tugging, and tucking,

Roger finishes the job. He steps back to examine his handiwork. Satis-fied, he starts his day.

It's summertime, and for Randall Hutchins, the driving is easy. Coast-ing, air-conditioned, through the simmering eastern Kentucky hills, he notices that the path ahead is an undulating green. Susan, Randall's wife of thirty-six years, relaxes in the passenger seat. As the miles roll by, she offers sandwiches, apple slices, and potato chips, then rests her head against the window and dozes. Mostly, as he drives, Randall scans the hillsides, woods, and palisades. Occasionally, he glances over at the graying, but still radiant, woman beside him and smiles.

Over the past fifty years, America has adopted a gold standard for mar-riage. A good relationship, we've been told, involves two partners who ex-press their emotions, talk about their hopes and fears, and show physical affection while not necessarily seeking sex.

In reality, this is marriage primarily from a woman's point of view. And it's only half the story. There's a masculine style of loving too. It's a style that may not always look like loving. As indicated by the vignettes above, it relies not on the direct sharing of feelings, not on emotional expression, not even on words themselves. But to practitioners of this style, it's an ap-proach to loving that reflects who they are and how they've learned to ex-perience closeness.

As Melvin Konner, author of *The Tangled Wing*, writes: "If a man for-gets an anniversary or neglects to say 'I love you,' it doesn't necessarily mean his heart is cold. If he finds conversations about 'the relationship' as enticing as fingernails on a blackboard, it doesn't mean he is psychologi-cally defective. At some level, it simply means he isn't female."

The female style of loving was not always the way in America. From colonial times through the Civil War, the nation was primarily agricul-tural, with couples working as teams to raise crops and livestock, as well as children. The feminist sociologist Francesca Cancian has conducted a careful study of this era. She found that on America's early farms, husbands and wives worked in tandem to sustain the economy of their families and to guide the next generation. In those times, Cancian maintains, "[L]ove was a complex whole that included feelings and working together."

The Industrial Revolution, with its emphasis on factory work, plucked men off their farms, away from their homes, wives, and children. Between the mid–nineteenth century and the mid–twentieth century, men increasingly came to specialize in making and selling goods. Women, meanwhile, unwelcome in most workplaces, focused their creative energies on maintaining their homes and family relationships. It was during this time, Cancian asserts, that women's way of loving became the standard. Cancian writes: "With the split between home and work, and the polarization of gender roles, love became a feminine quality. . . . [T]he cultural images of love shifted toward emphasizing tenderness, expression of emotion, and weakness."

This female-oriented notion of loving remained largely unchallenged until the 1960s, when social, economic, and political forces sent women flooding into the workplace. During this same period, men began moving back into the home, involving themselves increasingly in the daily household duties.

But just as women's business style has been resisted at work, men's style of loving has been treated skeptically at home. Most social scientists and marital therapists continue to promote the idea that good relationships require, primarily, direct verbal and emotional expression. As Cancian concludes, "Part of the reason that men seem so much less loving than women is that men's behavior is measured with a feminine ruler."

Given the prominence of the female style of loving, it's not surprising that men often blame themselves for the problems in their marriages and other relationships. "I don't share my feelings enough," one man told me in explaining the struggles in his twenty-year relationship. "I don't listen well," reported another.

There's no reason to doubt these men's assessments. But as often as not in my interviews, I found marriages that foundered because the husbands were being called upon to show love in a way that didn't suit them. Their own preferred style of loving was rejected as *not enough*.

When I speak of men's preferred style of loving, I do not mean this in solely biological terms. Certainly, the more we learn about the biology of gender, the more we see that men and women are wired differently. And those differences appear to have an impact on relationship skills. Sociobiologists point out, for example, that structural and chemical differences in male and female brains tend to make it easier for women to turn feelings into words and men to turn emotions into action.

These biological tendencies have, through the centuries, been reinforced in human societies. Because men are generally larger than women, for example, men have been assigned to the outskirts of their communities, hunting and protecting—two activities in which quietude and emotional control are highly valued. Women, grouped more closely together in the interior of the community, have trained in the arts of conversation and emotional sharing. It's no wonder that each gender has developed its own style of loving.

In my in-depth interviews with husbands, I asked each the same question: *When do you feel closest to your wife?* I wanted to know about the everyday moments during which men experienced a strong sense of connection. Based on these individual experiences, I sought to outline a distinctly masculine style of loving.

First, I found that a small but significant percentage of husbands described their "closest moments" with their wives in largely female terms. About one in five husbands reported that they felt closest when talking with their wives, expressing emotions, or engaging in nonsexual affection. Here's how some of the men put this.

- "I love it when I can share what's deep and she listens."
- "I feel closest when we have time to talk, fight, or express feelings [about] where we're at."
- "My favorite time is when we're snuggling half-asleep in the morning, slowly waking up to the day."

- "I love to sit on the couch with her. There's something about the feel of her hand in mine that makes me melt."

Not surprisingly, men who favored this approach to intimacy tended to report happy marriages. Their wives appreciated their openness, sensitivity, and ability to talk and listen. Interestingly, in a number of cases, these emotionally open husbands complained that their wives were too distant. One man said: "I wish I could open her up." Another reported: "I always have to be the one who pushes" to resolve problems. It seems that sometimes, both women and men select partners with a style of intimacy that contrasts with their own and then become frustrated with the difference.

So what is the predominant masculine style of intimacy? Based on men's reports of closest moments, I have identified three components. Although I will name them in contrast to women's style, the masculine and feminine styles are not mutually exclusive. Indeed, among the most happily married couples, husbands tended to see these differing styles as complementary and healthy. Here are the three components.

First, while the female style of loving emphasizes *sharing feelings,* the masculine style focuses on *sharing space.*

Jake Morrison, the man at the beginning of this chapter who put a hole in his living-room wall, is an example of a husband for whom sharing space is an intimate experience. He actually used the word "intimate" to describe the time he spends rehabbing his home with his wife, Diane. Jake told me that Diane would probably prefer to "crawl onto the couch and cuddle" when they have time alone. And sometimes, they do that. But, he adds, "I'm much more action-oriented than she is. I enjoy the feeling of accomplishment. I like to step back and say, 'Look what we've done today!' "

I asked him why the presence of his wife during these renovation projects was so important. He responded: "Working with her is soul-to-soul time. We get into a rhythm. We're a great team." When he described the hole-in-the-wall incident, he recalled how hard he and Diane had laughed once the shock of the moment wore off. Since then, they've had a good story to share with others. "I could have asked a friend" to help on the renovation, Jake says. "But I asked my wife. She's my person of choice."

Other husbands recalled intimate times with their wives when they had been hiking, camping, fishing, kayaking, walking, or running together. While conversations might break out during these space-sharing times, men said, talking was not the point. "I make no apology," one husband told me. "Words don't interest me much."

Overlapping with this first element, a second element of the masculine style of loving emerges: While the female style stresses *talking* as a way of improving a relationship, the male style emphasizes *doing* something to improve it.

Roger Warden, the husband who makes his marital bed every day, told me he had started doing this particular task soon after he and Janet married ten years ago. They were dividing up household duties, and he offhandedly volunteered to take care it.

After a few months, he admits, he began to resent having to make the bed every day. He thought about asking Janet to share the bed-making duties but realized that "the main thing my wife wants is a man who will do what he says he's going to do. One day, I said I was going to [make the bed]. By God, if I have to walk on glass, I'm going to follow through."

So he changed his attitude and began making the bed "the way a young man takes care of his first car. . . . I do it with intention. I view the bed as an altar. That's where [my wife] and I are together the most time. I can tend to be a perfectionist about it. But I do it out of reverence for the altar . . . of my marriage."

Of course, Janet also likes a well-made bed at the end of the day. And Roger likes to please Janet. As do many other husbands. A thirty-four-year-old man, for example, told me he felt closest to his wife on the twenty-third of every month. That's the day he brings home a bouquet of flowers and places it in the vase they received as a wedding gift. Other husbands spoke of expressing their love by planning surprise weekend getaways with their wife, leaving chocolates on her pillow, or drawing a bath for her when she returns from a hard day at work.

As with the bed-making, loving actions can be mundane ones. A retired editor told me that he felt closest to his wife every Tuesday afternoon. That's when he gathers together the household recycling—plastic, glass, newspaper, corrugated cardboard—and places it in boxes on the front lawn to be taken away. His wife is a passionate environmentalist but can no longer carry heavy loads. So by handling the recycling, this husband says, "I'm doing something for the two of us." He has come to believe that loving is "about deeds, not creeds. . . . What men *do* is often very deep, and reflects a devotion that they can't express in words."

One corporate executive said that when he works late into the evening, his wife often "takes it personally. She thinks it means that I love my job more than I love her." He contends that he's actually *showing* how much he loves his wife by working the extra time. "When I return home from eight hours [at work], my wife looks at me: 'What have you done for me today?'!As if the hours at work have nothing to do with the marriage."

Men's interest in doing can be seen in their approach to sex as well. While it may be difficult for some husbands to express love in words, many feel comfortable expressing it through sex. "I want her to enjoy sex as much as I do," one husband told me. "I want her to have the same kind of pleasure." This husband expressed frustration, however, that his wife sometimes thinks he's being self-centered when he initiates sex. "I don't get it," the husband told me. "A man who says 'I love you' [in words] is cheered; a man who says it in bed is selfish."

The third major component of the masculine style of loving is this: While women's way of loving tends to focus on *face-to-face* time, the masculine way emphasizes *side-by-side* experiences.

Randall Hutchins is the man at the beginning of the chapter who was on a road trip with his wife. He was one of many men I interviewed who named among their closest marital moments leisurely time spent with their wives in the front seat of a car. Randall explained why he likes it so much: "We can talk. We can be quiet. . . . There's no pressure to be there, and no one's going away."

Randall, who was sixty years old when I spoke with him, admits to being uncomfortable when his wife approaches him for face-to-face conversations about relationship issues. He said it reminds him of when he was a child and his mother lectured him about his bad behavior. Just as then, he tends to feel criticized and inept. However, pack up the car and hit the road, and the conversations are not nearly as threatening. "Her eyes aren't boring in on me," he said.

Indeed, eye contact has a very different meaning in the male community than it does for most women. While females express intimacy by holding eye contact with each other, among men direct eye contact may be construed as a challenge. One reason that many males enjoy playing sports is that they can communicate with other males in a way that's nonthreatening. Eye contact is fleeting. The competition has clear rules. When such safety is created, the players can communicate with one another (using words or not) in a way that's comfortable for them.

Even watching sports can be intimate time for a man and his wife. Many of the husbands I spoke with said they were thrilled when their wives accompanied them to football games or watched sports with them on TV. In these situations, they could sit next to their wives—share space—and communicate in a relaxed way.

So men and women tend to practice the art of loving in different ways. But this doesn't mean they have to clash over the differences. Indeed, most husbands told me that they generally liked the way their wives expressed love, even though it seemed foreign to them at times. The VoiceMale Survey bore out this attitude: 93 percent of husbands said that if given the chance, they'd marry the same woman again.

A Final Note

Researching and writing this book has been a fascinating journey for me. I have been privileged to gaze, with the help of hundreds of men, behind the veil of American marriage. And, admittedly, on some days I came away saddened.

Here, though, at the end, I'm optimistic. The women's movement of the 1960s and 1970s necessarily shook up the American marriage system. Some husbands reacted against this shake up. But today, most seem to agree that the weight of the changes has been for the better. By law and custom, marriage is no longer a relationship of domination and submission, but rather one edging toward equality. Men now have the opportunity to choose a partner rather than a subordinate.

Meanwhile, the rash of antimale stereotyping in the late 20th century seems to be on the wane too. Though they are still skeptical at times, women seem increasingly interested in what men think and feel. Perhaps not coincidentally, divorce rates have inched downward over the past decade.

My hope is that this book helps maintain that positive momentum. Clearly, as we've seen in these pages, men experience marriage differently, and express their love differently, than do women. Husbands and wives often talk in different tongues. But diversity need not be divisive. Indeed, if understood, tolerated, and ultimately embraced, diversity can do for marriage what it has done forever in the natural world: create a thing of endlessly expanding richness.

Acknowledgments

I am most grateful to you 358 husbands who opened your lives to help me with the research for this book. I thank each of you and hope that my retelling of your stories honors you and your relationships, as it was meant to do.

I also appreciate the immense support that I received from numerous friends, family members, and colleagues. These include, foremost, my wife, Kelly, and son, Evan. Also of great help were my parents, Morton and Beverly Chethik, who have been married for fifty-two years, and my siblings, Peter, Leigh, and Jessica. My friends John Lynch and Robert Ferguson were stalwarts in every way. So too were members of my Tuesday evening men's group (through the ManKind Project) and the Nonfiction Writing Group at the Carnegie Center for Literacy and Learning.

My agent, Alice Martell, steered me smartly, and with heart, through the business side of this project. Sydny Miner, my editor at Simon & Schuster, consistently improved the book through every stage of the process. And Debby Perry, my research assistant, helped keep me organized and optimistic. Thank you also to Sarah Hochman, Alexis Welby, Ken Cooke, and Linda Nielsen.

A number of other people were enormously helpful in developing the content of the book. They include Ronald Langley, Bill Paterson, Michael Gurian, Steven Nock, Frank Pittman, Bill Doherty, Sam Osherson, Terrence Real, Michael Meade, David Popenoe, Tim Schladand, Tony Lobianco, and Brian Throckmorton.

A Note on the Research

In writing this book, I have relied on two major pieces of research: (1) in-depth interviews, which I personally conducted, with seventy American husbands, and (2) a national, scientific survey of 288 husbands, which was carried out on my behalf by the University of Kentucky Survey Research Center (UKSRC).

The in-depth personal interviews generally lasted two to three hours each. The span in age of the interviewees was twenty-two to ninety-five, their length of marriage ranging from three months to seventy-two years. The interviewees included husbands from all regions of the country (twenty-two states) and most major ethnic groups. They had fathered anywhere from zero to eight children each and had been married between one and six times.

I identified men to interview through several sources: (1) religious organizations; (2) interest groups, including labor unions, ethnic-oriented associations, and professional organizations, and (3) personal contacts. In 2003 and 2004, I traveled to several regions of the country to conduct most of the interviews in person. I offered anonymity to the interviewees and tape-recorded most of the conversations.

In late 2003, I wrote a hundred-item questionnaire to be used by UKSRC to conduct a national, random telephone survey on my behalf. That survey was conducted in early 2004, overseen by Dr. Ronald E. Langley, director of UKSRC.

The sample for this telephone survey was selected using a modified list-assisted Waksberg Random Digit Dialing method. This means that every home telephone line in the continental United States had an equal probability of being selected. The margin of error for the 288-person sample size survey is ±5.8 percent at the 95 percent confidence level. The response rate for the survey, based on one of the standardized methods (known as RR4) developed by the American Association for Public Opinion Research, was 46.7 percent. That means that just less than half of the men contacted who were eligible to take the survey agreed to do so.

Respondents to this telephone survey ranged in age from nineteen to ninety. They had been married between two months and seventy years and had between zero and eight children each. Ninety percent of the respondents were white, 5 percent African-American, 4 percent Latino, and the rest Asian, Native American, or other.

In most respects, this survey captured a representative sample of the national population of married men. However, compared to U.S. Census data, the husbands who agreed to answer the survey had a higher income than average, and racial minorities were underrepresented. To mitigate these concerns, I specifically sought out low-income men and racial and ethnic minorities for my in-depth interviews. Their stories are related anecdotally throughout the book.

There are other limitations to my research. For example, married men who have only cell phones are underrepresented because current sampling programs do not include cell-only exchanges. Also, men who cannot communicate in English over the phone are not represented in the survey.

Overall, though, the combination of a quantitative survey and in-depth interviews offers a rare, multidimensional portrait of the American husband. I hope it will inspire other explorers of the male psyche to move forward with much-needed new research in this arena.

N.J.C.

Sources

Chapter One: The Spark

Barker, Olivia. "No Time for Dating?" *USA Today,* Nov. 13, 2003.

Brooks, David. "Love, Internet Style." *New York Times,* Nov. 8, 2003.

Buss, David M. "Desires in Human Mating." In Dori LeCroy and Peter Moller, eds., *Evolutionary Perspectives on Human Reproductive Behavior.* The New York Academy of Sciences, 2000.

Buss, David M.; Michael D. Botwin; and Todd K. Shackelford. "Personal and Mate Preferences," *Journal of Personality*, vol. 65 (Mar. 1997).

Buunk, Bram P., et al. "Age and Gender Differences in Mate Selection Criteria." *Personal Relationships*, vol. 9 (2002).

Fischman, Josh; Jia-Rui Chong; and Roberta Hotinski. "Why We Fall in Love." *U.S. News & World Report,* Feb. 7, 2000.

Furnham, A.; T. Tan; and C. McManus. "Waist-to-Hip Ratio and Preferences for Body Shape: A Replication and Extension." *Personal and Individual Differences*, vol. 22 (1997).

Grover, Kelly J., et al. "Mate Selection Processes and Marital Satisfaction." *Family Relations,* vol. 34 (1985).

Maisey, D. M., et al. "Characteristics of Male Attractiveness for Women." *Lancet,* vol. 353 (1999).

McKnight, Jim, et al. "Just How Good Are We at Estimating Attractiveness?" *Psychology, Evolution, and Gender,* vol. 1 (Dec. 1999).

Popenoe, David, and Barbara Dafoe Whitehead. *The State of Our Unions 2001.* National Marriage Project, Rutgers University, 2001.

Rock, Maxine. *The Marriage Map: Understanding and Surviving the Stages of Marriage.* Peachtree Publishers, 1986.

Schmitt, David P., et al. "Are Men Really More Oriented Toward Short-Term Mating than Women?" *Psychology, Evolution, and Gender,* vol. 3 (Dec. 2001).

Torte, Martin J., and Piers Cornelissen. "Female and Male Perceptions of Female Physical Attractiveness." *British Journal of Psychology,* vol. 92 (May 2001).

Chapter Two: The Decision

Buss, David M., et al. "A Half Century of Mate Preferences: The Cultural Evolution of Values." *Journal of Marriage and the Family,* vol. 63 (May 2001).

Cere, Daniel. "Courtship Today: The View from Academia." *Public Interest,* vol. 143 (Spring 2001).

Molloy, John. *Why Men Marry Some Women and Not Others.* Warner Books, 2003.

Murstein, Bernard I. *Who Will Marry Whom?* Spring Publishing Co., 1976.

Schoen, Robert. "Partner Choice in Marriages and Cohabitations." *Journal of Marriage and the Family,* vol. 55 (May 1993).

Sprecher, Susan, et al. "Mate Selection Preferences." *Journal of Personality and Social Psychology,* vol. 66 (1994).

Sternberg, Robert J. "A Triangular Theory of Love." *Psychological Review,* vol. 93 (1986).

Chapter Three: The Wedding

Barker, Olivia. "Engaged to Marry, Eventually." *USA Today,* Dec. 31, 2003.

Forbes, Gordon B., et al. *Sex Roles: A Journal of Research,* March 2002.

Gannon, Dr. Patrick, and Michelle Gannon. "Marriage-Bound or Just Living Together?" *Marriage Prep 101 Quarterly Newsletter* (www.marriageprep 101.com/generic2.html), Apr. 12, 2002.

Chapter Four: Newlyweds

Creighton University Center for Marriage and Family. "Time, Sex, and Money: The First Five Years of Marriage." Dec. 2000. (Available at www.creighton.edu/marriageandfamily.)

Gorman, Megan Othersen. "Do You Love Him?" *Prevention,* vol. 50 (March 1998).

Johnson, Jessica. "Just Married—and Panicking." *Globe and Mail* (Toronto), Nov. 22, 2003.

Kantrowitz, Barbara. "The Science of a Good Marriage." *Newsweek,* April 19, 1999.

Kurdek, Lawrence A. "The Nature and Predictors of the Trajectory of Change in Marital Quality for Husbands and Wives over the First 10 Years of Marriage." *Developmental Psychology,* vol. 35 (Sept. 1999).

———"The Nature and Predictors of the Trajectory of Change in Marital Quality over the First Four Years of Marriage for First-Married Husbands and Wives." *Journal of Family Psychology,* vol. 12 (1998).

McLaughlin, Lisa. "Personal Time/Your Family." *Time,* Dec. 11, 2000.

Nelson, Jennifer. "After the Wedding, a 'Familymoon.' " *Washington Post,* Nov. 11, 2003.

Pittman, Frank S. *Man Enough,* Berkley Publishing Group, 1993.

Schram, Rosalyn Weinman. "Marital Satisfaction over the Family Life Cycle: A Critique and Proposal." *Journal of Marriage and the Family,* Feb. 1979.

Chapter Five: Family Times

Adams, Brooke. "Marriage Is Becoming Less About Rearing Kids." *Salt Lake Tribune,* June 20, 2003.

Gottman, John, and Robert Wayne Levenson. "The Timing of Divorce." *Journal of Marriage and the Family,* vol. 62 (Aug. 2000).

Kantrowitz, Barbara. "The Science of a Good Marriage." *Newsweek,* Apr. 19, 1999.

McLaughlin, Lisa. "Personal Time/Your Family." *Time,* Dec. 11, 2000.

Rosenbluth, Susan C.; Janice M. Steil; and Juliet H. Whitcomb. "Marital Equality: What Does It Mean?" *Journal of Family Issues,* vol. 19 (May 1998).

Schram, Rosalyn Weinman. "Marital Satisfaction over the Family Life Cycle: A Critique and Proposal." *Journal of Marriage and the Family,* Feb. 1979.

Seccombe, Karen. "Assessing the Costs and Benefits of Children: Gender Comparisons Among Childfree Husbands and Wives." *Journal of Marriage and the Family,* vol. 53 (Feb. 1991).

Snarey, John. "Men Without Children." *Psychology Today,* March 1988.

Steinberg, Laurence, and Susan B. Silverberg. "Influences on Marital Satisfaction During the Middle States of the Family Life Cycle." *Journal of Marriage and the Family,* vol. 40 (Nov. 1987).

Chapter Six: The Empty Nest

Greeff, A. P. "Characteristics of Families That Function Well." *Journal of Family Issues,* vol. 21 (Nov. 2000).

Kovacs, Liberty. "A Conceptualization of Marital Development." *Family Therapy,* vol. 10 (1983).

Simpson, Eileen. *Late Love.* Houghton Mifflin, 1994.

Steinberg, Laurence, and Susan B. Silverberg. "Influences on Marital Satisfaction During the Middle States of the Family Life Cycle." *Journal of Marriage and the Family,* vol. 40 (Nov. 1987).

Chapter Seven: Mature Marriage

Cahill, Suzanne. "Elderly Husbands Caring at Home for Wives Diagnosed with Alzheimer's Disease." *Australian Journal of Social Issues,* vol. 35 (Feb. 2000).

Dickson, Fran C., and Kandi L. Walker. "The Expression of Emotion in Later-Life Married Men." *Communications Quarterly,* vol. 49 (Winter 2001).

Kirsi, Tapio, et al. "A Man's Gotta Do What a Man's Gotta Do: Husbands as

Caregivers to Their Demented Wives: A Discourse Analytic Approach." *Journal of Aging Studies,* vol. 14 (June 2000).

Kramer, Betty J. "Husbands Caring for Wives with Dementia: A Longitudinal Study of Continuity." *Health and Social Work,* vol. 25 (May 2000).

Lang, Susan S. "The Recipe for Happy, Retired Husbands." *Human Ecology Forum,* vol. 27 (Fall 1999).

Lauer, Robert H.; Janette C. Lauer; and Sarah T. Kerr. "The Long-Term Marriage: Perceptions of Stability and Satisfaction." *International Journal of Aging and Human Development,* vol. 31 (1990).

Weishaus, Sylvia, and Dorothy Field. "A Half Century of Marriage: Continuity or Change?" *Journal of Marriage and the Family,* vol. 50 (Aug. 1988).

Wilson, Barbara Foley, and Charlotte Schoenborn. "A Healthy Marriage." *American Demographics,* Nov. 1989.

Chapter Eight: Housework

Doherty, William J. *Take Back Your Marriage.* Guilford Press, 2001.

Gurian, Michael. *What Could He Be Thinking?* St. Martin's Press, 2003.

Morris, Betsy. "Trophy Husbands: Arm Candy?" *Fortune,* Oct. 14, 2002.

Nock, Steven L. "Turn-Taking as Relational Behavior." *Social Science Research,* vol. 27 (1998).

Rosenbluth, Susan C.; Janice M. Steil; and Juliet H. Whitcomb. "Marital Equality: What Does It Mean?" *Journal of Family Issues,* vol. 19 (May 1998).

Suttor, J. Jill. "Marital Quality and Satisfaction with the Division of Household Labor Across the Family Life Cycle." *Journal of Marriage and the Family,* vol. 53 (Feb. 1991).

"U.S. Husbands Are Doing More Housework While Wives Are Doing Less, University of Michigan Time-Use Study Shows." *Ascribe Higher Education News Service,* March 12, 2002.

Chapter Nine: Sex

Call, Vaughn, et al. "The Incidence and Frequency of Marital Sex in a National Sample." *Journal of Marriage and the Family,* vol. 57 (Aug. 1995).

Cavanagh, Michael E. *Before the Wedding: Look Before You Leap.* Westminster/John Knox Press, 1994.

Deveny, Kathleen. "We're Not in the Mood." *Newsweek,* June 30, 2003.

Gaillardetz, Richard R. "Learning from Marriage: The Sacrament That Just Won't Quit." *Commonweal,* vol. 127 (Sept. 8, 2000).

Gilder, George. *Men and Marriage.* Pelican Publishing Co., 1986.

Langer, Gary, et al. "A Peek Beneath the Sheets." ABC News Internet Ventures, Oct. 21, 2004.

Richardson, John H. "Sex with One Woman (My Wife)." *Esquire*, Feb. 2001.

Young, Toby. "Confessions of a Porn Addict." *Spectator Ltd.* (UK), Nov. 10, 2001.

Chapter Ten: Affairs

Anonymous. "Six Women Who Were Not My Wife: A True Story of Adultery." *Esquire,* Feb. 2001.

Buss, D. M. "The Evolutionary Psychology of Human Social Strategies." In E. T. Higgins and A. W. Kruglanski, eds., *Social Psychology: Handbook of Basic Principles*. Guilford Press, 1996.

Buss, D. M., et al. "Sex Differences in Jealousy." *Psychological Science*, vol. 7 (1996).

Daly, M., et al. "Male Sexual Jealousy." *Ethology and Sociobiology*, vol. 3 (1982).

Glass, Ira. "The Doctor of the Dalliance." *New York Times,* Dec. 28, 2003.

Shackelford, T. K., et al. "Emotional Reactions to Infidelity." *Cognition and Emotion*, vol. 14 (2000).

Storey, Celia. "Surviving the Affair." *Arkansas Democrat-Gazette,* Nov. 12, 2003.

Chapter Eleven: Money and Work

Barnett, Rosaline, and Caryl Rivers. *She Works, He Works.* HarperSanFrancisco, 1996.

Braverman, Amy M. "Healthy, Wealthy, and Wed." *University of Chicago Magazine*, vol. 96 (Oct. 2003).

Deutsch, Francine M., et al. "How Gender Counts When Couples Count Their Money." *Sex Roles: A Journal of Research,* Apr. 2003.

Ealy, C. Diane, and Kay Lesh. *Our Money, Ourselves for Couples*. Capital Books, 2003.

Ehrenreich, Barbara. *The Hearts of Men: American Dreams and the Flight from Commitment*. Doubleday, 1983.

Kaufman, Gayle, and Peter Uhlenberg. "The Influence of Parenthood on the Work Effort of Married Men and Women." *Social Forces,* vol. 78 (Mar. 2000).

Macdonald, Jay. "Gender Spender: Sex Sets Your Money DNA." www.bankrate.com, Dec. 13, 2002.

Mellan, Olivia. *Money Harmony*. Walker & Co., 1994.

Shellenbarger, Sue. "Work and Family." *Wall Street Journal,* Nov. 12, 2003.

Tyre, Peg, and Daniel McGinn. "She Works, He Doesn't." *Newsweek,* May 12, 2003.

Chapter Twelve: Arguing

Doheny, Kathleen. " 'We're Done' Can Be Predicted Before 'I Do,' " www.drkoop.com, Aug. 19, 2004.

Kurdek, Lawrence A. "Predicting Change in Marital Satisfaction from Husbands' and Wives' Conflict Resolution Styles." *Journal of Marriage and the Family,* vol. 57 (Feb. 1995).

Popcak, Gregory K. *The Exceptional Seven Percent.* Citadel Press, 2000.

Real, Terrence. *How Can I Get Through to You?* Scribner, 2002.

Rodriguez, Rod. "A Study of Anger Arousal in Married Men." *Male Health Weekly Plus,* June 22, 1998.

Stout, Hilary. "The Key to a Lasting Marriage: Combat." *Wall Street Journal,* Nov. 3, 2004.

Chapter Thirteen: How to Change a Man

Arndt, Bettina. "Till Therapy Do Us Part." www.smartmarriage.com, July 5, 2003.

Buss, Dale. "Let No Man Put Asunder." *Wall Street Journal,* May 21, 2004.

Price, Joyce. "Studies Indicate That Married Men Live Longer." *Insight on the News,* vol. 12 (Feb. 26, 1996).

Shellenbarger, Sue. "Can This Marriage Be Saved?" *Wall Street Journal,* Jan. 8, 2004.

Snyder, Leah. "United Way Making Investment in Healthy Marriages." *Journal* (Johnson County, Indiana), May 25, 2004.

Chapter Fourteen: Parents and In-Laws

Forward, Susan, and Donna Frazier. *Toxic In-laws.* HarperCollins, 2001.

Rock, Maxine. *The Marriage Map: Understanding and Surviving the Stages of Marriage.* Peachtree Publishers, 1986.

Chapter Fifteen: Second Marriages

Albrecht, Stanley. "Correlates of Marital Happiness Among the Remarried." *Journal of Marriage and the Family,* vol. 41 (1979).

Felker, Jennifer A., et al. "A Qualitative Analysis of Stepfamilies." *Journal of Divorce and Remarriage,* vol. 38 (2002).

Hetherington, E. Mavis. "Marriage and Divorce American Style: A Destructive Marriage Is Not a Happy Family." *American Prospect,* vol. 13 (Apr. 8, 2002).

Kelley, Susan, and Dale Burg. *The Second Time Around.* Morrow, 2000.

Marks, Nadine F., and James David Lambert. "Marital Status Continuity and Change Among Young and Midlife Adults: Longitudinal Effects on Psychological Well-Being." *Journal of Family Issues,* vol. 19 (Nov. 1998).

Maudlin, Karen L. "Succeeding at Second Marriages." *Marriage Partnership,* vol. 18 (Fall 2001).

Rosin, Mark Bruce. *Step-Fathering.* Simon & Schuster, 1987.

Stokes, Sean B., et al. "Remarried Clients." *Journal of Divorce and Remarriage,* vol. 38 (2002).

Chapter Sixteen: Husbandly Advice

Bramlett, Matthew D., and William D. Mosher. "Cohabitation, Marriage, Divorce, and Remarriage in the United States." *Vital and Health Statistics,* vol. 23 (2002).

Chapter Seventeen: The Male Style of Loving

Bradbury, Thomas N.; Frank D. Fincham; and Steven R. H. Beach. "Research on the Nature and Determinants of Marital Satisfaction: A Decade in Review." *Journal of Marriage and Family,* vol. 62 (Nov. 2000).

Cancian, Francesca M. *Love in America: Gender and Self-Development.* Cambridge University Press, 1987.

Crain, Rance. "Husbands Are Boys and Wives Their Mothers in the Land of Ads." *Advertising Age,* Mar. 26, 2001.

de Vaus, David. "Marriage and Mental Health: Does Marriage Improve the Mental Health of Men at the Expense of Women?" *Family Matters,* Winter 2002.

Gray, John. *Men Are from Mars, Women Are from Venus.* HarperCollins, 1992.

Konner, Melvin, M.D. "Bridging Our Differences." *Newsweek,* June 16, 2003.

Simon, Robin W. "Revisiting the Relationships Among Gender, Marital Status, and Mental Health." *American Journal of Sociology,* January 2002.

Vogler, Candace. "Sex and Talk." *Critical Inquiry,* vol. 24 (Winter 1998).

Yolom, Marilyn. *A History of the Wife.* HarperCollins, 2001.

Index

arguments *(cont.)*
  escape from, 176–77, 181–82
  expressing oneself in, 180–81
  in family years, 81–82, 84, 175, 205
  giving in, 68
  intellectualizing in, 176, 189
  lack of skill in, 67, 175–76
  in mature marriages, 175
  on money issues, 160, 161–69
  with mother-in-law, 199
  of newlyweds, 67, 175
  reaching out to one another in, 182
  and sex, 105–8, 128–29
  Smith, 174
  strategies of, 175–78, 189
  verbal abuse in, 177, 182
  violence in, 67, 177–80, 190
  winning, 181

bachelor life, 35
bachelor parties, 41–42
bankruptcy, 167
beauty, 14, 16, 211, 218
biology, role of, 39–40, 122
birth-control pill, 31, 129
bisexuality, 36–37, 143
bridal registries, 44
Buss, David M., 14

Cancian, Francesca, 228–29
caregiving, 110–11
change, 183–90
  as disrespectful, 184
  evolving, 185
  Hudson, 184
  modeling behavior for, 187–88
  motivation for, 183, 185–86, 187–88
  professional counseling for, 188–89
  readiness for, 183–84
  and religion, 186–87
  resistance to, 186
  societal, 30–31
  threatening to leave, 189, 190
  of unhealthy behaviors, 184–85, 187–88, 189–90
character, 14, 20
charm, 17
chastity, 18
childlessness, 82–83
children:
  adolescent, 80, 132, 195
  adoption of, 82, 130
  adult, 88, 210
  birth of, 65, 69–71, 135
  born out of wedlock, 31, 184
  breast-feeding, 73
  coparenting, 65, 81, 86, 172
  cost of, 73
  crying infants, 77–78
  custody of, 64–65, 208
  disciplining of, 77, 78–80, 205, 207
  end of child-raising, 87–89
  expectations from, 79–80, 217
  fairness with, 209
  fears of, 67–68
  financial support of, 75
  as focus of relationship, 81
  generational issues about, 81–82
  girl vs. boy culture of, 66–68
  and grandchildren, 88, 94, 110
  husband as jealous of, 70, 73
  individuation of, 196
  inheritance of, 210
  marriage relationship changed by, 70, 102, 106, 147, 204–5
  number of, 72–73, 81–82, 84, 98
  obligation to have, 72, 97–98
  other people's, 82–83, 130
  positive impact of, 80–81, 86
  readiness to have, 71–72, 211
  ready-made family, 19
  reality of, 73
  as reason to marry, 35–37, 72
  responsibility for, 73, 77–80, 81, 172

mothers:
abuse from, 212
influence of, 196–97
relationship with, 151, 191, 192, 197
separation from, 196
smothering, 197
standards set by, 196–97
temperaments of, 15
values of, 194
Murstein, Bernard I., 29

nagging, 124
negative interactions, 182
neglect, 63, 217
newlyweds, 57–68
adjustments of, 58
affairs of, 66, 96
arguments of, 67, 175
conflicts of, 58–61, 66–68
disillusionment of, 59, 131
as honeymoon phase, 58
and in-laws, 64
money issues of, 58, 59–61
neglect, 63
power struggles of, 59–61
practical daily issues of, 58–59
in second marriages, 64–65
sex lives of, 65–66, 106, 131
sharing housework in, 57–58
transition period of, 58–59
work-family balance, 61–63
Nock, Steven, 118, 185

online cybersex, 157
online dating, 23–24
opposites, attraction of, 24
optimism, 15–16

panic attacks, 39
parents, 191–201
abandonment by, 152
divorced, 197–98
honoring, 48
relationship with father, 191–96

relationship with mother, 151, 191, 192, 197
relationships between, 197–98
of wife, see in-laws
partners:
in equal relationship, 115
search for, see search
spouses as, 25
passive-aggressive behavior, 177
perfection, fantasy of, 59
performance anxiety, 140
"Perhaps Love" (Denver), 50
personal ads, 57
personality, 15–16, 211
phone sex, 157
Pittman, Frank, 152, 157, 180, 192–93
Popenoe, David, 25
positive attitude, 15–16, 184
positive contact, 80–81, 182
possessiveness, 149
postpartum depression, 70
power struggles, 59–61
pregnancy:
of adult daughter, 88
anger about, 71–72
and mistreating women, 194
physical problems with, 106
as reason to marry, 35–36, 47–48
premarital sex, 31, 32, 100, 129
prisoners, interviews with, 193
proposal:
creative approaches to, 38–39
negative reactions to, 39
romantic, 146
from women, 29
see also decision to propose; spark

quickie wedding, 47–48

race:
civil-rights movement, 31
and in-laws, 199–201
interracial marriage, 24, 49, 100

rape, victims of, 212
readiness:
  and age, 24
  for change, 183–84
  to have children, 71–72, 211
  for marriage, 14–15, 24, 32, 34,
    109, 161, 215–16
Real, Terrence, 180
relationship:
  comfort in, 34, 218
  continued investment in, 96
  equal, 115
  long- vs. short-term, 14–15, 35
religion, 20, 23, 221
  and change, 186–87
  and Establishment wedding style,
    48–49
  reaffirmation of faith, 49
rescuers, 213
research methods, 237–38
responsibility:
  for housework, *see* housework
  for money matters, 165
  of parenting, 73, 77–80, 81, 172
  as sought-after quality, 19
retirement:
  in empty-nest years, 94
  in mature marriage, 102–3
  plans for, 62
  role shifts in, 103, 171
  saving for, 164–65
rites of passage, 53
romance, keeping it alive, 219
romantic love, 30, 130, 146
roommates, 84

search, 11–27, 34
  at a bar, 23
  for compatibility, 14
  at a dance, 30
  friends' introductions, 22, 23
  grew up together, 30
  in Laundromat, 11–13, 16, 22
  online, 23–24
  in personal ads, 57

  in religious setting, 23
  on the road, 17, 22
  at school, 11, 22, 59, 148
  for short-term connection, 15
  in singles scene, 14, 22–23
  at social events, 22, 97
  at work, 22, 162
second marriages, 202–14
  and adult children, 210
  and affairs, 204
  better choices in, 210–11, 214
  blended families of, 208–9
  children in, 64–65, 202–9
  and ex-husbands, 205–7
  and ex-wives, 208, 212
  fear of failure in, 45
  lessons from previous marriages,
    203
  multiple, 212–14
  newlyweds in, 64–65
  reasons for, 213
  and sexual compatibility, 211–12
  statistics on, 204
  and stepchildren, 202–9
  transition period in, 206
secularism, 49
security, 166
self-confidence, 16–18
separation, loneliness of, 107
serial monogamists, 151
sex, 128–45
  and aging, 138–39, 141
  arguments about, 105–8, 128–29
  availability, 211
  as barometer of marriage health,
    144–45
  communication about, 136, 138
  compatibility in, 211–12
  compromise in, 134
  desire to experience, 31
  disparity of desire for, 65, 74–77,
    105, 107, 129, 131, 133,
    136–38, 142–43, 147
  dissatisfaction with, 147–48
  and divorce, 212–13